LS Swaps

How to Swap GM LS ENGINES into *Almost ANYTHING*

Jefferson Bryant

CarTech®

CarTech®

CarTech®, Inc.
6118 Main Street
North Branch, MN 55056
Phone: 651-277-1200 or 800-551-4754
Fax: 651-277-1203
www.cartechbooks.com

Edit by Paul Johnson
Layout by Monica Seiberlich

ISBN978-1-61325-093-8
Item No. SA156

Library of Congress Cataloging-in-Publication Data

Bryant, Jefferson.
LS swaps / by Jefferson Bryant.
pages cm
ISBN 978-1-61325-093-8
1. General Motors automobiles–Motors–Modification. 2. General Motors automobiles–Parts. 3. General Motors automobiles–Performance. I. Title.
TL215.G4B793 2014
629.25›04–dc23
2013040498

Written, edited, and designed in the U.S.A.
Printed in China
15 14 13 12

Front Cover: *The LS engine is suitable for swapping into many different cars, and installing it in a second-generation Corvette Stingray is straightforward. A typical install requires motor mounts, fuel-line upgrade, return fuel line to tank, adapting the wiring harness, installing the drive-by-wire gas pedal, and other miscellaneous items. (Photo Courtesy Tony Huntimer)*

Title Page: *Vorshlag Motorsports makes many LS swap kits for BMWs. This one is designed to swap Gen III/IV engines into E36 BMWs (E-series). The kit is available in many stages from bare-bones engine and transmission mounts to everything you need, including headers and driveshaft.*

Back Cover Photos

Top Left: *A stock harness can be used "as-is" in the swap, or can be given the "wire diet" by cutting off the loom and removing the wires that are not needed. This is a great way to get to know the engine's wiring in detail. Keeping track of each wire can be a bit of a headache, though.*

Top Right: *These AN-style lines on the Rock Valley tanks are a little larger than a hose with a clamp. The fuel-sending unit was wired up as well. (Photo Courtesy Street & Performance)*

Middle Left: *Rather than purchase pre-made motor mounts, Mike Magnuson fabricated a set using 1/8-inch plate steel.*

Middle Right: *Install the collar on the hose. The hose should be 1/16 inch from the threads on the inside of the collar. Wrap tape around the hose at flush with the base of the collar.*

Bottom Left: *Bolting the adapters to the engine is pretty simple: four socket head bolts and you are done. Make sure to use some anti-seize compound to prevent galling of the different metals.*

Bottom Right: *For autocross and road-race applications, you need a well-designed pan to ensure that the engine has a constant supply of oil. This pan fabricated by Canton features a front sump as well, which makes it a good choice for rear-steer vehicles. (Photo Courtesy Blane Burnett)*

DISTRIBUTION BY:

Europe
PGUK
63 Hatton Garden
London EC1N 8LE, England
Phone: 020 7061 1980 • Fax: 020 7242 3725
www.pguk.co.uk

Australia
Renniks Publications Ltd.
3/37-39 Green Street
Banksmeadow, NSW 2109, Australia
Phone: 2 9695 7055
Fax: 2 9695 7355
www.renniks.com

Canada
Login Canada
300 Saulteaux Crescent
Winnipeg, MB, R3J 3T2 Canada
Phone: 800 665 1148 • Fax: 800 665 0103
www.lb.ca

CONTENTS

Dedication

To my wife and kids, thank you for dealing with all the late nights.
This book is for the all of the gearheads, who like me,
can never seem to leave well enough alone.

Acknowledgments

Without the help of the following people, this book would not have been possible: Dr. Jamie Meyer of Chevrolet Performance; Tom Read of GM Powertrain; Tom Henderson of GM Communications; Mark Campbell of Street & Performance; Rick Maechler of Street & Performance; Trent Goodwin of Comp Cams Group; Chris Douglas of Comp Cams Group; Bill Tichenor of Holley Performance; Blane Burnett of Holley Performance; Smitty Smith of Edelbrock; Matt Diamond of Gearhead Garage; Max Wyman of DiabloSport; LS1Tech.com; Doug Strickler; Summit Racing; ATS; AutoKraft; Vorshlag; Magnuson Products; Automedia2000; HP Tuners; Painless Performance; Fred, Kim, and Corey Mufin of Red Line Auto Sports; Ken Wolkens; Mike Magnuson; and Pat McElreath and Clayton Howard of Red Dirt Rodz. All of your hard work is greatly appreciated.

Introduction

The goal of most engine swaps is to increase performance, and in almost all cases the LS engines meet that goal. The Gen III/IV engine platform represents the largest-growing segment of the performance automotive aftermarket, so there are many options for increasing the performance of an LS-series engine. There are simple bolt-on components such as larger throttle bodies or high-flow intakes, and there are serious performance upgrades such as high-lift camshafts and large-port cylinder heads.

Although the factory fits its high-performance LS engines with superchargers, the most popular big-boost upgrade is adding a turbocharger. Driven off the exhaust rather than the drive belts, a turbo provides "free" horsepower. A single turbo fitted to the 5.3 Vortec engine can make more than 500 hp with no additional mods, other than a properly calibrated ignition map.

With all of these options, Gen III/IV engine swaps have become more and more popular. This book gives you the knowledge of where to find the engine that best suits your needs and covers all the details of performing the swap. Although every car and swap is different, there are quite a few common aspects.

An LS swapping project is fairly easy if it is carefully conceived, researched, and planned. The Gen III/IV engine families have a similar footprint with the original small-block Chevy. If a traditional small-block Chevy can be swapped into a particular vehicle, you can certainly install an LS engine as well, but some minor adjustments, such as re-arranging the drive pulleys and other components may be required. The possibilities are endless.

Many creative builders have swapped LS engines into everything from Volvos to BMWs to Honda Civics, and even a Honda S2000, which is sure to be a scary ride. Although most builders are familiar with carburetors and how they work, fuel-injection systems, computers, and wiring harness hookups intimidate many swappers. The electronics are an integral component of a swap and a particular car or other vehicle can be adapted to run the engine's vital electronic systems. In most cases, the wiring harness, connectors, and wiring must be carefully modified, or the correct aftermarket components for plugging in a particular engine to a specific car can be purchased. Shops such as Street & Performance and Painless Performance provide the products and support to help simplify the wiring harness. Tuning companies such as HP Tuners and EFI Live can reprogram the electronic control module (ECM) to adapt it for a swap. In the end, you get a more efficient power plant for your vehicle, with the ability to tune it better and faster.

For simplicity's sake, many electronic controls can be eliminated by installing a carburetor on an LS engine, as is the case with the LS364. In addition, an aftermarket carbureted intake designed for the LS-series engines can be used. These engines are just as powerful and still take advantage of the electronic spark distribution, using the one-coil-per-cylinder design. A spark controller is still necessary, as these engines do not have a provision for a traditional distributor, but these control boxes are very easy to wire.

One of the biggest benefits of the new Gen III/IV engines is efficiency. These engines were designed to meet the strict Corporate Average Fuel Economy (CAFE) standards for new vehicles. This means that the Gen III/IV engines must meet the fuel-economy ratings, all while making significant horsepower numbers. In the past, making 400 hp and getting 20 mpg with a small-block Chevy was an impossible proposition. With an LS engine, it is not only achievable, it's standard. The 2013 ZR1 Corvette cranks out 638 hp from the LS9 and maintains 21 mpg highway, 14 mpg city. A Gen I small-block Chevy cannot even get close to those numbers. A stock Vortec 5.3 liter with an overdrive automatic can produce 350 hp and attain 20 mpg with a custom ECM tune.

All of these factors together add up to make the Gen III/IV engines the most popular swap since the original small-block Chevy hit the dealers in 1955. With so many variations, there is sure to be a Gen III/IV engine to suit your application.

CHAPTER 1

What You Need to Know about LS-Series Engines

Development for the Gen III engine began after the short-lived LT1/LT4 (1992–1997) engine failed to meet GM's performance expectations. General Motors essentially started from square one and created the new Gen III V-8 engine, which shared very little with the original small-block Chevy LT1/LT4 platform that it replaced. A phenomenal high-performance engine, the Gen III LS1 showcased modern engine technology while retaining the traditional pushrod valvetrain. The engine first appeared as the flagship engine in the 1997 Corvette, generating a groundswell of enthusiast interest, and a whole series of high-performance Gen III/Gen IV engines followed it.

Although many consider these "LS" engines, the official nomenclature is Gen III and Gen IV. These remarkable engines produced class-leading performance and fuel efficiency. As a result, street rodders, muscle car enthusiasts, and even sports car aficionados recognized the potential of the potent, compact V-8 engines and sought out Gen III/IV engines for swapping into a wide range of vehicles. The factory small-block engines pushed out 350 hp at the low end of the scale and reached more than 500 hp at the top end of the spectrum. It seemed the horsepower wars from the late 1960s were back again. In addition, Gen III/IV engines transformed GM's performance business, now called Chevrolet Performance, and released a full complement of high-performance parts for the powerhouse engine.

The Gen III platform began life as the replacement for the LTI/LT4 engines, and it was first installed between the frame rails of the 1997 Corvette. It was also installed in the 1998 Camaro/Firebird models as well as the truck and SUV lines. (Photo Courtesy General Motors)

The desire to swap these engines into other vehicles is at an all-time high. Finding an LS engine for your project can be as simple as strolling through the local wrecking yard, visiting a website, or making a single phone call to your local dealer. Furthermore, you have quite a few versions of these venerable engines to choose from.

All Gen III/IV engines are distributorless, and all but one is fuel injected. If you're buying a used engine, retain all the wiring and electronics for almost every engine swap, unless you're using an aftermarket controller. (Photo Courtesy General Motors)

The scalloped holes (top right) at the side of the main webs on this block are the crankcase breathing holes. This promotes proper ventilation for the air and oil vapor in Gen III/IV engines. (Photo Courtesy General Motors)

Gen III: A Revolution in V-8 Performance

All-aluminum or cast-iron blocks built from 1997 through 2004 are basically the same. However, there are some minor differences, including an important internal difference. The outside diameter (OD) of the camshaft bore was changed in 2004. Although the cam itself remained the same, only the bearing OD changed, and as such it required a different set of cam bearings.

General Motors utilized the Gen III platform for the full range of GM trucks as well. With two years of experience under its belt, General Motors replaced the aging Gen I 305 and 350 small-block truck engine platform with Gen III engines. The new truck and SUV powertrain was offered in three displacements: 4.8-, 5.3-, and 6.0-liter. These V-8 engines were installed in every GM truck and SUV from 1999 to 2007. The 4.8- and 5.3-liter engines share aluminum cylinder head design; the larger 6.0-liter engines have their own aluminum head design. The heads do, however, swap across all blocks. The Vortec truck engines have proven to be a very popular swap candidate due to sheer volume and low cost.

Gen IV: Improving the Legend

In 2005, when the Gen IV platform began replacing the popular Gen III, the evolution in pushrod engine technology took another step forward. Based on Gen III architecture, these new engines took advantage of

The LS7 was the first dry-sump LS engine, introduced in the 2006 Z06 Corvette, making 505 hp. The LS7 ushered in a new era of ultra-performance engines for General Motors, bringing race technology to street-driven vehicles. (Photo Courtesy General Motors)

Cadillac and Chevrolet needed an engine to turn the CTS-V and ZL1 Camaro into street demons, so General Motors came up with the LSA. The slightly smaller Eaton supercharger reduces the overall output to 556 hp compared to the LS9. The LSA is also available as a crate engine. (Photo Courtesy General Motors)

displacement-on-demand (DoD) technology, which General Motors called Active Fuel Management (AFM). AFM allows the engine to alternately fire the pistons between all eight or as few as four pistons, saving fuel and reducing emissions. This technology has been offered on the Gen IV platform; this engine series was even designed to accept variable valve timing (VVT) and three valves per cylinder. The first Gen IVs were the LS2 and the front-wheel-drive V-8 LS4.

However, the Gen III production engines didn't disappear in 2005. They were still in production for the Holden VE and W models and the LS6-powered Cadillac CTS-V, while the Chevrolet Performance division continued to offer both engines. In fact, Gen III engine production continued for new vehicles through 2007, so General Motors offered both the Gen III and IV engines during the mid-2000s.

In 2006, the ultimate Gen IV engine, the LS7 installed in the Corvette Z06, took to the streets. This fire-breathing small-block produced 505 hp and earned the distinction as the most powerful naturally aspirated production small-block Chevy engine ever built. In 2005, the truck engine line changed over to the Gen IV platform, adding six new Gen IV blocks. By 2008, the 6.0-liter L76 and the 6.2-liter LS3 joined the Gen IV line. With the popularity of the Gen III and Gen IV engines, General Motors developed (for the aftermarket) the LS364 carbureted Gen IV engine and the LSX bare block for retrofitting and swapping.

To further push the Gen IV platform, General Motors stepped up the game with two new ultra-high-performance engines in an effort to stay on top of the late-model horsepower wars: the LSA and the LS9, both based on the LS3 block. The LSA is a supercharged 6.2-liter that utilizes a 1.9-liter Roots-type Eaton supercharger to build 556 bhp (flywheel) and 551 ft-lbs of torque. The LSA is available in the 2009–up Cadillac CTS-V models as well as the 2012–up ZL1 Camaro. The LS9 also measures 6.2 liters, but uses a 2.3-liter Eaton Roots blower to generate the 638 bhp and 604 ft-lbs of torque, making it the most powerful GM V-8 ever produced. Just like the LS7, the LS9 features a 10.75-quart dry-sump oiling system. The LS9 is used in the 2009–2013 Corvette ZR1.

In 2013, General Motors released the Gen V platform, which will eventually replace the LS-series engine. The Gen V shares the same bellhousing and motor mounts, but just about everything else is different. General Motors is committed to LS-series performance, however, and it will be at least 2015 before the Gen V sees production in anything other than the C7 Corvette.

The LS9 is the bad boy from the Gen IV line, making 638 hp with the intercooled supercharger. The 6.2-liter engine is available as a crate engine from GM Performance. (Photo Courtesy General Motors)

Feature Vehicle

1996 Nissan 240SX SE

Photos courtesy Blane Burnett

Proving to be a popular swap platform, this Nissan 240SX owned by Blane Burnett devours any autocross course and track upon which it is unleashed. This is due in part to the performance heritage of the S14 platform, but the real reason is the LS2 stuffed between the fender wells. This Nissan was used in the development of the LS swap kit that Holley Performance now offers as an off-the-shelf system.

The goal was to build the Nissan into a potent autocross car that was affordable, had good handling out of the box, and was easy to work on. The factory weight bias of the 240SX is 60/40, but the LS2 only added 50 pounds to the nose of the car. With the addition of a rollbar in the back, the bias remained the same. The aluminum-block engines offer weight savings over the iron blocks of the Gen III Vortecs. An LS7 certainly swaps into the Nissan, but the dry-sump oiling system can create some fitment issues due to the smaller engine bay. Supercharged versions of the LS engines would have been an excellent option for the 240, but hood clearance might be an issue. Keeping the stock hood adds to the sleeper effect of the project.

The beauty of the LS platform is that it is almost like Legos for gearheads. You can start with just about any base engine and swap parts back and forth until you get what you want. You are not stuck with one particular accessory drive, oil pan, or induction system with any one particular block. Most of the parts swap across all generations and sizes of LS-series engines.

This LS2 was sourced from a salvage yard 2005 GTO. The GTO accessory drive was swapped out for the Cadillac CTS-V drive. The GTO drive has a wide A/C compressor position, and although the CTS-V drive is very similar, the A/C compressor position is much tighter to the block, allowing for more chassis clearance. The water outlet also moves to the upper driver's side of the water pump. One other benefit of the CTS-V drive is that the pulleys are closer to the engine, increasing the front clearance by 3/4 inch. The stock T56 transmission is mated to an LS2 engine.

Installing the LS2 was a straightforward process using Holley-designed components. The motor mounts are a two-piece design. The block mounts have a raised platform for the intermediate bushings. The mounts are connected to the factory chassis mounts using cylindrical intermediate polyurethane bushings, which are made by Creative Steel. Out back, the Holley-fabricated transmission mount for the T56 transmission bolts directly to the chassis.

Above: *Nissan's 240SX is a popular swap platform because of its rear-wheel drive, and the chassis has a good balance. The installation of a high-horsepower LS engine is a definite benefit. The 240SX's nimble handling makes it perfect for autocrossing, road racing, and drifting. The stock naturally aspirated 2.4L engine produces 150 hp or less, so the stock engine is by no means a powerhouse.*

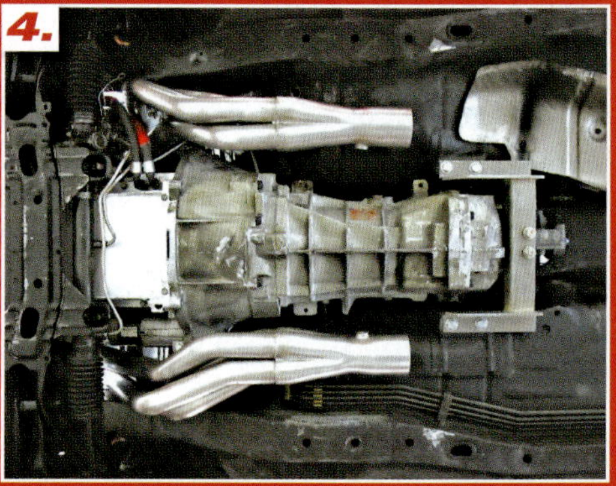

The transmission was converted to the F-Body shifter using the internal shifter receiver inside the T56. An LS7 clutch kit and RAM 19.2-pound flywheel were used to connect the T56 to the LS2 for spirited shifts on and off the track. The clutch is operated through a Wilwood 3/4-inch master cylinder with an adapter kit from Street Elite Performance.

To adequately cool the LS2, Blane installed a Hinson LS aluminum radiator. This radiator is a drop-in for the 240SX, maintaining accessory drive and hose clearance. It uses a set of electric fans to supplement cooling.

To complete the project, he upgraded the suspension with SPL Pro Suspension components, including tension rods, tie-rods, and a set of Stance GR+ Pro coil-over shocks. The 240SX rides on Nitto NT-05 tires with 17x10s out back and 17x8s in front.

The 240SX is now quite quick on the autocross. In its first outing at LSFest, it ran a 44.59 in the autocross. For comparison, Randy Johnson's pro-touring Camaro ran a best lap of 43.90, and that is a dialed-in track car. Only .69 second separate the two, and the 240SX had not been dialed in. That is one slick Nissan.

Photo 1: *The LS2, like all LS engines, is a compact V-8. Although it appeared that the LS2 was much larger than the stock Nissan 2.4L 4-cylinder, the physical dimensions were similar. Once the LS2 was on the hoist and lowered into the chassis, it fit into the engine bay. The exhaust, steering rod, and all other components cleared the chassis. No chassis mods were required to get the engine to fit.* **2.** *These CAD-designed Hooker motor mount adapters are steel and position the engine over the factory frame mounts; they are secured here with a solid block. These particular adapters are only compatible with the Tremec T56 manual transmission. The adapters do not come with engine-to-frame connections.* **3.** *To eliminate the harsh vibrations from a solid-mount engine, the block mounts were replaced with a set of polyurethane bushings from Creative Steel, and are actually for a 1997–2004 C5 Corvette (SKU #6). These mounts provide adequate stiffness and feature a two-part interlocking steel structure that's surrounded by polyurethane. They are designed to counteract the torsional forces placed on the mounts.* **4.** *The Hooker transmission mount included in the kit was used to install the T56 in the chassis. The kit is designed to handle an LS-series engine with a manual T56 transmission only. These headers are also made by Hooker for the Nissan LS swap. All of these components were developed using Blane's 240.* **5.** *Ground clearance is critical for an autocross vehicle, and there is plenty of room for suspension travel. Even if it's used as a street car, you also need to make sure the headers and oil pan have plenty of ground clearance. Typically, you should have 1 to 3 inches of ground clearance for the street.* **6.** *Holley's Dominator EFI ECU controls the fuel system of the LS2 by activating the factory sensors and components. It is also capable of handling the electronic controls of an automatic transmission. The Dominator is a static system, and therefore it does not have the learning feature of the lower-level versions from Holley. That means that the engine must be tuned by the user. The Holley Terminator and HP ECUs have self-learning tuning capabilities. That makes them better suited for the average builder who does not have the skills for EFI tuning.*

CHAPTER 2

Engine and Driveline

The first piece of the puzzle of any engine swap is to actually mount the engine into the chassis. This can be as simple as bolting a set of adapter plates to the block or as complicated as fabricating an entirely new pair of frame stands. It all depends on the chassis. This chapter covers the gamut, from simple to complex fabrication of motor mounts and transmission mounts to making the connection from the transmission to the rear differential.

Motor Mounts

The key to any swap is installing the engine in the chassis. This can be easy or it can take weeks to figure out: it all depends on the car. General Motors certainly helped swappers by using the same motor mount design for all Gen III/IV engines, with the exception of the LS4, which is a front-wheel-drive platform.

The LS engine uses a four-bolt mount that installs on the side of the engine block. The typical solution for this change is simply converting the LS engine to the more common early-style three-bolt motor mounts. The original 1955 small-block featured the three-bolt mount configuration, and the same pattern continued in production through the second-generation small-block: the LT1 and LT4 engines.

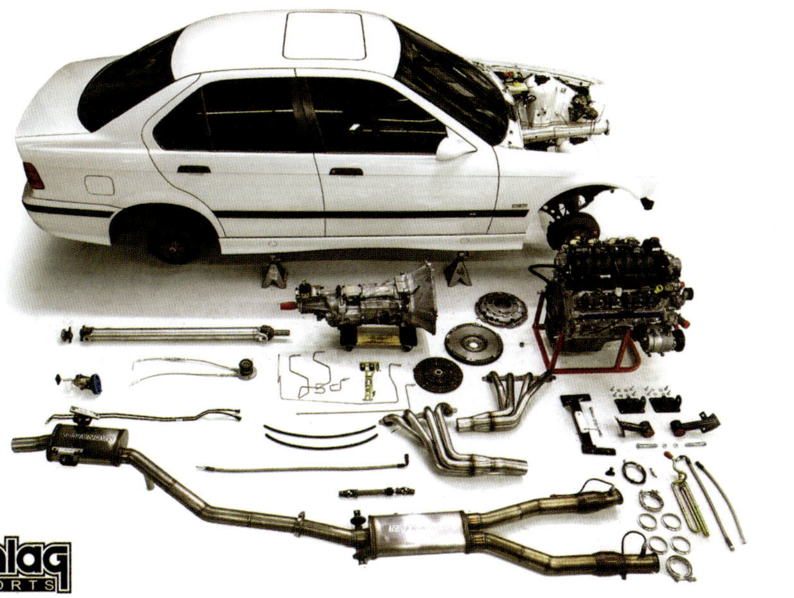

Vorshlag Motorsports makes many LS swap kits for BMWs. This one is designed to swap Gen III/IV engines into E36 BMWs (E-series). The kit is available in many stages from bare-bones engine and transmission mounts to everything you need, including headers and driveshaft. (Photo Courtesy Vorshlag Motorsports)

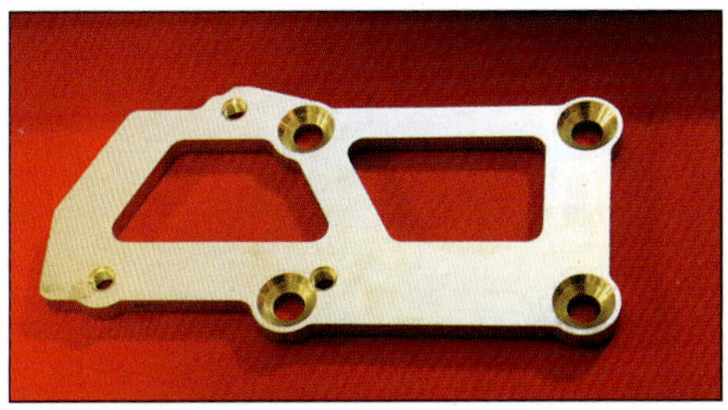

Basic adapter plates are the most common solution for LS engine swaps. They bolt to the Gen III/IV four-bolt motor mount pad and allow a three-bolt GM motor mount to bolt on, and they work with most headers. Made of rugged 3/8-inch-thick hot-rolled steel, they are zinc plated and include countersunk machine screws.

Installing adapters to an engine block is rather simple. Torque the four socket head bolts into the block using an Allen key socket. Most motor mount brackets are torqued to 37 to 43 ft-lbs, but follow the specific recommendations from the motor mount manufacturer. In addition, use some anti-seize compound to prevent galling of the different metals.

The GM three-bolt motor mount bolts to the upper studs, and the lower mount uses the stock LS bolt hole. There are different designs, and some adapters shift position on the engine front or rear depending on the application. These Speed Hound Performance mounts are designed for the C2/C3 Corvette. Using a stock small-block Chevy motor mount, they bolt directly to the factory frame stands.

LS-series engines are similar dimensionally to the classic small-block Chevy engine, so they fit anywhere a small-block Chevy does. The conversion from a small-block Chevy to an LS can be as simple as using adapter plates.

Adapter Plates

Many companies make adapter plates to convert the LS mount to accept a small-block Chevy three-bolt mount. With so many adapters available (there are literally hundreds of different brands), deciding which one to use is the tough part. The stock LS engine motor mounts are located farther back toward the bellhousing than on the Gen I/II blocks. If a motor mount is bolted to the frame using these holes, in most vehicles, the engine sits too far forward. This increases the nose weight of the car, causing instability. Some adapter mounts are for specific applications, such as the GM first-generation F-Body or A-Body cars. Some manufacturers, such as Holley, offer different adapters with offset mount locations such as "1.25 forward" and ".5 up" to better facilitate engine placement for chassis and body clearance. Other manufacturers have adjustable adapter plates, so you can get the positioning just right for your application.

Depending on the style of mount, the motor mount cup may have a hump that must be removed to attain the correct amount of clearance. A disc sander or grinder quickly removes it.

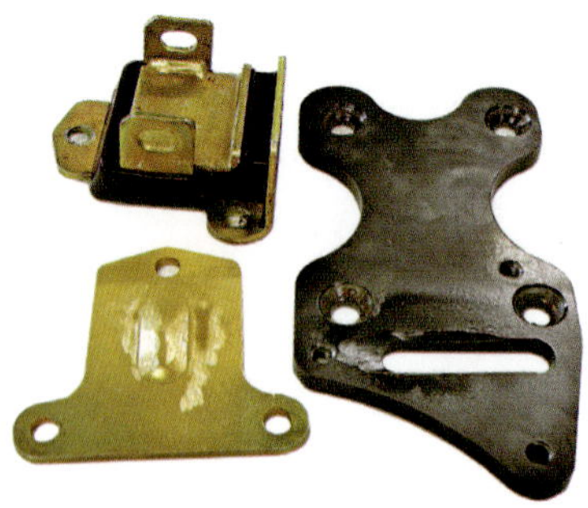

Once the center hump has been removed, the small-block Chevy mount should bolt up to the adapter. The clamshell-type mounts typically need to be ground down to the proper clearance.

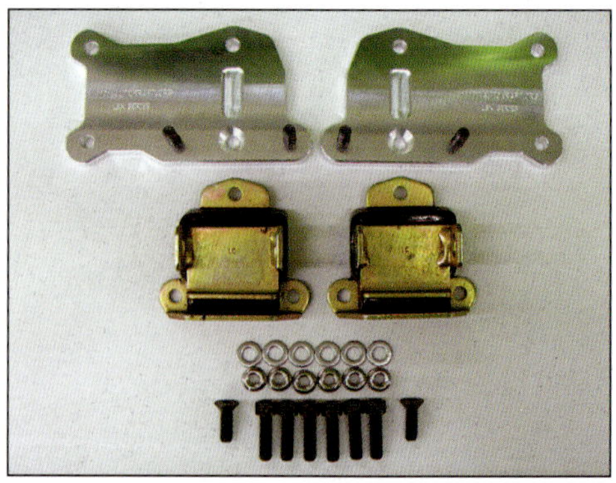

These mounts from Autokraft feature a recessed area milled into the adapter plate, allowing the hump on some small-block Chevy motor mounts to fit without any additional work.

All adapters are not the same. This kit from ATS flips the small-block Chevy mounts upside down to position the engine lower in the chassis. These are designed to fit the first-generation Camaro and the GM A-Body, but they are compatible with other chassis and LS engine combinations. (Photo Courtesy ATS Performance)

Some adapters require a lock nut on the back side of the plate, such as these Trans-Dapt mounts. The external webbing makes these adapters a bit more difficult to install. The locking nuts are recommended to add extra security.

Once the locking nuts have been installed on the back side of the plate, the bolt is tightened in the threaded plate and then the lock nut is tightened.

By simply bolting the adapter plate to the engine block, you have mounting provisions for the old-style three-bolt motor mount. For GM vehicles or cars that have already been converted to a small-block Chevy, this allows the LS-series engine to drop right into the chassis with no re-engineering.

Street & Performance offers many different adapter plates to correctly position the engine in different chassis designs. These plates fit the Tri-Five GM cars. This is called a biscuit mount, and many early GM V-8 chassis use this style of mount. (Photo Courtesy Street & Performance)

Swap Kits

American Touring Specialties (ATS) offers a set of LS adapter plates that feature an early-style motor mount in an upside-down configuration. ATS offers this arrangement so the engine is able to sit lower in the car and farther back from the firewall, allowing for better stability and a lower center of gravity. With these ATS mounts, an LS engine can be swapped into most any GM muscle car.

That is not to say that every GM car fits the same way. Vehicles such as the 1994–1996 Impala SS originally had an LT1. The stock LT1 motor mounts on these vehicles are set a little farther back than the Gen I small-block. To compensate for engine position, the Impala mount from Street & Performance (for example) moves the motor mounts on the LS adapter plates back 1 inch, so the engine is correctly positioned in the frame while maintaining proper weight distribution. The Corvette has always been the flagship model for Chevrolet and General Motors. When the Corvette received the first LS1 in 1997, owners of older Corvettes wanted one also. Unlike other GM vehicles, however, Corvettes have a few additional impediments for an LS swap. Although you can make a standard LS adapter plate work, you have to modify engine components, which is expensive and time consuming. Speed Hound Performance has the solution: a specialized motor mount designed specifically for the 1968–1982 and 1984–1996 Corvettes; they also work great in the C2 (1963–1967) chassis.

Another staple for LS engine swaps is the classic Tri-Five Chevy, otherwise known as the 1955–1957 Chevrolet. Other GM offerings from the Tri-Five era include Buick,

Many LS engines do not clear the brake booster and other accessories in certain chassis; therefore, you need to find a smaller, compact brake booster to install. This is a stock full-size 9-inch booster. (Photo Courtesy Street & Performance)

You may need a smaller brake booster to overcome the fit challenge. Make sure it provides enough braking power for your particular application. A smaller booster often mean less braking power. This is a 7-inch booster. (Photo Courtesy Street & Performance)

Pontiac, and Oldsmobile. These cars used a different-style motor mount called a "biscuit" mount. These early-style mounts bolt to upright pads near the front of the engine on the frame. A steel bracket then reaches from the motor mount pads to the uprights. A rubber disc, referred to as the "biscuit," rests between the pads and the uprights to absorb the twists and shock from the running engine. These mounts easily bolt to the adapter plates to make an LS swap simpler and more convenient.

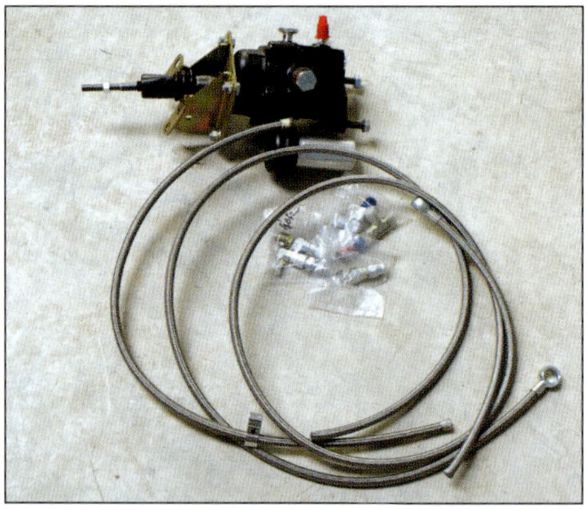

This hydroboost from Power Brake Service is an alternative to the vacuum power booster. It not only provides the needed clearance, it also delivers exceptional braking power. The braking force with a hydroboost is impressive; even stock brakes see a serious increase in performance. The hydroboost gets its power from the power steering pump, which is more reliable than simple vacuum.

Non-GM Swap Kits

It isn't just muscle cars and GM vehicles that are candidates for LS swaps. LS-series engines have been installed into BMWs, Volvos, Hondas, even Fox-Body Ford Mustangs and Mazda Rx-7s. Non-traditional LS swaps require more effort, so it pays to do your homework and research what others have done.

It is imperative to check for proper fitment of all aspects of the swap: engine/transmission, brake control, steering, and cooling all must be considered. You must verify that the engine bay can hold the engine; if not, you have to modify it. If any of the chassis components (brakes, steering, etc.) have to be relocated, that adds complexity to the swap.

The transmission and drivetrain must be compatible as well. Installing an LS3 into an S10 chassis is fairly easy, but the stock 7.5-inch rear end

Most LS engine adapters position the engine closer to the radiator. Many owners opt to use an electric fan so this clearance is not needed. (Photo Courtesy Street & Performance)

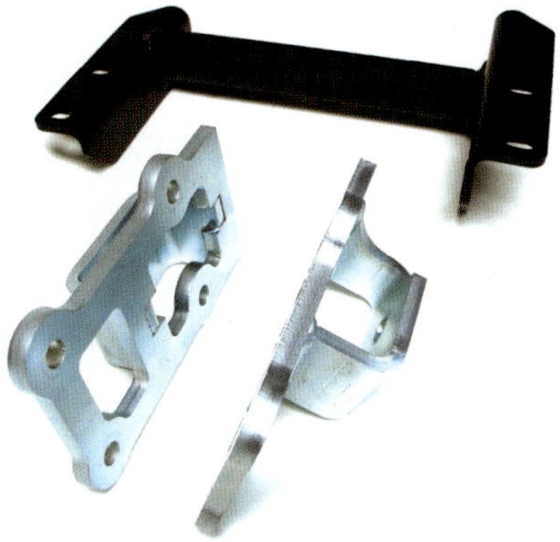

Hooker's LS swap kit for the Nissan 240SX features a transmission crossmember bracket and motor mounts. These allow the installation of an LS engine into an S13 Nissan body along with a T56 manual transmission. This kit is compatible with the Canton Racing oil pan, expressly designed to fit in the S14 Nissan chassis. (Photo Courtesy Holley Performance Products)

Some vehicles readily accept the LS engine because the chassis, frame rails, and mount system are similar to the stock setup. Other vehicles are dissimilar and require custom fabrication. This twin-turbo LS-powered Volvo wagon needs a completely new front crossmember. (Photo Courtesy Doug Strickler)

is not going to last very long with that kind of power. These are some of the considerations you need to keep in mind when looking at an LS swap for a non-GM vehicle.

LS swaps have become so popular that companies are building kits for many of these vehicles. Vorshlag Motorsports manufactures an LS swap kit for 1991–1999 BMW E36 (3-series) models, complete with all the components required for installation. This complete kit contains motor mounts, transmission crossmember, headers, steering shaft, driveshaft, and all the necessary hardware. It also includes optional components: a hydraulic throw-out bearing kit for manual transmissions, radiator, coolant lines, power steering, and fuel pump.

Another excellent resource for non-GM swap kits and components is Hinson Supercars. Hinson has the components for most imports such as the Mazda Rx7s and Rx8, Honda S2000, and Nissan Z-cars.

Transmission Mounts

Mounting an LS engine between the frame rails is only one part of the job; you also need to support the rear of the transmission. With the exception of an extra bolt at the top, the bellhousing pattern on the LS engines is the same as on the small-block Chevy. This allows just about any traditional Chevy bolt-pattern bellhousing to bolt to an LS engine. Adapting the transmission

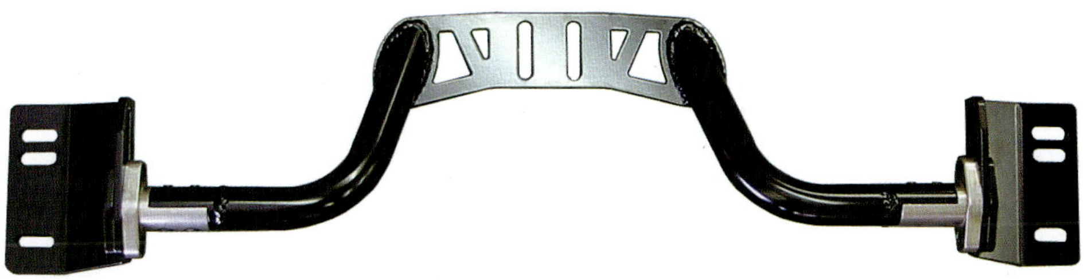

ATS offers this adjustable transmission crossmember for the first-generation Camaro/Firebird. It allows the location of the transmission mount to shift, accommodating different transmissions and different engine setback/forward specs. (Photo Courtesy ATS Performance)

If you have a GM A-Body, you may be able to reposition the factory crossmember to another set of holes. Remember, an early transmission sits about 2 inches back from the LS engine. This is due to the lack of extra material on the back of the LS block.

When building a custom transmission mount, be sure to center the transmission in the frame. Measure the transmission centerline. Follow the input shaft to the output shaft along the length of the case and start from there. On this 1963 Buick Wagon (which has an X-frame), the transmission mount started with a piece of angle steel bolted to the factory locations, extending about 6 inches past them.

Use an angle finder to set the transmission at the proper 3-degree downward angle for proper driveline adjustment. The rear end should have a matching upward angle. The U-joints must be "working" to last. If the joints are positioned at 0 degrees, there is no load on the bearings, which allows them to move around, generating excess heat and causing premature wear. Therefore they wear out much faster.

mount to each vehicle usually requires a combination of stock components modified with new mounts.

Interchangeability

For most GM chassis, there are simple adapters available to fit most GM transmissions, particularly with 1964-later cars. Before 1964, each GM division was separate; they shared a few core items, including the frame, and sometimes basic component design, but the details changed.

For example, a 1960 Chevy B-Body (Impala, Biscayne) used the same frame as the Buick B-Body (Le Sabre, Wildcat), but none of the parts interchange, not even the rear end. They look similar, but the parts don't fit. This is important for swappers to know. In the case of transmission mounts, a Buick Dynaflow is completely different from a Chevy Powerglide.

In 1964, General Motors started using "corporate" parts, so a control arm for a 1964 Pontiac LeMans fits a 1964 Chevy Chevelle or Oldsmobile F85. The bigger cars started using corporate parts a few years later, as the body styles expired and new styles were rolled out.

For most GM muscle cars, the stock crossmember can be modified to fit late-model transmissions, such as the T56 manual transmission and the 4L60E automatic. With the engine mounted to the frame, the transmission must be supported in front of its mount for access during the fabrication process. For example, you can use a block of wood to keep the transmission oil pan from buckling under the weight.

Clearance

Firewall clearance must also be considered when using an older GM transmission with an LS engine. The Gen I small-block was designed with offset cylinder heads. As a result, there are about 2 inches of space between the bellhousing mounting pad and the back of the cylinder heads.

Keep this in mind when deciding whether to use the stock transmission in a GM muscle car or truck: the Gen III/IV engines do not have offset cylinder heads, and therefore do not have any space between the bellhousing and the cylinder heads. The cylinder heads are flush with the back of the block. The heads are not necessarily longer, but the back of the block is actually a little shorter.

Most adapter plates provide a space of about 2 inches between the back of the engine and the stock transmission in the stock location. As a result, it's often necessary to relocate the transmission mount and/or

Custom Mount Fabrication

Custom frame stands can easily be made using a few pieces of scrap steel, but you need to have some welding and fabricating experience to make them. ■

1 *This mount was fabricated for a Buick wagon. Use an angle grinder to cut two pieces of angle iron and then place them into the motor mount. Then cut a piece of tubing to fit between the channels.*

2 *Chamfer the tubing so it fits tight to the bottom of the angle in the channel. The angle steel has a rounded inner edge; chamfering the edges allows the tube to sit flush on both flat surfaces, yielding a better fit.*

3 *With the fit set, mark the bolt location on the new metal and drill out to the correct 1/2-inch bolt size. Drilling it before it is welded allows for the hole placement to be adjusted, so the two holes line up with each other.*

4 *Using the drill bit to maintain the channel's location, weld up the mount, including the tubing. Even though the metal is 1/8 inch thick, it is important to weld the joints in short sections to avoid warpage.*

5 *Position the completed frame mount in the car and weld it to the frame. Before welding the mount to the frame, it is a good idea to paint the back side with a high-zinc weld-through coating to protect the metal from rust.*

Custom Mount Fabrication *CONTINUED*

6 *Cut another piece of angle steel to size and position it between the side mounts. Using the transmission as a guide, note the position for the transmission mount. The steel is 10 gauge (1/8 inch thick).*

7 *Place the cross beam on the side beams. If it sits a little high, mark and notch the side beams so you tack weld the cross beam in the correct position.*

8 *Remove the entire assembly from the chassis and fully weld it. Make sure that you get good penetration of the metal for the welds. Place beads of weld in lengths of 1 inch or less to avoid warpage.*

9 *The transmission mount hole usually requires a little play, so they typically have a short slot for adjustment. Note that the ends are boxed in to the main tube, which adds support to the mount plate.*

10 *When using box tubing for any type of mount, it is always a good idea to make a support tube inside. This keeps the tubing from crushing under the stress of the bolt and the weight of the transmission.*

11 *The 4L80E in this 1962 Comet wagon required a 3-degree down angle, and that meant it needed a dropped crossmember. This was made with five sections of 1x2 tubing cut to the proper angles and welded together. Each section was fully boxed.*

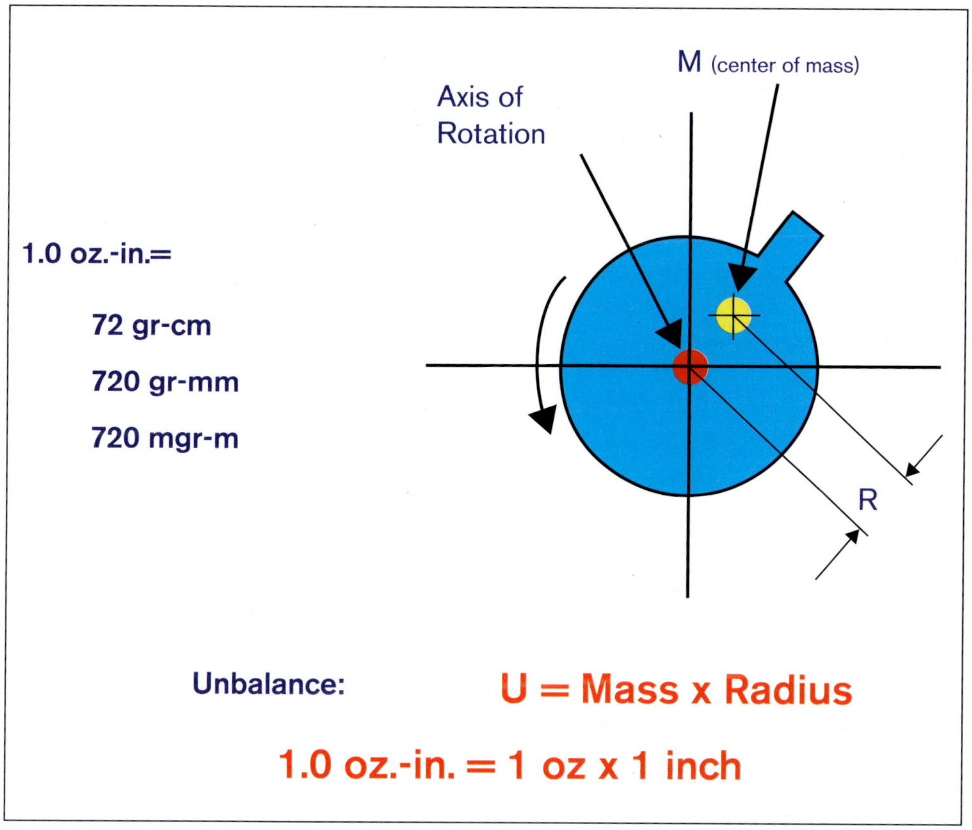

This diagram shows the formula for balancing. The red dot in the center is the actual rotational center; the yellow dot shows the center of mass. This represents an unbalanced shaft. The distance between the rotational center and the center mass determines how much weight needs to be added to shift the center mass to the rotational mass.

This cast-steel Dana slip yoke is a high-strength unit that withstands up to 800 hp, depending on the application. Although a stock-type slip yoke can transmit up to 500 hp, a 40-year-old yoke may have many micro-cracks and weak spots that can become a failure point at far lower power levels. You can Magnaflux the U-joint, or you may determine that the U-joint has reached the end of its service life and needs to be replaced. (Photo Courtesy Dana Spicer)

move the transmission crossmember to bring the two components together.

Driveline Angle and Crossmember Modification

When installing an LS engine, getting the driveline angle correct is critical in terms of strength and reliability. The transmission *must be* angled between 1 and 5 degrees downward on the yoke. For performance applications, 2 degrees is optimal. An angle finder (available at most hardware stores) can determine this angle. Place it against the tailshaft and let the needle rest until it points to the drive angle. If the stock crossmember bolts to the engine and the drive angle is between 1 and 5 degrees, it works.

If the drive angle is not between 1 and 5 degrees, the crossmember must be modified. There are several methods to attack this problem; it all depends on the crossmember. If the crossmember is removable, it can be lowered with spacers, or the transmission itself raised with spacers placed under the mount. Sometimes the crossmember must be modified by cutting and welding new tabs or mounts.

For example, the C2 Chevy Corvette does not have a removable crossmember, and the mount is not adjustable. The mount must be cut out and a recessed mount welded into the crossmember.

With many non-GM vehicles, the stock transmission crossmember can be retained and modified. If that's not possible, a new crossmember is required. The key here is the driveline angles and keeping the tailshaft square between the frame rails.

When approaching the 800-hp mark, look into billet slip yokes. Machined from a single block of billet steel, these yokes can handle just about any power level. (Photo Courtesy Dynotech Engineering)

Once welded, the driveshaft must be balanced. This Balance Engineering balancer spins the shaft to 5,000 rpm, ensuring a proper balance for high-performance applications. This machine has the capability of revving to 7,500 rpm.

The final piece of the driveline puzzle is the pinion yoke. The chances of breaking one are small. The compact design means more meat in the important places, yielding a strong component. A cast yoke is not bulletproof, but a billet steel yoke, such as this one from Mark Williams, is pretty close. New yokes also usually come with better joint caps rather than lighter-weight stock-style U-bolts, which are prone to distorting the U-joint bearing caps. (Photo Courtesy Dynotech Engineering)

The driveshaft is a critical component of the vehicle, and you cannot risk a driveline failure because you may lose control of the car. When shortening and re-welding a driveshaft, you should rely on a professional shop to perform the work. Choosing a qualified driveline shop is important. Dynotech Engineering uses CNC-operated welders to ensure a perfect weld every time.

When fabricating crossmembers to support the transmission, it is important to note that the materials used must be strong enough to hold the weight and torque of the transmission. Tubing (round or square) is a good material to use, as the tubing provides structural stability with less overall material thickness and weight. Using flat plate steel requires thicker material to achieve the same structural integrity. Angle steel is another excellent material for custom transmission crossmembers.

Choosing a Driveline

When performing an engine swap, the driveshaft often needs to be replaced. Simply shortening the stock driveshaft is not really the best solution. With all of the engineering, time, and effort you are putting into an LS engine swap, why use the same old driveshaft that will never work like a properly designed custom unit?

A design is only as good as the workmanship that goes into it. Building the right driveshaft for the application is critical; every high-performance vehicle should have a driveshaft professionally built by a shop that specializes in high-performance drivelines. Or, you can order a driveshaft from a reputable high-performance builder.

Either way, be sure to specify it is for a high-performance application, which is very different from a stock driveshaft, and needs to be held to a higher standard.

In the end, the driveline is perfect for a swap.

Driveshaft Balance

In most cases, installing an LS engine in a vehicle increases the torque and horsepower output. Anytime power output to the stock driveline is increased, the impact of that increase on the stock driveshaft must be taken into account. Most factory driveshafts are balanced between 3,000 and 3,500 rpm, which means spinning the driveshaft faster than 3,500 rpm can have a parasitic effect. In fact, Steve Raymond, from Dynotech Engineering said, "We have had several NASCAR teams tell us that our driveshaft saves them 3 to 7 hp on their chassis dynamometers. That's why balance is important and why we manufacture shafts for about 85 to 90 percent of the NASCAR teams." The stock balance on the stock driveshaft is not good enough for anything but a stock engine.

Dynotech uses Balance Engineering's driveshaft balancers, which are considered to be the best for accuracy. Dynotech recommends balancing a performance driveshaft at a minimum of 5,000 rpm, and as high as 7,500 rpm. This ensures a properly tuned driveshaft that reduces parasitic loss of horsepower through harmonics and vibration.

Both slip and pinion yokes are critical driveline components. They physically connect the transmission, driveshaft, and differential. Break one of these and you have a disaster on your hands. That being said, a cast yoke is usually good enough to handle up to 800 hp in most applications. That number has some fudge room, though, as a lightweight hot rod with street tires and 800 hp puts less strain on the driveline than a 4,000-pound Chevelle with slicks and 500 hp.

Another option when using a cast pinion yoke is to use U-joint caps instead of the weaker stock-style U-bolt retainers. This increases the holding power and eliminates the possibility of distorting the caps. New billet yokes typically come with the proper retaining caps.

Driveshaft Length and Diameter

Other than balance, the length and diameter of the driveshaft directly affect the performance of the unit. Determining the required length for a driveshaft necessitates looking at several factors. The distance from the rear yoke to the transmission seal is the most

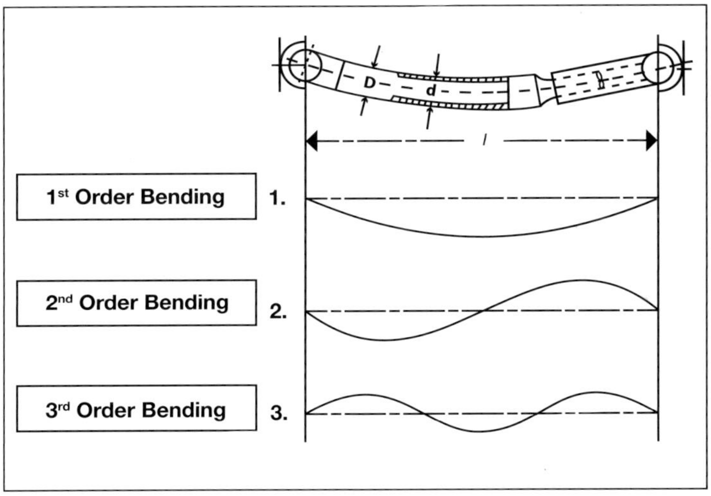

A driveshaft that is too small in diameter for its length is often inefficient. It can bend and produce parasitic drag on the drivetrain, eating up horsepower. The first type of bend is referred to as first-order bending. Once this starts, the shaft begins to flex up and down, and it "jump ropes." When driving the car, you feel a significant vibration that will eventually fatigue the shaft and U-joints. (Photo Courtesy Dynotech Engineering)

$$\left(\frac{923.44}{\text{Driveshaft Length}}\right)\sqrt{\left(\frac{\text{Module of Elasticity}}{(\text{Mat'l Density})(100)}\right)(10^8)\left(\left(\frac{\text{Tube Dia.}}{2}\right)^2+\left(\frac{\text{Tube Dia.}}{2}-\text{Wall Thickness}\right)^2\right)}$$

Attachment No. 1 – Critical Speed Calculation

Reaching critical speed causes first-order bending. This complex formula is used to calculate the critical speed for every driveshaft. All driveshafts have a critical speed, depending on their length and diameter. The shaft material elasticity is an important part of the equation. This is the material's ability to resist non-permanent elastic deformation. For a driveshaft, this translates into bending. The higher the modulus of elasticity (MOE), the less it bends.

Getting these numbers can be a little tricky because most shops keep the specific numbers they use as trade secrets. For steel, the basic MOE is 30, aluminum is 10, and carbon fiber depends on the manufacturing processes used, so no general numbers are available.

Here is a fully welded aluminum shaft and yoke. Note the clean CNC-welded joint. You cannot achieve this level of welding at home, so it's best to leave this work to a professional shop. (Photo Courtesy Dynotech Engineering)

important measurement. In turn, it is important to measure this length with the pinion yoke installed and set (and the car sitting at ride height). Changing to a billet pinion yoke can alter the length by as much as 3/4 inch.

With this measurement, the driveshaft shop can create the complete shaft with the required slip yoke and pre-determined run-out for the slip yoke. For most applications, slip yoke run-out (the length of yoke shaft that extends out of the transmission) of 1 inch is more than enough to provide the play needed for suspension travel.

Do not let a shop talk you into leaving more run-out than that. Some transmission shops insist on running out 1.5 inches, which could be disastrous. With that much of the slip yoke hanging out of the transmission, there could be fewer than 3 inches of splined yoke in the transmission, thus creating a wobble in the yoke, which causes a heavy vibration at various RPM. Stick with the 1-inch rule and always measure the driveshaft length at drive height.

If the vehicle is too low to get under it on the ground, jack up both ends and use jack stands under the rear end and front suspension, and be careful to make sure all the stands are at the same height. The slightest variation can throw off the measurement, resulting in a driveshaft that does not fit.

Driveshaft Critical Speed

Critical speed (CS) is the RPM at which the driveshaft becomes unstable and begins to bend in the middle. This is also known as "jump roping" (because it actually looks like a jumping rope). The longer and smaller (diameter) a driveshaft is, the slower its critical speed. CS is felt as excessive vibration, and if run at CS too long, the unit fails.

To calculate critical speed, the length, diameter, wall thickness, and the material module of elasticity must first be identified. Then, using the critical speed calculation formula on page 21, you can plug in your numbers to determine the driveshaft's critical speed.

For trucks and exceptionally long vehicles, consider using a carrier bearing. It essentially cuts the driveshaft into two pieces. One half is in a fixed position (it neither moves up/down nor does it slide in/out with suspension movement) to the transmission, and only the carrier unit rotates. The other half uses a slip yoke to the carrier unit and mounts to the differential.

Although most full-size trucks use carrier bearings to minimize vibrations and reduce the overall diameter of the driveshaft, they are definitely not as strong as a one-piece unit. Given that a two-piece shaft has twice as many connections and U-joints, the opportunities for failure are twice as high.

The type of U-joint is more important than most people think. A "lubed for life" Spicer U-joint (left) is stronger than its same-size greaseable counterpart (right). (Photo Courtesy Dynotech Engineering)

Here are three common sizes of U-joints, from the left: 1350, 1330, and 1310. The 1310 is the most common U-joint, found in most cars. Performance yokes are made of the 1350 series U-joint, although larger and smaller units can be found. Make sure to use the same-series joint throughout the entire driveline. A drivetrain is only as strong as its weakest link. (Photo Courtesy Dynotech Engineering)

Driveshaft Material

The composition of the driveshaft is just as important as the length and diameter.

Steel: OEM steel driveshafts are for just that, OEM power. An OEM shaft is rated for no more than 350 ft-lbs, or 350 to 400 hp. For high-performance use, drawn over mandrel (DOM) seamless tubing and chrome-moly steel are the two preferred types used.

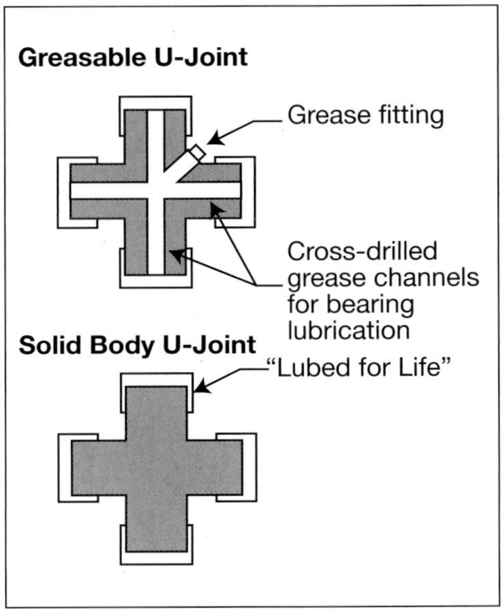

This diagram shows the difference between the two types of joints. The greaseable version (top) has less material in the center of the joint, reducing its strength and torque rating. A solid U-joint (bottom) does not require maintenance and is much stronger.

DOM steel is better than OEM steel, handling much more torque, up to 1,300 ft-lbs, and 1,000 to 1,300 hp. DOM steel can be spun faster as well with its higher RPM rating. This is a good choice for any car that does not need a lightweight unit.

The step up from a DOM steel shaft is chrome-moly, which is the strongest material available. Pro Stock cars run it with 3,000 hp. Chrome-moly steel tubing can be heat treated as well, raising the torsional strength 22 percent and increasing the critical speed 19 percent. Steel is heavy, which increases the load on the engine and the length of time the engine needs to get to speed.

Aluminum: This is the most common performance driveshaft material. A lightweight aluminum shaft has less rotational mass and frees up horsepower from the engine, reducing parasitic loss. Aluminum driveshafts are strong but cannot withstand as much torque as steel. Therefore, some custom driveshaft shops do not have "twist" guarantees on aluminum driveshafts. An aluminum driveshaft supports up to 900 ft-lbs, or 900 to 1,000 hp, making it a great lightweight choice for most muscle cars.

Carbon fiber: It is the most efficient, but it is also the most expensive. For up to 1,200 ft-lbs or 900 to 1,500 hp, carbon fiber is a great choice. Carbon fiber driveshafts are not only strong, but have a surprisingly high torsional strength, resisting twisting and reducing the shock factor on the rear end. Carbon fiber also has the highest CS, meaning the shaft doesn't flex at slower speeds, unlike other component material. With the highest CS factors and the lowest weight, a carbon fiber driveshaft can free up as much as 5 hp over a stock steel driveshaft. When winning is everything, 5 hp might make the difference.

U-Joints

Once the driveshaft is measured and ready to build, there are a few other issues to consider. Phasing the U-joints with the weld-in yokes is an important part of the equation. With every rotation of a U-joint at any degree other than zero, a fourth-order vibration is generated. This shows up as a torsional pulse, which is felt as a significant vibration. By phasing the weld-in yokes to minimize the combined degrees of rotation, any fourth-order vibration is drastically reduced. The weld-in yokes need to be installed on the same plane; they can't be rotated off axis from one another.

U-joint quality also makes a difference, and not just the brand. U-joint design and its load capacity must also be considered. For most cars, 1310-series U-joints are the typical choice, but for performance applications, the rugged 1350-series joints are preferred. The larger the series number, the larger the trunnion.

Trunnions are the protruding shafts under the caps. Larger trunnions equate to more torsional strength, which makes them more resistant to twisting motion. Changing to a larger U-joint is not a simple task; you can't just buy bigger joints. All yokes (slip, bolt-on, and weld-in) must match the desired joint size.

Crossover U-joints are also an option, but they tend not to be as strong, and they don't last as long. However, they do allow a larger U-joint to be mated to a smaller U-joint, or vice versa. For example, a new driveshaft comes with 1350 weld-in yokes, but the car has 1310-sized yokes for the transmission and rear differential. A 1350-to-1310 joint has a 1350 on one side and a 1310 on the other, allowing you to install the driveshaft until the slip and bolt-on yokes are replaced.

Although it can be done, using crossover U-joints is not suggested as a long-term solution. The smaller size breaks eventually.

Additionally, the type of joint (solid-body versus greaseable) is important as well. The Spicer-style, solid-body U-joint comes "lubed for life," and does not have grease zerk fittings. This makes them a little stronger because they do not have the stress risers created by the opening for the zerk fitting in a greaseable U-joint.

Feature Vehicle

1967 Corvette C2 Stingray

There are few GM cars more beautiful than a C2 Stingray, from the elusive 1963 split window to the 1967, which many claim to be the ultimate Corvette. Under that fiberglass body shell, however, lies a classic drivetrain and transverse leaf-spring rear suspension, and the dual-arm coil spring does not provide a modern level of comfort. For this Red Line Muscle Cars 1967 roadster, owner Fred and Kim Murfin wanted a classic Corvette but with modern ride quality, performance, and reliability.

Parts Compatibility

The only choice for the drivetrain was an LS1. Swapping an LS-series engine into a C2 Corvette is not routine and is certainly not as common as an LS swap into a Camaro or Firebird. Yet the LS swap into a C2 is much easier because the aftermarket now offers many of the required parts to complete the job. Companies such as Street & Performance, Speed Hound, and others now offer the vital parts you need so you don't have to fabricate or adapt parts to complete the swap.

Of course, manufacturers also offer other parts, such as motor and transmission mounts. Some are compatible among manufacturer, but some are not compatible. I recommend that you select a kit or buy your parts from the same source because the parts are designed to work together. At least 20 different types of motor mounts are offered for the first-generation F-Body cars. But the aftermarket currently does not offer nearly as many motor mounts for the C2 (1963–1967) Corvette. You do not need all these options to complete the LS swap, however. The key to any LS swap is to avoid adding complications.

A set of Speed Hound C2/C3 Corvette motor mount adapters and the correct oil pan make installing an LS engine in the chassis a simple bolt endeavor. No fabrication of the original body work or extensive modifications are necessary. The factory F-Body oil pan works quite well in the C2–C3 chassis without any modifications. There are lots of choices for aftermarket pans, but the Holley LS swap oil pan is a good fit.

Above: *The C2 is the most valuable of all Corvette generations, and it's also a popular platform for an LS swap. The frame is exactly the same from 1963 through 1982, covering the C2 and C3 generations. The Gen III/IV engines are dimensionally similar to the small-block Chevy engines, which were originally installed in the C2. Therefore, an LS engine swap into a C2 does not require many modifications. Motor mounts are readily available, and most of the other modifications are required for all LS engine swaps.*

Here, the body has been separated from the birdcage frame. Although the body does not need to be off the frame for the swap, you have greater access to all components and it makes the process easier.

Photo 1: *These Speed Hound mounts were bolted to the 2000 Camaro LS1 and then bolted to the original 327 frame stands. The F-Body oil pan worked perfectly in the C2 chassis, and it even clears the Steeroids rack-and-pinion.* **2.** *One issue is the clearance of the water pump heater outlets. They have to be removed and replaced with 90-degree barbs or AN-style fittings.* **3.** *The 4L60E fit the factory transmission crossmember. It was marked for the location of the factory-style mount then the engine and transmission were removed.* **4.** *I recommend using a reciprocating saw with the correct blade to quickly cut through the factory steel frame. You can also use a pneumatic die grinder. But I do not recommend using a plasma torch because it's very difficult to achieve clean, precise cuts.* **5.** *Use a die grinder to clean up the work area and square off the corners and edges. This modification looks clean and professional.* **6.** *Use a MIG welder on 1/8-inch plate steel and box the area that was cut out. Make sure not to apply too much heat in any one area to achieve ideal weld penetration. The area must be completely welded to prevent any moisture or contaminants from entering the frame, which eventually cause rusting. The crossmember remains strong once the boxing process has been completed.* **7.** *Place the transmission into the chassis and test fit. You must make sure that the transmission and engine maintain the proper angle in the chassis. If the transmission has adequate clearance and lines up properly with the engine, no further modifications are necessary.*

The Murfins are not using a T56 manual transmission. Instead, they opted to install a 4L60E automatic transmission in their 1967 Stingray, which is the most common transmission bolted to LS engines from the factory. This choice complicated the installation, however, because most swap kits are designed to use a manual transmission. In order to mount the 4L60E, some chassis modifications needed to be done.

The LS1 engine came out of a 1999 Camaro, complete with the harness, computer, transmission, and accessory drive. Although the F-Body (Camaro/Firebird) oil pan and accessory drive works well in the C2 chassis, the newer, better-fitting A/C and power steering components from Street & Performance replaced the stock components.

Motor Mounts

Speed Hound Performance motor mount adapter plates for the Gen III/IV engines position the engine correctly in the chassis to clear all body and chassis components. These plates do not fit the C2 chassis with parts-store motor mounts. Those cheap overseas brands use thinner metal and that is a problem because they do not quite reach the engine.

However, a set of Energy Suspension polyurethane mounts come with a thick spacer plate that allows the engine to sit neatly on the stock frame stands without any issue, although you may have to grind a little on both the motor mounts and the Speed Hound adapter plates where they bolt together to get the fit just right.

Headers

A set of Street & Performance mid-length headers for the Corvette were added to make everything work. These headers come with the correct flange adapters to mount the exhaust pipe. This roadster runs a set of factory-style side pipes, which do not bolt up to the new headers.

To make this combination work, approximately 1½ feet of pipe was cut off the side pipes (starting at the header flange), and then a custom pipe was bent around the Steeroids rack-and-pinion steering shaft to meet up with the remaining side-pipe exhaust.

There are bolt-on side-pipe kits for LS swaps, but, depending on your adapter plates, they may or may not fit. The factory pipes can be adapted to an LS engine; it just requires a trip to the muffler shop for the final connections.

Transmission Mounting Location

With the engine resting in place, the 4L60E transmission clearly does not fit in the stock transmission mounting location. The C2 chassis was originally a 4-speed car and had a stock welded-in crossmember. In order to set a suitable driveshaft angle and correctly mount the transmission, the crossmember needed to be notched and a support plate welded in. This is necessary because the angle of the rear pinion yoke dictates the angle of the transmission tailshaft, and pinion yoke angle is not adjustable.

The Corvette uses a fixed-position center section for the independent rear suspension (IRS); the pinion angle is relatively fixed as well. It can be shimmed, but in most cases the transmission can be adjusted to match it just as easily. The angle should be between 1 and 5 degrees down on the transmission (the pinion angle should match

*Photo **8:** With the fit nice and neat, fully weld the notch. Weld short sections and then move on to minimize warping. Make sure that the welds penetrate the steel for strength. **9.** Use a grinder to smooth the fresh welds. The trick here is to remove just the top layer to get a flush seam. If your welds do not penetrate well, there are cracks in the joint and the modification is not strong. **10.** You can use some Eastwood Extreme Chassis Black to paint the new mount notch. This specialized paint protects the metal from rust and leaves a clean, durable finish.*

that in an upward angle): the optimum angle is 2 degrees. A magnetic angle finder is used to determine the angles.

A piece of 4 x 3¼-inch angle steel about 8 inches long was used for the notch insert and to fill in the boxed section, making for a nice, clean install. The crew at Red Line Muscle Cars mocked up the mounts, fabricated the mounts, welded in the mounts, and dropped in the engine in a single day, so you could easily do it in a lazy weekend.

Wiring

The LS1 was wired using a pre-made harness from Street & Performance connected to the factory ECM, which had been tuned by Street & Performance. The rest of the chassis was wired with Painless Performance wiring products, including a Phantom Key setup that eliminates the ignition key in favor of a transponder and a push-to-start button.

Fuel System

The fuel system was converted to electric using a Walbro external in-line pump with a C6 Corvette single-output pressure regulator return-style filter. This eliminated the need for a second fuel line from the engine. The factory tank was converted to accept the short return line from the regulator filter, which was mounted under the body near the tank (see Chapter 8).

Shifter

In order to shift the 4L60E transmission, the stock shifter was swapped out for a Shiftworks conversion unit. This maintains the look and feel of the factory shifter with the correct detents for the overdrive automatic.

Brake Booster

One aspect that was a real bear on this conversion was the power brake booster. LS engines are wider than first-generation Chevy small-block engines. A typical 11-inch power booster crowds the coil packs on the valve covers. To resolve the fitment issue, you can install custom mounts and move the coil packs underneath the engine or you can use a smaller brake booster.

The Murfins decided to install a 7-inch power brake booster and a cast-iron master cylinder. In order to clear the Stinger hood, the master cylinder was machined on a mill to remove about 1/2 inch from the reservoir.

In hindsight, moving the coil packs would have been a better option, because the smaller 7-inch brake booster did not afford as much room. Yes, the booster fit, but it was a very tight fit with the coil packs. Also, the plastic engine cover had to be trimmed to clear the booster.

Gauges

The factory Corvette gauges look good, but they don't work with modern electronic senders. Mechanical sending units could be used on the LS, but that is taking a step backward. For this 1967, a set of AutoMeter Sport Comp gauges with black bezels and red numbers were ordered. Using 5-inch gauges for the speedometer and tach, and 2⅝-inch gauges for the rest, they fit right into the factory bezel with no mods required.

If you just can't do without the factory look, companies such as Redline Gauge Works can replace the mechanical guts with new electronics using the factory gauge faces.

Performance Mods

The end result of this build was a clean Stingray that has the power to back up the look. With no performance mods beyond the ECM tune, the LS1 can break the tires loose in third gear. The Sharkbite front coil-over suspension and rocker-arm-style rear suspension provide the ride and handling that will give a C6 a run for its money, with better styling to boot.

Set the transmission and engine back into the chassis. When the transmission is bolted to the crossmember and the engine is bolted in place on the front subframe, the bellhousing on the transmission should line up with the engine. If it does not, you need to remove the engine and transmission and additional modifications. In this case, everything lined up nice and neat.

CHAPTER 3

Oil Pan

Once the motor mounts have been sorted out, the next step is to choose an oil pan. Many stock oil pans are available for LS engines, each one designed for a specific chassis. With so many different oil-pan options, there is confusion as to which oil pans fit which chassis.

The relationship between the front crossmember and the motor mounts determines the fit of the oil pan. Each brand of motor mount is different, and the engine-mount towers used on the frames can differ by application as well. Although there are several stock pans that fit certain vehicles, they don't always fit as is, and there are different depths and clearances. In the end, there will probably be some trial-and-error test fitting to find just the right pan.

Usually, a stock oil pan and stock crossmember can be modified to a particular chassis. In many cases, cutting a small notch on the back side of the crossmember, then filling it with 1/4-inch steel (boxing it in), reinforces and strengthens the crossmember while allowing the engine to sit in place. However, this does not work for every application.

Stock Oil Pans

Using a stock oil pan can greatly simplify the installation, provided it's the right one. There are many designs, but only a few are desirable for engine swaps. These are the 1998–2002 Camaro, the 2002–2006 truck, the C5 Corvette "Y" (also referred to as the "batwing" due to the dual kickouts on the sides), and the Cadillac CTS-V pans. These stock oil pans have proven to be the most versatile and fit many vehicles without modifications. There are, of course, many other pans that might fit.

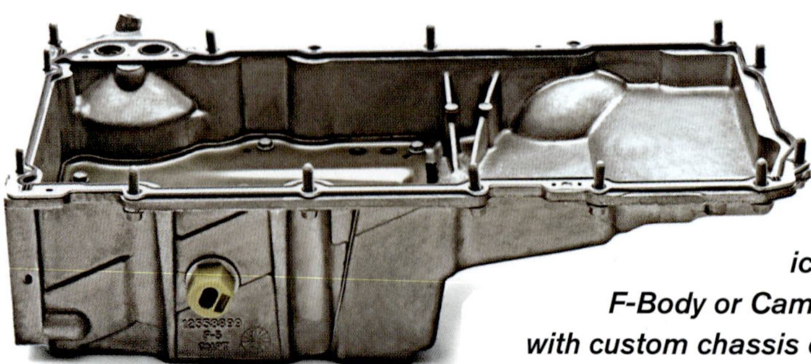

The 1998–2002 F-Body LS1 pan is the most commonly used LS oil pan. Typically referred to as the F-Body or Camaro pan, it works well with custom chassis crossmembers, and it is also the most frequently modified pan. It fits most 1958–1964 GM cars without any modifications. (Photo Courtesy Chevrolet Performance)

Popular LS swap platforms have had the oil-pan fitment issue hashed and re-hashed since the first LS swap was done. The problems arise when you swap an LS engine into something that is not a typical GM A-Body, truck, or F-Body. These issues must be addressed when mocking up the motor mounts and modifying or building the front crossmember. Sump depth also needs to be considered, as several stock pans may clear the chassis itself, but ground clearance can become an issue when the sump hangs below the crossmember, especially on lowered vehicles.

In a typical installation, more than one pan probably fits the vehicle. Case in point: the LH8 oil pan (a special pan for the 5.3-powered Hummer H3) easily fits GM A-Body cars. However, with a typical adapter plate and motor mount installed, the LH8 pan rear sump hangs about 1½ inches below the engine crossmember. This is acceptable for standard-suspension-height cars, but

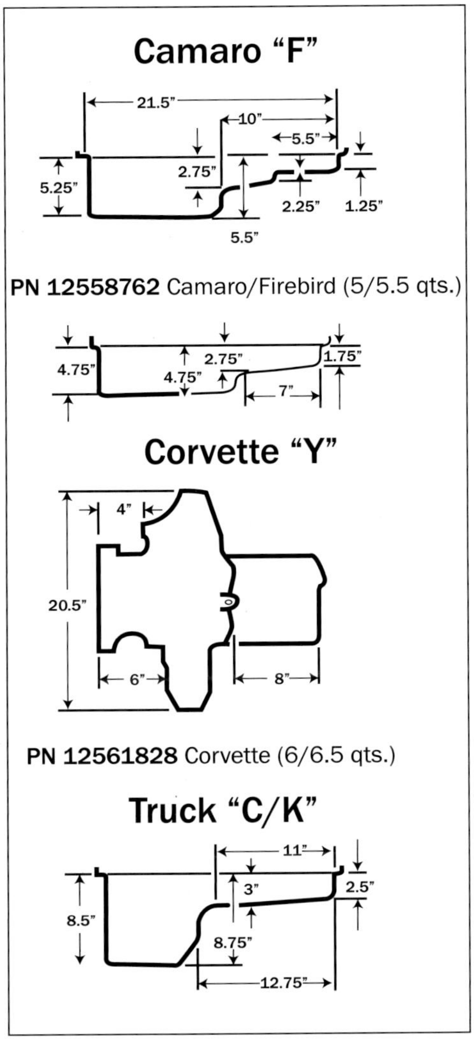

This diagram shows the three most common LS pans and their measurements. In order to select the right pan for your swap, consider the engine bay, crossmember, and steering clearances. Each pan requires a dedicated pick-up tube and windage tray. (Photo Courtesy Street & Performance)

if the car has a low ride height (especially an air-ride suspension) there may not be enough clearance between the pan and the pavement, and it could be damaged.

The Brewer's Restoration and Performance motor mount kits use the LH8 oil pan, but the motor mounts are specialized and position the engine differently in the car than most other adapter kit installations, allowing the LH8 pan to work quite well. Additionally, each oil pan requires its own specific windage tray, pick-up tube, and dipstick. When selecting an oil pan, make sure it comes with these parts so they don't have to be purchased later.

Several blocks and oil-pan configurations place the dipstick tube in the pan rather than in the block. In order to use a non-dipstick tube pan on these engines, the machined boss on the passenger's side of the block must be drilled out. Using a 3/8-inch drill bit, drill it through (about 1/8 inch of material), and slide the tube right in.

One more note on factory oil pans: they can be swapped from engine to engine, but there are a few points that need to be considered. The pick-up tube and windage tray go with the oil pan, not the engine. These items are a matched set, so anytime an oil pan is swapped, the correct tube and windage tray must be swapped as well.

Additionally, displacement on demand (DoD) engines have an oil-pressure bypass valve built into the oil pan. If the DoD system isn't going to be used, then it doesn't matter. For engine swaps using the DoD system, however, an oil pan with the bypass valve must be used.

F-Body Camaro/Firebird Oil Pan (PN 12558762)

The most commonly used stock oil pan is the Camaro/Firebird pan. According to Street & Performance, the 1998–2002 Camaro/Firebird IROC pan fits 1958–1964 GM cars without modification, though the fit is tight.

All 1955–1957 and 1965–up GM cars require modifications to the Camaro oil pan. The problem here is that the oil pan interferes with the front crossmember, keeping the engine from sitting down on the mounts. About 2 inches of depth must be removed from the front edge of the rear sump, along with a large section of the front of the sump. The aluminum oil pan must be tungsten inert gas (TIG) welded, and even an experienced welder can quickly ruin an oil pan. Therefore, consider buying a modified or custom aftermarket oil pan.

Some builders have used the Camaro pan in 1965-up GM muscle cars without modification. They used their own custom-built motor mounts. It depends on the particular engine/transmission package and chassis as to whether this pan fits unmodified.

The Camaro oil pan also fits well, unmodified, in the C2 (1962–1967) and C3 (1968–1982) Corvettes. The F-Body oil pan's rear sump measures 5 inches deep, 11½ inches long, and 9½ inches wide. The shallow front section is where most of the interference occurs. The frontmost section is flat for 4¼ inches, and then slopes at a steep angle for 4¾ inches. About 1½ inches of the sump's depth must be removed from the first 4 inches of the front section of the rear sump to allow it to fit into the 1967–1969 F-Body.

Many swappers use this pan in stock form for Fox-Body Mustang swaps.

2002–2006 C/K Truck Oil Pan (PN 12579273)

This oil pan is fitted to all 4.8-, 5.3-, and 6.0-liter C/K trucks and Escalades. This pan features a long, shallow front section (12¼ inches) with a crossmember-friendly, short, 8¾-inch-long rear sump. The rear

Early Vortec oil pans fit many vehicles, but the deep rear sump can be problematic due to lack of ground clearance. Most trucks accept this pan with ease. (Photo Courtesy Street & Performance)

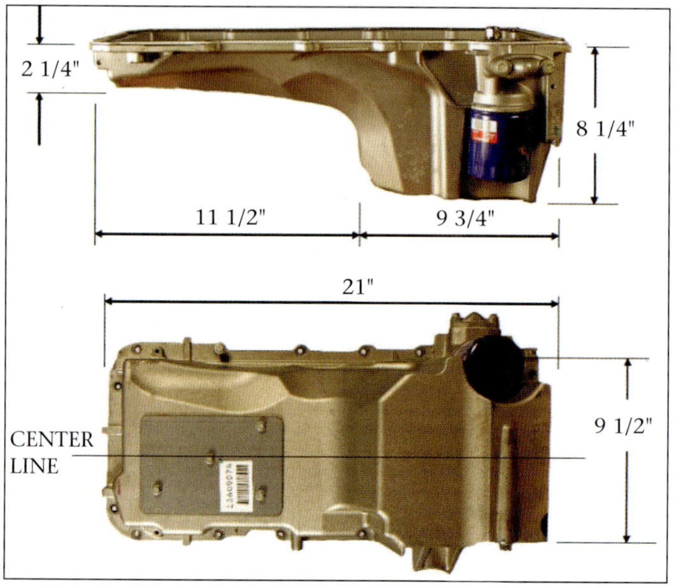

The 2007-up Vortec pan works well in the 1960-up GM truck swaps, but the deeper pan can be an issue for lowered trucks and cars. (Photo Courtesy Paul Chiver)

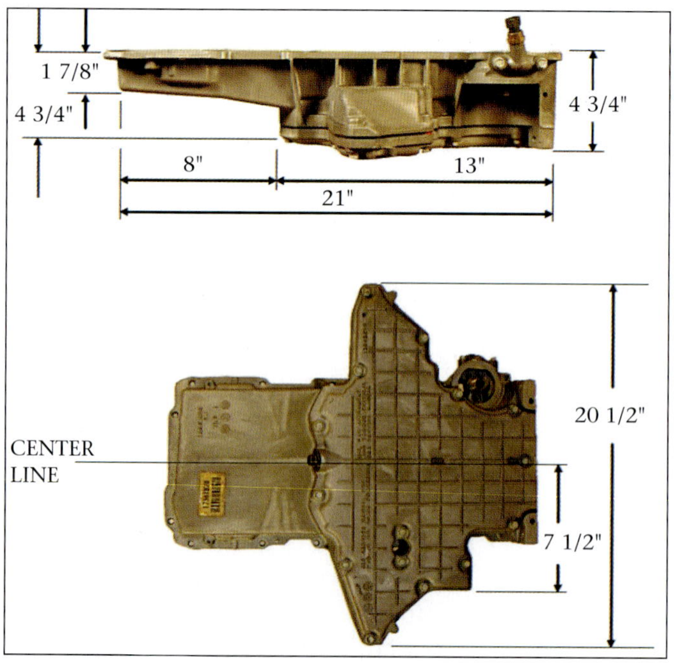

The famous batwing oil pan works well for street rods, early Corvettes (C1, C2, and C3), and just about anything using a Mustang-II-style front crossmember and suspension. (Photo Courtesy Paul Chiver)

sump is quite deep (8¼ inches), making it a poor candidate for most car applications. It is, however, a great pan for trucks, and it fits without modification in 1960–up Chevy and GMC trucks and SUVs (Blazer, Suburban, etc.).

This pan can be used in GM A-Body cars (Chevelle, GTO, Buick GS, etc.), but has a tendency to become a victim of road debris due to the deep sump and resulting low ground clearance.

2007–Up GM Truck Oil Pan (PN 12609074)

The 2007–up GM trucks with the 4.8-, 5.3-, 6.0-, and 6.2-liter Gen IV engines come with this oil pan. Basically the same as the 2002–2006 C/K truck pan, it has a shorter, shallow front section at 11½ inches, and a slightly longer rear sump at 9¾ inches. The rear sump depth remains the same at 8¼ inches. This pan fits all 1960-up Chevy and GMC trucks.

Like the earlier truck pans, these have a deep rear sump, which tends to hang down past the crossmember in muscle cars and other cars. Modifying them is a budget alternative to purchasing a new pan.

C5 Corvette "Y" Oil Pan (PN 12561828)

With one kickout on each side, this pan is typically referred to as the "batwing" pan because the kickouts resemble wings. This race-inspired design allows for consistent pick-up coverage under high lateral g-force turns. The pan is very shallow (4¾ inches top to bottom) and has 20½-inch-wide kickouts that prevent it from working in most stock muscle cars.

This pan is widely used in any car with a Mustang II–style suspension,

The CTS-V Cadillac oil pan works well in trucks and muscle cars, although the rear sump is deeper than an F-Body pan. This means the pan might hang below the crossmember, depending on the motor mounts, but it is still a great option for a stock pan. (Photo Courtesy Street & Performance)

Some manufacturers have used the LH8 oil pan for all of their LS swap kits. For the universal-style adapter plates, it may or may not hang too low under the crossmember. Lowered muscle cars should stay away from this pan unless it is specifically required for a kit. (Photo Courtesy Paul Chiver)

one of the most popular suspension swaps. Most aftermarket street rod frames (TCI, Heidts, Fat Man Fabrications, etc.) use a Mustang II suspension, so this is the pan of choice.

This pan also fits the C4 Corvette (1984–1996), simplifying the LS swap for C4 Corvettes.

Cadillac CTS-V Oil Pan 2004–2007, 2009–up

Available on the Cadillac CTS-V, this oil pan is basically a cross between the F-Body and the C/K truck pans. The rear sump is 5½ inches deep, 3 inches less than the truck pan and 1/2 inch deeper than the F-Body pan. The shallow front section is 11 inches long, which is shorter than the truck pan, but longer than the F-Body.

Standard adapter plates can be used, setting the motor low in the car and clearing the engine crossmember. The CTS-V pan hangs below the front crossmember by about 1 inch on 1965–1972 GM A-Bodies (Chevy Chevelle, Buick Gran Sport, Pontiac GTO, etc.) and 1978–1988 G-Bodies (Buick Regal, Chevy Monte Carlo). It depends on which motor mounts are used, as some mounts such as the Trans-Dapt adapter plates place the engine slightly higher in the car, reducing the amount of overhang.

This is an excellent pan for Fox-Body Mustang swaps using the stock K-member. Later-model CTS-V cars with an LSA use a similar oil pan, with a few minor differences. The external dimensions are the same; however, the LSA pan has larger oil filter threads, a different oil-pressure sending unit boss, and oil cooler bosses.

Hummer H3 Alpha 5.3 Oil Pan (PN 12614821)

The H3 oil pan is commonly referred to as the LH8 (for the Hummer H3 5.3L LS engine code). First available in late 2007, its measurements caused quite a stir in the LS swap community because the long, 13-inch shallow front section allows this pan to clear most stock GM crossmembers without modification. Again, though, this pan has a 7½-inch-deep rear sump, making it hang about 1½ to 2 inches below the crossmember. A stock suspension on a car is able to clear the road, but any lowering and this pan could be an issue.

Corvette LS2 Oil Pan (PN 12581810)

The LS2 Corvette oil pan falls in the "maybe" category of fitment. Its 5-inch-deep rear sump certainly clears the road, but the 13½-inch length of the sump prevents this pan from being used in most muscle car chassis. Although it can be modified for a particular vehicle, thanks to the relatively flat and square rear sump, it might not be worth it to buy this pan for a muscle car application.

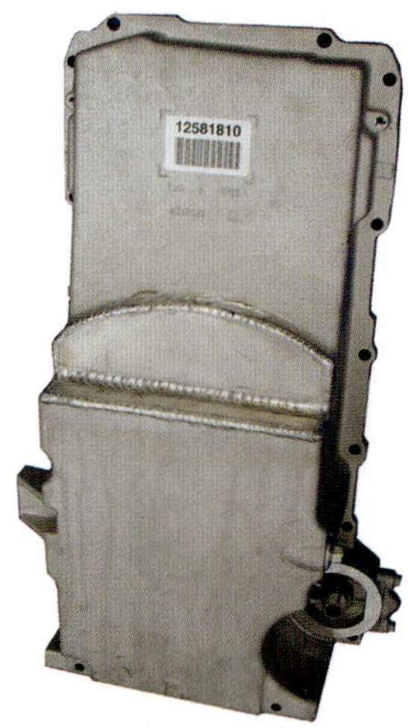

The LS2 Corvette oil pan must be modified to fit GM muscle car chassis designs, which is relatively simple because it's mostly flat. The modifications depend on the specific application. Keep in mind that any modification to the depth or sidewall of the pan requires modifying the pick-up tube. (Photo Courtesy Street & Performance)

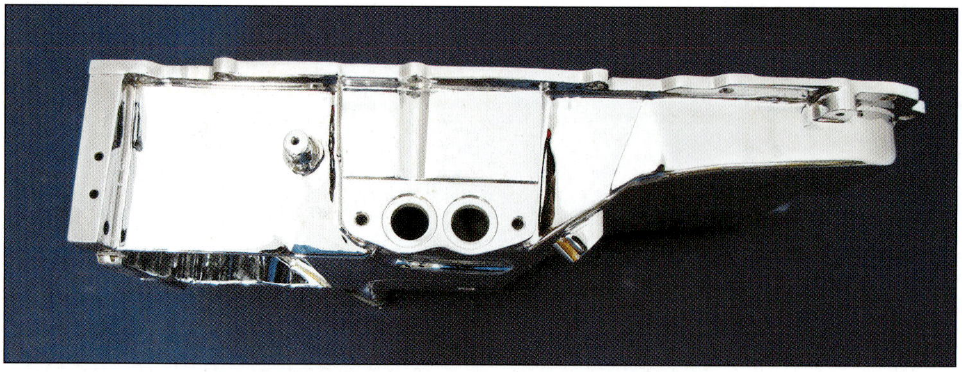

This polished LS7 oil pan shows the dry-sump output lines, which must run to the dry-sump oil tank. The tank can be mounted in almost any convenient location under the hood. (Photo Courtesy Street & Performance)

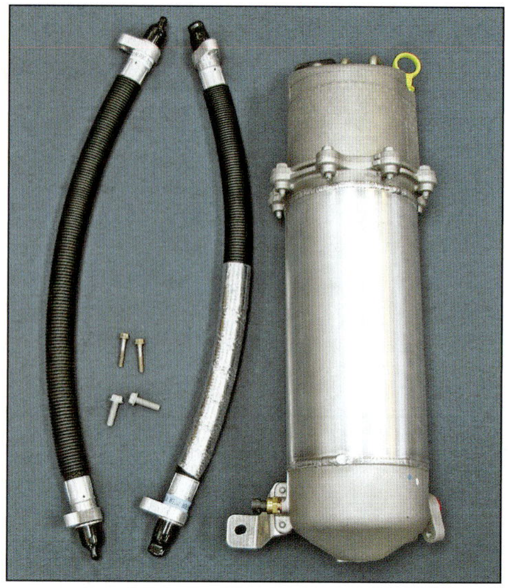

Many different oil tanks are available. This is the stock LS7 oil tank and its lines. It can be polished for show vehicles or hidden away, but must be easily accessed. (Photo Courtesy Street & Performance)

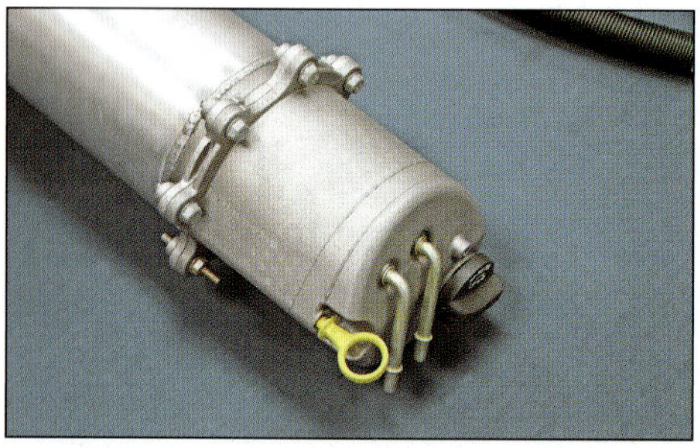

On LS7 engines, the dipstick is located in the oil tank. All of the engine's oil is stored in this tank. A secure mount is of critical importance. (Photo Courtesy Street & Performance)

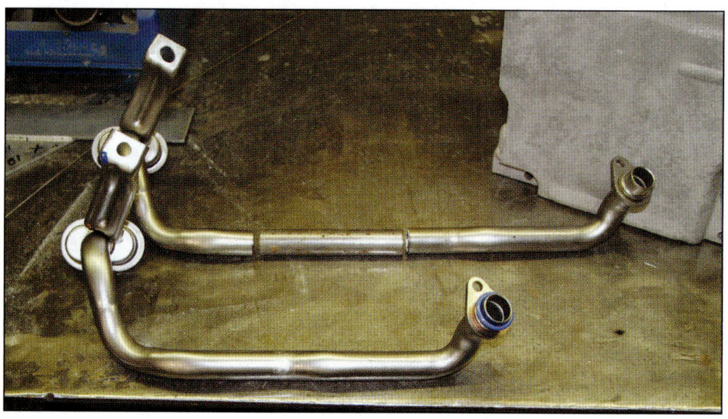

Each oil pan also requires its own specific pick-up tube. Shown are a modified F-Body pick-up tube (top) and a stock F-Body tube (bottom). (Photo Courtesy Street & Performance)

Corvette LS7 Dry-Sump Oil Pan

The LS7 is a specialized pan that only fits the LS7. This is a dry-sump oiling system and requires a lot of special consideration. For swapping an LS7 into a GM muscle car, an aftermarket oil pan is required. Modifying the stock pan is not a simple task because of the internal oil-routing design. ATS offers a sheet-metal oil pan for the LS7 that fits the first-generation F-Body (1967–1969 Chevy Camaro/Pontiac Firebird). Although this pan was designed for the F-Body, it fits most GM muscle cars as well.

GTO LS3 Oil Pan

Many swap platforms require a front-sump oil pan in order to clear the crossmember or rear-steer steering links or racks. The GTO pan works well in these situations. The early Mustangs and Nissan/Datsun Z-cars typically work with a GTO pan.

LS3/LSA 2010–Up Camaro

The fifth-generation Camaro uses a different oil pan than the fourth-generation F-Body. The newest Camaro pan has a long rear sump that doesn't clear the front crossmember on many muscle cars, leaving it out as a versatile pan for swappers.

LS9 Corvette ZR1

Like the LS7, the LS9 in the ZR1 Corvette is a dry-sump design. It can be retrofitted to other blocks, but considering the money necessary to buy the factory unit, an aftermarket dry-sump pan likely fits better and costs less.

Aftermarket Gen III/IV Oil Pans

With so many options and potential pitfalls, many builders choose an aftermarket oil pan that fits specific vehicles. There are many versions, and most are one of two platforms:

Oil-Pressure Sending Unit

Gauges need to monitor the vital functions of every engine. The Gen III/IV engines are certainly no exception. The stock oil-pressure sending unit works for the factory-type gauges only. All stock oil pans, however, feature a factory bypass plug, which may or may not be already drilled and tapped for a sending unit. ■

1 *These two plugs represent the two main versions of factory bypass plugs. Both can be drilled and tapped.*

2 *In order to install an aftermarket oil-pressure sending unit, the plug needs to be drilled to match the thread size on the oil-pressure sending unit. The most common thread size is 1/4-inch NPT, but the hole can be drilled much smaller if necessary.*

3 *Next, you tap the plug for 1/4-inch NPT threads. When tapping a hole, always work slowly; don't use a drill to drive the tap; it can break the tap or crack the part. Cutting fluid should be used as well. If you don't have any, penetrating oil is an alternative.*

4 *Install the bypass adapter. This boss can also be swapped out for an oil cooler bypass regulator.*

The 2010–up Camaro uses this oil pan for the LS3 and LSA engines. It has provisions for mounting an oil cooler. Its odd shape makes it a tricky pan for swappers. Improved Racing made the internal baffling in this pan. (Photo Courtesy Improved Racing)

the first-generation F-Body 1967–1969 Chevy Camaro and Pontiac Firebird; and the 1965–1972 GM A-Body cars, such as the Chevy Chevelle, Pontiac GTO, Buick GS/Skylark, and Oldsmobile Cutlass/442.

Most fabricated (meaning welded steel or aluminum, not cast) aftermarket oil pans require the use of a remote oil filter. This is a major drawback for some builders, as a suitable location for the filter and lines must

Modifying a Stock Oil Pan

Because there isn't a fix-all version of the LS oil pan, sometimes there is no other choice than to modify a stock pan. All factory oil pans are made from cast aluminum, which can be welded through the TIG process with relative ease, or with a metal inert gas (MIG) welder using a spool gun.

Welding aluminum requires special techniques, unlike welding steel. Aluminum oxidizes almost instantly and this oxidation layer is very hard. It melts at a much higher temperature than the actual aluminum, so by the time the oxidation melts, the aluminum underneath has already melted, flowing out from under the oxidation.

The solution is to remove the layer through mechanical or chemical means. Usually, a stiff stainless-steel wire brush works great. There are also chemicals that dissolve the layer but welding aluminum is not easy, and it takes some practice and technique. If an oil pan requires modification, take it to a professional. Blowing big holes in an oil pan is not a good way to keep an engine alive.

One of the benefits of an aftermarket pan is that many of them have internal baffles designed to keep the oil surrounding the pick-up tube at all times, even under severe g-forces. The baffles trap the oil so it doesn't slosh around inside the pan, potentially uncovering the pick-up tube. There are some options for modifying a factory pan with an internal baffle.

The F-Body oil pan is one of the biggest culprits for high-g oil starvation. Improved Racing designed a bolt-in baffle for the F-Body pan (they also offer them for the fifth-generation Camaro and GTO pans) that is a direct bolt-in; no welding required. By reducing the sloshing and aeration of the oil, the engine can maintain oil pressure and eliminate oil starvation. ■

1 ***Street & Performance (S&P) modified oil pans allow the use of the stock oil filter location and fit the application needed. From left to right: Tri-Five Chevy/Buick/Olds; first-generation F-Body; 1964–1972 GM A-Body and 1978–1987 GM G-Body. (Photo Courtesy Street & Performance)***

2 ***Comparing an S&P modified pan (top) to a stock F-Body pan (bottom) shows the alterations to increase clearance. The modified pan has been cut down on the front side of the sump, moving it back to clear the crossmember. (Photo Courtesy Street & Performance)***

3 ***S&P uses a jig to cut off the offending sections of the stock pan. It is important that the cuts are clean and even to help make a solid seal when it's all welded back up. (Photo Courtesy Street & Performance)***

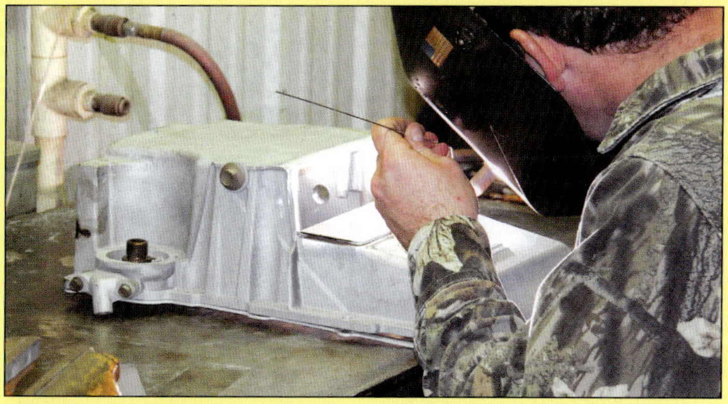

4 *These S&P oil pans are cast aluminum, which must be TIG-welded. TIG welding aluminum is difficult, so be sure all welding is done by a professional. (Photo Courtesy Street & Performance)*

5 *Once finished, the completed S&P pan is ready for use. The pick-up tube must also be modified because it previously ran along the bottom of the pan and does not fit with the modifications. (Photo Courtesy Street & Performance)*

6 *Mounted into a Buick Grand National (G-Body), the S&P pan clears the crossmember with not an inch to spare. (Photo Courtesy Street & Performance)*

7 *Modified S&P oil pans also work great for first-generation F-Body cars with rack-and-pinion steering because the pan provides ample clearance for the rack and steering components. (Photo Courtesy Street & Performance)*

now be considered. This is not always the case, however, as there are several aftermarket pans that maintain the pan-mounted filter, such as the Holley LSX-swap cast-aluminum pan.

Oil Coolers

Oil temperature is important, especially for road racing or running superchargers and turbos. Maintaining proper engine oil temperature is critical to the life of the engine and the usable life of the oil. Chevrolet suggests running your engine oil between 220 and 240 degrees F at full warm-up. This is higher than the previously acceptable range of 190 to 220, and is a point of contention among experts. That doesn't change the fact that anything over 250 degrees begins to break down the oil, dramatically reducing its usable life.

Colder oil temperatures are also an issue and rob the engine of power. The cooler the oil, the thicker it is, and LS engines run tighter tolerances than the old small-block Chevy. That means there is less oil inside the bearings, increasing friction and costing more power. Heat the oil a little more and it flows better, reducing the friction and freeing up a little extra power, not to mention adding life to the engine.

Another side effect of running the engine oil too cool is the lack of sufficient burn-off temperature. Engine oil becomes contaminated with fuel and water through condensation. When the oil reaches 200 degrees F, the fuel and water begin to burn off. Although this is necessary for a naturally aspirated engine, it is critical for a turbocharged engine as the turbos are cooled through the engine oil system. Water and fuel in the oil can destroy turbo bearings in a hurry.

Thermostatic Bypass

Adding an oil cooler is an easy way to maintain the correct engine oil temperatures, but simply adding an in-line cooler is not the answer. If the oil is allowed to flow through the cooler, it takes longer to warm up and runs cooler overall. The key to a proper oil cooling system is thermostatic bypass.

All factory LS engine oil pans have an oil bypass port built right into the side of the pan above the oil filter. These ports can be used for the oil cooler lines (as well as the oil-pressure sending unit, more on that later) or an oil filter sandwich-type adapter. A thermostatic bypass port allows the engine oil to circulate through the cooler only after it reaches a certain temperature, allowing the oil to warm up faster. If it cools too quickly in the cooler the bypass closes, maintaining a consistent minimum temperature. These types of valves can be found in adjustable versions, but are typically sold as static versions, usually opening at 180 degrees and fully open at 200 degrees.

Several Gen III/IV LS engines even have oil coolers built into them, namely the high-performance versions and some of the Vortec heavy-duty applications. If you choose to run an aftermarket oil pan with a remote oil filter, the plumbing allows you to add an in-line cooler. There are thermostatic bypasses available for this design as well.

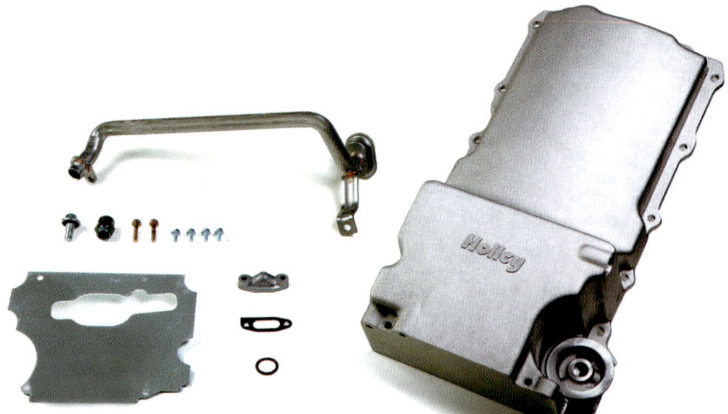

Holley came into the oil pan market with its LSX retrofit pan. This aluminum oil pan features a stock-style oil filter mount and has adequate clearance for most popular swaps. It is also a beefy design, with thick casting ridges for strength. (Photo Courtesy Holley Performance Products)

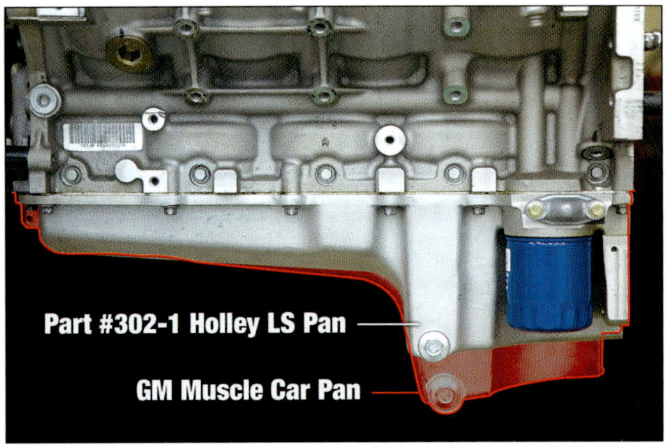

Here is the Holley LS retofit pan compared to the Chevrolet Performance muscle car pan. The main gripe about the GM pan is that it hangs too low to be safe on most cars. The Holley pan corrected that problem. (Photo Courtesy Holley Performance Products)

Cooler Location

Locating the cooler is fairly simple, most of the time. The cooler is mounted in front of the radiator or A/C condenser, but it doesn't have to go there. It can be mounted just about anywhere as long as it gets enough airflow. "Hot rod"–style coolers mount on the frame itself. Some even have 12-volt fans for forced-air cooling. There are a lot of options, but the simplest solution is a radiator front mount.

Oil Filter

As previously mentioned, many aftermarket oil pans do not have factory-style oil filter mounts, only ports for the oil feed and return lines. This means you must run a remote oil filter. Locating the oil filter can be a challenge in many applications, but it is a necessary component. If you use an oil cooler, the filter can be located in the same location.

The key here is to have easy access to the filter and protection from road debris. If the filter is hanging too low, it could get damaged, resulting in a shattered engine. The lines for the oil filter do not have to be high-pressure, but braided lines certainly look good and reduce the chances for leaks or blowouts from cut or damaged lines.

Also keep in mind that the ports are not labeled on LS engines, and some oil pans do not include instructions indicating what port is pressure/return. The pressure port is the front (toward the belts) one; the return is the rearmost port.

LS Oil Pan Options

Each LS engine swap has its own particular set of challenges. A common one is oil pan fitment. The oil pan must clear the transmission crossmember and the subframe, and also allow for adequate ground clearance. Holley, Canton, Moroso, and others offer high-performance oil pans for most Gen III/IV engines for swaps into popular models, such as the GM A-, F-, Y-, and X-Body. You need to select a pan for the specific application of your car. Some have internal baffles and some don't. If you autocross or road race your vehicle, you need sufficient baffling to keep the oil pickup submerged in oil. Sheet-metal pans do not have built-in oil filters mounts, so they require a remote oil filter. ■

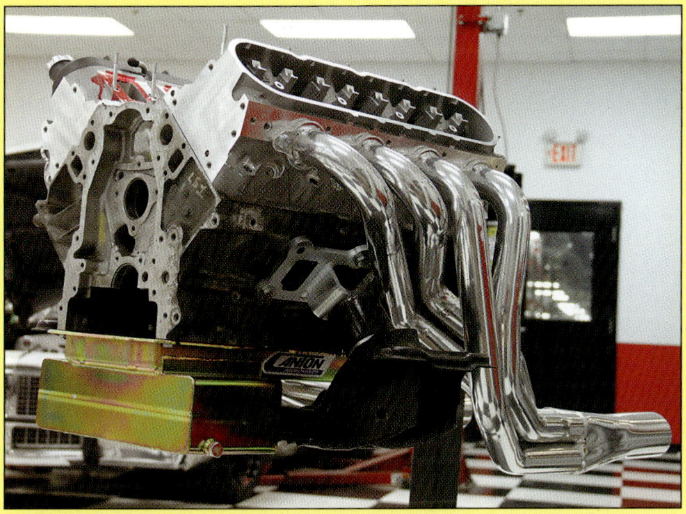

For autocross and road race applications, you need a well-designed pan that has sufficient baffling. This ensures the engine has a constant supply of oil. This Canton pan features a front sump as well, so the front subframe can be equipped for rear steer. With rear steer, the steering arms are behind the spindle center rather than in front of it. (Photo Courtesy Blane Burnett)

The Canton aluminum drag race oil pan for LS engine swaps fits GM A-, F-, Y-, and 1970s X- (Nova) Body cars. It is an aluminum sheet-metal pan, with trap-door baffles for oil control. The required remote filter adapter is included. (Photo Courtesy Canton Racing Products)

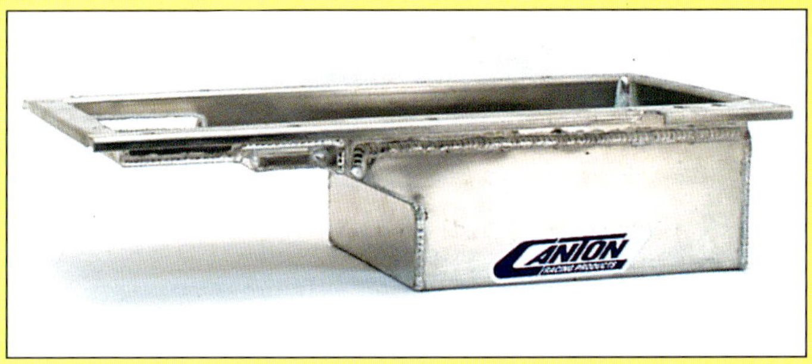

This aluminum drag race oil pan from Canton is designed for 1998-up F-Body chassis. It features fully fabricated aluminum construction, which is significantly lighter than cast pan designs, and road-race-style trap-door baffles for oil control. It works with OEM windage trays but requires the use of a remote filter adapter, which is included. It works in any chassis that the factory F-Body pan fits. (Photo Courtesy Canton Racing Products)

This Moroso panfeatures a deep-angled front sump section, which helps expedite the oil's return to the sump. (Photo Courtesy Moroso Performance Products)

LS Oil Pan Options *CONTINUED*

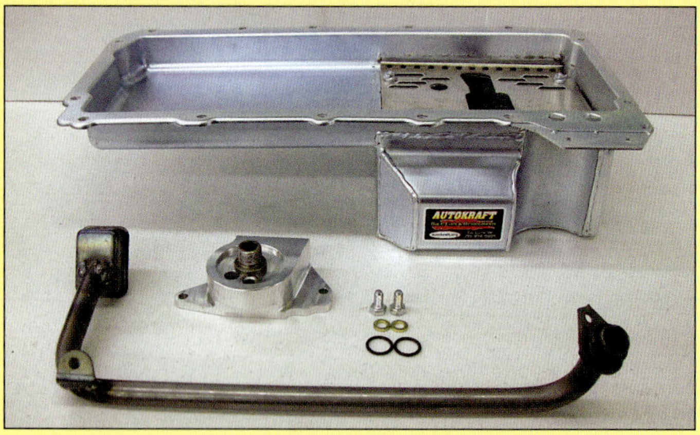

Autokraft uses stamped-steel and sheet-metal fabrication on their LS swap oil pan. This pan was designed for road race applications and uses a four-corner baffling design. It also can be installed with the oil filter adapter, allowing the filter to remain in the stock location. (Photo Courtesy Autokraft)

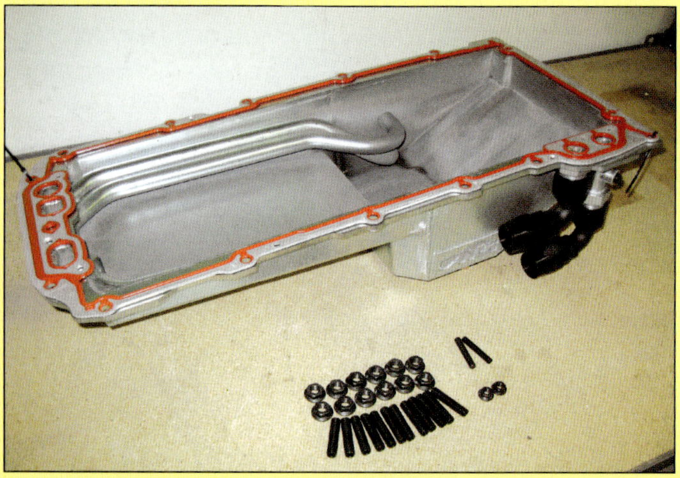

For the LS7, ATS offers this pan for the 1967–1969 F-Body cars with ATS motor mounts. If the ATS motor mounts are flipped upside down, this pan can be used in 1964–1967 GM A-Body cars as well. (Photo Courtesy American Touring Specialties)

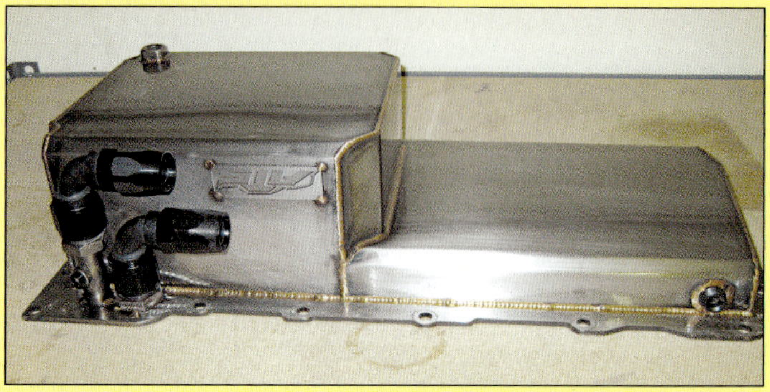

The ATS sheet-metal road race pan fits first-generation F-Body cars with ATS motor mounts. This pan also works well with GM A-Body cars. (Photo Courtesy American Touring Specialties)

The ATS baffling design keeps the oil directly around the oil pick-up, ensuring that there is no loss of oil pressure. (Photo Courtesy American Touring Specialties)

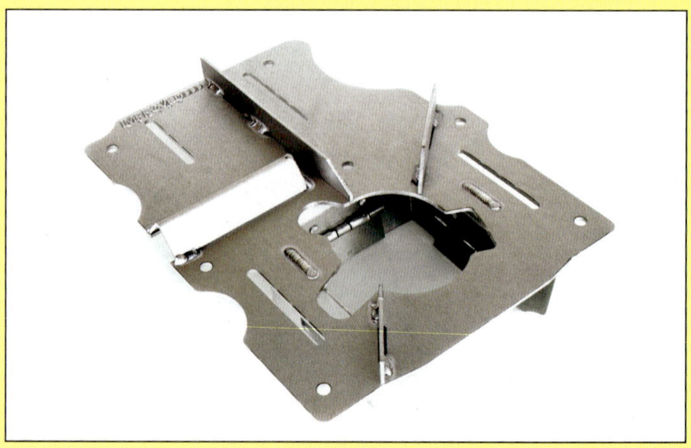

Improved Racing's bolt-in baffles can be purchased for the 2010 Camaro, GTO, and F-Body pans. These baffles ensure the oil pump pick-up remains submerged in oil during hard cornering so the engine always receives a strong supply of oil from the pan. (Photo Courtesy Improved Racing)

Feature Vehicle

BMW E36

Photos courtesy Vorshlag Motorsports and Brandon LaJoie

The team at Vorshlag combined the most popular BMW of all time, the E36 3-Series sport coupe platform, with one of the most popular GM engine series, the LS Gen III/IV, to create a winner. This kit helps to build one of the most agile and powerful European sports coupes ever. The lightweight BMW E36 (2,500 to 3,500 pounds) and the powerful Gen III/IV engines make the possibilities endless. The Vorshlag components are essential for packaging the LS engine and front subframe components.

This kit allows the BMW rack-and-pinion steering and anti-locking braking system (ABS) to remain in the vehicle, unlike some other kits. The entire process has been reduced to a simple matter of following instructions, thereby reducing the fabrication time and cost. The basics (motor mounts, transmission crossmember, headers, steering shaft, driveshaft) are all included in the Stage 0 kit. (The Stage 1 kit includes the radiator, coolant hoses, power steering hoses, fuel line connections, fuel pump, custom T56 hydraulic throw-out bearing, and remote bleed).

The basic Stage 0 kit provides all the parts to make the engine and transmission fit and function correctly. The round polyurethane motor mounts are powdercoated. The mounts are a bolt-in item, and the frame stands bolt to the BMW chassis. The upper clamshell bolts to the engine, then the two pieces are mated as the engine is lowered into place. The transmission crossmember is also a bolt-in item.

The kit is designed for a T56 manual transmission. An automatic can fit in the BMW chassis, but that requires you to build a custom crossmember. The floorpan opening is very close to matching the T56 shifter location, and a bit of trimming is usually required to get it just right. There are multiple shifter configurations, so this process varies by each build.

The kit was designed to use an F-Body oil pan, either factory or aftermarket. One of the issues with an LS swap on the BMW is the ABS manifold. The F-Body accessory drive fits the chassis the best, but the power steering pump is dangerously close to the ABS unit. Using the supplied relocation bracket, you move the ABS manifold, providing the necessary clearance.

Above: *The BMW E36 series (1990–1999) is probably the most popular BMW ever produced. With a vast aftermarket dedicated to E36 performance, many suspension and chassis parts are available to upgrade performance. The team at Vorshlag Motorsports set out to drop an LS1 in an E36, and they built a kit while they were at it.*

Photo 1: *Remove the stock BMW 2.5-liter engine and the engine bay can be cleaned up in preparation for the LS1. Remove all non-essential components, such as wiring harnesses and washer pump/motor.* ***2.*** *Set the LS1 and T56 transmission in place and keep it level. Place a straightedge across the top of the engine from strut tower to strut tower to ensure the engine sits below this line for clearance.* ***3.*** *A jack under the car supports the transmission. You need to properly support the transmission and make sure it's in the correct location so it doesn't throw off the motor mounts' correct placement.* ***4.*** *The shifter location of the transmission has moved back several inches. At this point, a decision needs to be made to resolve this issue. You can install an adjustable shifter kit and retain the stock BWM console, or you can remove the interior, cut a new opening for the shifter, weld in a patch panel for the old transmission hump hole, and install a custom console. Obviously, installing an adjustable shifter is far less complicated and time consuming.* ***5.*** *With the engine stand in place, the motor mount brackets slide into place with the engine in the air and then bolt to the engine. Vorshlag makes a high-quality motor mount kit for the LS swap. These mounts are hand-fabricated, TIG-welded components that bolt to the frame. The motor mounts are made of powdercoated alloy steel. The kit uses Grade-8 hardware and provides a precise fit.* ***6.*** *The Vorshlag oil pan is based on the F-Body oil pan, and it allows the engine to fit over the subframe crossmember.*

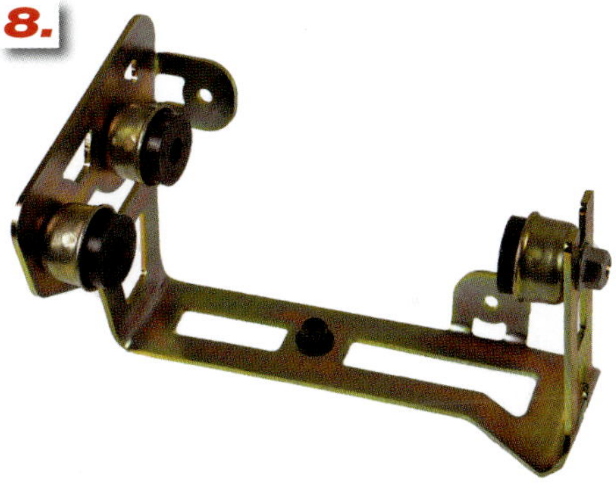

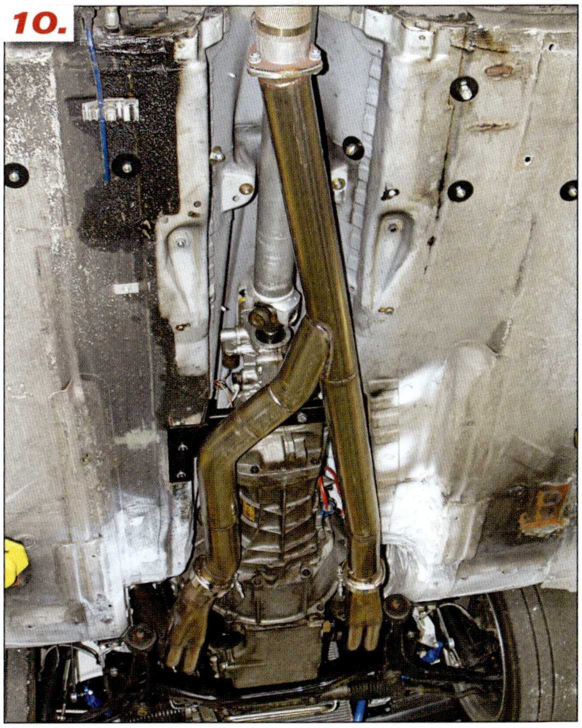

The ABS and steering systems are a major part of what makes the E36 BMW handle so well; this kit retains those factory systems, keeping the “BMW” in the car. You replace the steering shaft with a new unit that allows clearance for the headers and motor mounts.

One of the most contentious components of any engine swap is the exhaust. Headers are always a difficult endeavor. These are no exception. Instead of a traditional header collector flange, these headers feature a round pipe with no flange at all. That is because there simply is not enough room to slide the headers into the car with a flange installed—it’s a tight fit. To connect the headers to the rest of the exhaust, you use a set of included V-band clamps. These clamps have a double-wall design to seal the tubing from the inside and the outside, which is a unique design that greatly benefits this swap.

The last piece of the Stage 0 puzzle is the custom aluminum driveshaft. Again, this fits the T56 transmissions, not an automatic.

This basic kit can be upgraded with items such as new custom-fit brake lines, a drop-in fuel system upgrade, and a six-bolt axle drive flange conversion to handle the increased power.

The installation of the Vorshlag kit is straightforward, with only minor modifications to the chassis itself. All of the kit’s components are designed to work together, not as mix-and-match components. This is an LS swap system, not just a kit.

7. *The BMW E36 chassis was not designed for the Tremec manual transmissions or the GM AOD automatic transmissions. When installing either transmission, you need to install a custom-fabricated transmission crossmember. This crossmember supports the T56 manual transmission on this E36.* ***8.*** *The power steering pump is too close to the ABS unit, so you relocate the ABS pump to afford the power steering pump enough room. The Vorshlag ABS pump relocation bracket features three holes so you can drill and bolt the bracket and pump to the chassis. The bracket is often attached to inner-fender sheet metal.* ***9.*** *A custom radiator is required for this swap. This radiator was built at a local radiator shop.* ***10.*** *The headers on this E36 were custom designed and fabricated, which resulted in an exhaust that fits perfectly. Some non-traditional swaps require custom headers.* ***11.*** *Route the air cleaner to the passenger’s side of the engine bay using custom tubing. You can re-use the stock MAF sensor.*

CHAPTER 4

Accessory Drives and Cooling System

Stock accessory drives were designed to fit in late-model vehicles with modern frames and spacing. Depending on which accessory drives are retained, clearance may or may not be an issue. However, the A/C compressor constantly presents an issue. It's typically mounted low on the passenger's side of the engine, and it tends to hit the frame rail or the upper A-arm on the suspension at this location.

On the other side of the engine, power steering pump and alternator placement becomes an issue. The stock recirculating-ball steering gearbox gets in the way. Each chassis is different and each accessory drive is different.

Stock Accessory Drives

Specific stock accessory drives work on specific chassis. If the drive system doesn't fit your car, there are several options. The first is to find a stock drive that fits your chassis, but these can be difficult to find, especially the older 1998–2002 F-Body drives. There are also quite a few aftermarket drive kits that not only relocate the offending components, but also add some flash to the install. The last solution, relocating the problem component with a home-fabricated bracket, requires a little more ingenuity and fabrication. When swapping an LS into a less traditional vehicle, the possibilities are endless. In many cases, the chassis and suspension is modified to accept the LS engine. In addition, each vehicle's purpose helps determine the accessory drive choice. Vehicles that do not run A/C or power steering are certainly easier to fit and modify than a project that requires all of the accessories: keep that in mind when choosing your accessory drive. An alternator alone is much easier to relocate than three components.

The accessory drives on Gen III/IV engines are interchangeable throughout the product line. However, each accessory drive is based on two components: the water pump and the harmonic dampener (or harmonic balancer; LS engines are internally balanced, so it is technically a harmonic dampener, but commonly referred to as a balancer).

Engine-to-radiator clearance is a primary consideration when installing an LS engine into a non-GM vehicle. The LS engine may be physically larger than the engine it is replacing, or you may move the engine farther forward. In each of these cases, clearance may be reduced, so selecting compatible accessory pulleys is imperative. With many swap projects in which clearance is minimal, an electric fan must be used. (Photo Courtesy Blane Burnett)

Water Pumps

You have three water pump offset options: the 1998–2002 F-Body, the Corvette, and the C/K trucks. Within these types are subgroups. The F-Body water pump remained the same throughout its production run, from 1998 to 2002.

The Corvette (also GTO in 2004) used one water pump design with some internal differences. The 2005-up Corvette/GTO water pump for the LS2, LS7, and LS3 used the same offset, but contained a different internal design.

The same is true for the C/K truck pumps. The 1999–2005 trucks use a specific water pump, but in 2007 the design changed to DoD. Not all 2007 C/K engines use this pump. The offset remains the same as with early pumps, but you do not want to swap a DoD pump onto a non-DoD engine. The LS1/LS3 pumps are interchangeable; the LS3 pump uses a lighter pulley, with about 4 pounds of weight savings.

The main difference between these two water pumps is the length of the pulley bell. The Corvette-style pump (top) has a longer bell because the Corvette accessories run on two belts. The F-Body pump (bottom) uses a single belt. (Photo Courtesy Street & Performance)

Harmonic Dampeners

The crank pulley is part of the dampener; it is one piece as opposed to a separate pulley that bolts to the balancer. There are three balancer designs for the LS engines.

The Corvette (Y-Body) dampener is the shortest of the three, placing the drive belt close to the engine.

The F-Body (also GTO) dampener is 3/4 inch longer than the Corvette engine.

The C/K (GM truck engine's 4.8-. 5.3-, and 6.0-liter) unit is 1½ inches longer than the Corvette unit.

This correlates to the water pump as well.

GM Vehicles

Each GM vehicle accepts a certain stock drive. Matching the drive to the car saves money in the long run and probably some headaches as well. The following breakdown refers to fully accessorized engines running A/C and power steering. If you are not running A/C or power steering, other drives may work; it depends on the vehicle and the drive system.

1958–1972 GM Muscle Cars and Early Corvettes

The C5 Corvette (Y-Body) accessory drive fits most GM muscle cars; C2, C3, and C4 Corvettes; and clears the stock chassis and stock chassis components with most

This is the 1998–2002 LS1 F-Body drive system. The accessories fit somewhat tight to the engine, but the A/C compressor and alternator can still be difficult to fit to the chassis. (Photo Courtesy Street & Performance)

The 1997–2004 Corvette has a dual-belt drive. The alternator is raised so it clears narrower frames. (Photo Courtesy Street & Performance)

The 2005–2006 GTO accessory drive system features an A/C compressor that hangs fairly wide, so it's more difficult to fit between the frame rails. (Photo Courtesy Blane Burnett)

motor mount adapters. The C5 uses a variable clutch-speed compressor that rides low on the smaller secondary four-rib belt. Depending on the motor mounts used, there can be clearance issues.

A Sanden 508 A/C compressor on a Street & Performance bracket positions the compressor forward to clear the chassis and puts the A/C compressor on the larger six-rib belt. You can run other accessory drives in these cars, but the engine crossmember must be notched to clear the A/C compressor, and the alternator hits the frame and steering gearbox.

A rack-and-pinion conversion simplifies the installation. This drive places the A/C compressor low and pushed back on the passenger's side. The power steering pump mounts in front of the driver-side cylinder head, and the alternator rides up and over the power steering pump.

1967–1969 Camaro, Firebird, 1978–1988 G-Body

The classic Camaro and G-Body cars require the 1998–2002 F-Body accessory drive to clear the chassis. This drive system places the A/C compressor very low and tight to the block, with the compressor centerline just below that of the crank. The alternator is tucked to the driver's side of the crank pulley and the power steering pump is mounted directly above the alternator.

A Corvette/CTS-V crank balancer is on the left; a mid-length F-Body/GTO is on the right. The rest of the accessory system must match the water pump and balancer.

Tri-Five Chevy, Buick and Oldsmobile

For the classic Tri-Fives, things get a little difficult. The C5 Corvette (1997–2004) accessory drive fits, depending on the chassis and the motor mounts. For a stock chassis using draglink steering, the C5 drive clears if the engine frame mounts set the engine forward.

Street & Performance suggests the Chassis Engineering V-8 engine stand, which sets the engine 3/4 inch forward. If the engine stand positions the engine rearward, you need a custom drive.

C1, C2, C3, C4 Corvette

The C5 Corvette drive system works well in the C2, C3, and C4 chassis without much modification. The C1 Corvette, however, typically requires an aftermarket accessory drive. An LS swap into a C1 also requires converting to a rack-and-pinion steering system, as the factory steering box doesn't clear the engine itself.

1960–1966 Chevy and GMC Trucks, SUVs

The F-Body and C/K accessory drives work well for this increasingly

Vortec engines have the longest pulley setup because trucks have more room to run the belts. Many Vortec engines also use a mechanical cooling fan. (Photo Courtesy Holley Performance Products)

The 1999–up Vortec drive fits all classic truck applications with the exception of the A/C compressor in the 1967–up trucks because the compressor hits the crossmember. You can relocate the A/C compressor or notch the crossmember. (Photo Courtesy Street & Performance)

popular truck line. The C/K accessory drive positions the A/C compressor just below the crank centerline, tucked in really tight to the passenger's side of the block. The power steering pump mounts tight to the block, midway between the crank and water pump. The alternator is out of the way at the top of the engine, above the power steering pump, next to the throttle body. This keeps everything nice and clean for these trucks.

1967–Up Chevy and GMC Trucks, SUVs

In stock form, with all the accessories, the F-Body and C5 drive accessories fit the rest of the GM truck line, but the C/K accessory drive does not fit in completely stock trim. The A/C compressor is the problem and can fail in the C/K drive of these trucks. If you do not use A/C, it fits.

If you do use A/C, the solutions are pretty simple. Either fabricate a custom bracket or purchase an aftermarket A/C relocation bracket for the C/K drive. Place the compressor on top, where it clears everything. Using a Sanden compressor makes the install nice and clean.

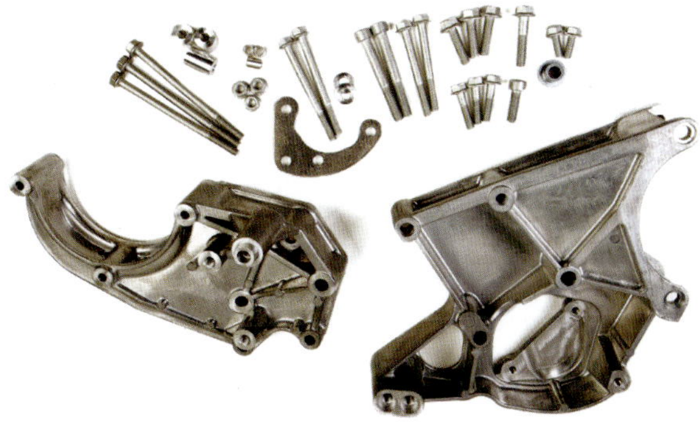

The Holley LSX accessory drive system comes in all three pulley lengths, and several options are available for positioning the accessories for maximum clearance. It is also available for the factory R4 A/C compressor or Sanden-style units. (Photo Courtesy Holley Performance Products)

Ford Mustangs

Although it might seem like Blue Oval blasphemy, the LS engine is often swapped into the Ford Mustang. The LS is a compact power plant, which makes the swapping process much easier than with many other engines, including the Ford Modular 4.6L and Coyote 5.0 engines. Every model is capable of taking an LS between the fenders; the Fox body is the most popular as well as the simplest.

The CTS-V drive system pulls the A/C compressor in tighter to the block than the GTO, and it uses the shortest crank pulley design for the most room. (Photo Courtesy Blane Burnett)

Sometimes a power steering pump with a built-in reservoir is too large to accommodate a particular swap. A Summit Racing GM Type-II mini-pump is a viable option because it is considerably smaller than the reservoir pumps, although it does require a remote reservoir.

1964–1973

Early Mustangs have very tight engine compartments; the stock shock towers are just in the way. The good news, however, is that the front area of the chassis is relatively clear of obstacles that the accessory drives can hit. The Corvette, CTS-V, and F-Body drives all work well here.

1979–1993 Fox-Body

Swapping an LS into a Ford may seem like sacrilege to some, but it is nonetheless a popular swap. The F-Body drive works well without any modifications, but they are getting hard to find. The ever-present Vortec drive, however, is available on the cheap and it works with a cowl hood. It can work with a stock hood with some modifications.

1994–2004 Mustang (SN95 Body)

For later-model Mustangs, the Corvette and CTS-V drives work well.

Nissan 240SX

The main issue with the 240SX is the limited space between the engine and the radiator and the lower subframe rails. The CTS-V drive works well in this regard, pulling the A/C pump tighter to the block and using the short pump design, maximizing the radiator-to-engine clearance.

Jeep CJ, YJ, TJ, XJ

All Jeeps can be fitted with F-Body brackets. The Vortec drive can be made to work; however, the alternator is really high and on some bodies it sticks out beyond the hood. There are modifications to re-position the alternator, which means custom fabrication.

Mazda

There are two popular LS swap platforms in the Mazda lineup: the RX-7 and the road race legend, the Miata. The lightweight aluminum-block engines work best.

Mazda Miata

As an increasingly popular swap platform, the Mazda Miata has a fair number of LS swap followers. The CTS-V accessory drive has proven to be the best drive for the Miata chassis. The CTS-V drive uses the shorter dampener, so it pulls the belts closer to the block. This saves a lot of room between the radiator and the engine, plus it retains the factory GM power steering pump.

Mazda RX-7

Late-model RX-7s take the CTS-V accessories with only a slight adjustment. The stock power steering pump sits a little high, causing interference with the hood. One solution is an LS2 GTO pump. Another option is to convert to a remote reservoir pump.

The CTS-V pump also requires a pressure reduction kit as the pump creates too much pressure for the Mazda rack, leading to over-assisted steering. As a result the steering is way too fast for safe driving.

This Holley power steering pump reservoir is small and compact for discreet installations. LS engines use a GM Type-II pump, some of which have a built-in reservoir, but most do not. (Photo Courtesy Holley Performance Products)

For a little bit of show, this Street & Performance dual-reservoir tank can be used for power steering and any number of other fluids, such as radiator overflow, windshield washers, etc. (Photo Courtesy Street & Performance)

The factory A/C compressor is a climate-control unit, and it runs regardless of whether the A/C is on or off. This style of compressor only works with the late-model factory-style A/C system. Running the stock compressor on an aftermarket A/C system doesn't work correctly, and likely freezes the lines. The only option is to use a Sanden compressor. (Photo Courtesy Street & Performance)

Running the stock accessory drive is a cheap solution. That does not mean it is the best solution. Stock drives are not aesthetic. Sure, the brackets are aluminum and can be polished, which looks nice, but that requires a tremendous amount of work and upkeep. Polished aluminum fades and oxidizes pretty quickly, and requires constant attention to retain a mirror finish if it is not anodized to protect it.

In addition, there is no guarantee that the stock drive will fit. The particular install depends on what mounts are used and how the engine is set up; there are always tolerances that may not work in some circumstances. An aftermarket accessory drive simplifies the install, removes the guesswork, and makes sure everything clears.

Cooling System

Swapping LS engines into non-GM vehicles can raise some challenges. For cars that were available with small-block V-8s, the radiator is not that big an issue, but more radical swaps sometimes require custom radiators. In addition, the Gen III/IV car engines were designed for electric cooling fans; only the Vortec engines have mechanical fans.

With a radiator and a fan, there can still be a few more issues. In many cases, the more radical swaps end up with a radiator that sits below the engine, creating air pockets in the cooling system and leading to overheating issues. These issues are easily remedied, but you need the right parts.

Radiators

Gen III/IV engines are typical V-8s with respect to the cooling system,

Aluminum radiators come in a million shapes and sizes. Choosing which one is right for your swap can be frustrating. The key is not necessarily to spend the most money. Budget-priced aluminum radiators such as those from Griffin, Summit Racing, and Howe are often just as good as more expensive units. (Photo Courtesy Summit Racing)

This Flex-a-lite aluminum radiator features a built-in overflow canister. Having a custom crossover radiator built with the inlet and outlet on both sides gives you a lot of hose-routing options during an LS swap. However, in some cases the expense is prohibitive. Since most LS engines do not use mechanical fans, routing a hose across the front of the engine is not an issue. (Photo Courtesy Flex-a-lite)

You can also buy a radiator with built-in electric fans. This ensures the fans are properly shrouded, which is an important element for achieving optimal cooling efficiency. (Photo Courtesy Flex-a-lite)

This sacrificial anode from Flex-a-lite gives up its material in the event of electrolysis, saving your valuable components. Electrolysis is known to destroy aluminum heads. (Photo Courtesy Flex-a-lite)

so they do not require huge radiators or special metals. What they do require is a radiator that is rated for the job. With the smallest LS engines easily making 300 hp, you don't want to use a stock 4-cylinder or V-6 radiator. Making horsepower means making heat as a byproduct, although the LS engines are pretty efficient when it comes to that.

Considering that the most popular GM muscle car and truck swaps had V-8s available from the factory, V-8 radiators are easy to find. And of course with a massive aftermarket catering to these vehicles, there are more than enough choices.

Aluminum versus Brass/Copper: In most 1970s vehicles, OEM radiators are constructed of a mixture of brass and copper. The brass components in radiators (typically the tubes) are expensive and the least effective at cooling an engine. The copper components (the header, and sometimes the tubes), however, quickly absorb and dissipate heat more quickly than aluminum components. Aluminum radiators absorb and dissipate heat better than brass, but at a slower rate than copper.

Copper, therefore, absorbs and dissipates heat at the fastest rate, cooling the engine more effectively than aluminum, right? Not exactly. Aluminum is stronger, which allows for thin-walled cooling tubes, which allows for more cores and rows than a traditional copper/brass radiator for increased cooling surface area. All of this translates into increased cooling capacity. In addition, aluminum is cheaper than brass, which certainly plays a part.

A further issue with brass/copper radiators is that they are soldered together with lead solder. The chemical reaction between the metals leads to contamination and build up inside the radiator. Solder also insulates the tank from the tubes, reducing the heat transfer between them, further reducing the effectiveness.

In reality, both radiators are useful, but the performance nod is typically given to the aluminum unit.

Electrolysis: Whenever there are two different metals in a coolant system, there is the potential for electrolysis. Electrolysis happens when one material is eaten away and deposited on the other. This can be disastrous for an aluminum engine because aluminum is generally the sacrificed material. When running a copper/brass radiator, there is potential to ruin aluminum components on the engine.

The simple solution is to install an anode kit in the radiator. Anodes are used in machinery and marine applications to protect the cooling systems and other components from damage due to electrolysis (or coolant additive failure and breakdown). Flex-a-lite offers a zinc anode kit (PN 32060) for installation as a replacement drain petcock in radiators that are equipped with a 1/4-inch NPT bushing welded into the tank.

The anode may also be installed in any 1/4-inch NPT hole that is available in the cooling system. The introduction of the zinc anode protects the cooling system from galvanic action as electrolysis eats away at the zinc rather than the aluminum.

Coolant: There has been much discussion about which coolant is best for LS engines, particularly in engine swaps. Dex-Cool is the factory engine coolant and is recommended by General Motors. That being said, those recommendations are for stock vehicles using all-stock components.

Dex-Cool is specifically designed for aluminum radiators, *not* for copper/brass radiators. Dex-Cool's harsh and resilient organic acids can attack the solder in copper radiators, eventually causing the radiator to leak.

Dex-Cool also has a tendency to sludge up in the system over time due to contaminants that find their way into the system. When swapping an LS engine, most builders suggest flushing the engine with water three or four times until it comes out clear and there are no more hints of orange.

Once the coolant system is clean, it's time to add new coolant. Most builders agree that the aftermarket (non-GM) orange long-life equivalent works well in systems with copper/brass radiators. Make sure that the coolant being used says it is compatible with both types of coolant (Prestone, for example).

Of course the good old green antifreeze provides more than adequate performance so long as the system has been properly flushed. Dex-Cool and the standard green antifreeze can be mixed; however, the green antifreeze counteracts the long-life properties of Dex-Cool.

Inlet/Outlet Positioning: All LS engines have the same inlet and outlet position: on the passenger's side of the engine. In most cases, the easiest solution is to purchase a radiator with passenger-side inlets and outlets. Because there is no mechanical fan in the way, running the upper return hose to the driver's side is a pretty simple solution if the stock radiator has a driver-side upper mount.

The lower feed hose is more difficult to cross over to the driver's side, depending on the distance between the engine and radiator. It is possible to have the inlets and outlets moved, but the expense is likely just as much as purchasing a new radiator.

Aftermarket Options: Each of the many aftermarket radiators has its own benefits. The easiest option is to order an off-the-shelf unit with the inlets and outlets as the manufacturer placed them. New aftermarket radiators that mount in the stock location are available for most popular cars.

You can also save some cash by purchasing a universal or "custom fit" radiator, typically sold in terms of dimension. For example, a four-core 20 x 16-inch radiator indicates a 20-inch-wide by 16-inch-tall radiator. Often, these radiators fit in the stock location using the stock or slightly modified mounting hardware and can cost as much as 30 percent less.

Custom Options: Ordering a custom radiator usually involves filling out a form and sending it in, along with a phone call or e-mail to discuss your specific needs. Griffin and Ron Davis, for example, have custom-build capabilities.

The ideal radiator configuration for a Gen III/IV is to have both outlets on the passenger's side and a divider placed in the middle of the tank. However, converting to a crossover-style simplifies the installation.

Crossover-style tanks also ensure the coolant takes a longer route through the tubes as all the coolant must pass through the top rows then through the bottom, doubling the surface area the coolant must pass through. Radiators built in this manner cost between $600 and $1,200, depending on the size, configuration, and manufacturer.

A transmission cooler can be run in the radiator also, which keeps the transmission the same temperature without being affected by ambient temperature. This maintains a much more consistent transmission temperature over an external transmission cooler, which allows the transmission to run cooler in the winter and warmer in the summer. Gen III/IV engines do not tend to run hot, so if your LS is running much hotter than the thermostat installed, there's a problem.

Mounting: Mounting the radiator below the engine is a common LS engine swap procedure that produces ineffective cooling and excessive heat. This is not an issue in most muscle cars and trucks, but on many other vehicles the radiator simply doesn't have clearance to be mounted in a position higher than the engine. In this scenario, the engines tend to hold air pockets that lead to overheating.

There are a couple of solutions for bleeding air out of a cooling system. The first is to use the upper radiator hose to fill the engine. This allows the coolant to fill the engine from the top down, helping to force the air out. Once the upper hose overflows, connect it to the radiator and fill the remainder of the radiator. Fill the overflow tank to half full. Then the engine should be run with the heater at full blast and brought up to temperature. The overflow tank drains into the radiator. Once the cap is removed and more coolant is added, the overflow tank should remain at about one-quarter full when the engine is cool. If there is air in the system, the tank drains and more should be added until the tank remains at one-quarter full.

This does not always work. Jaguars That Run offers a specialized part that installs in line with the upper radiator hose. This piece contains a valve that allows the system to be purged of any remaining air.

Water Necks

The stock cast-aluminum water neck (also called the thermostat housing) points at a 90-degree angle toward the passenger's side. This position works fine for many installations, but you may need a non-stock unit to accommodate a different

This straight water neck is best for Corvette applications. Corvettes typically have less radiator clearance; the straight outlet provides a quick shot to the radiator with fewer bends. (Photo Courtesy Street & Performance)

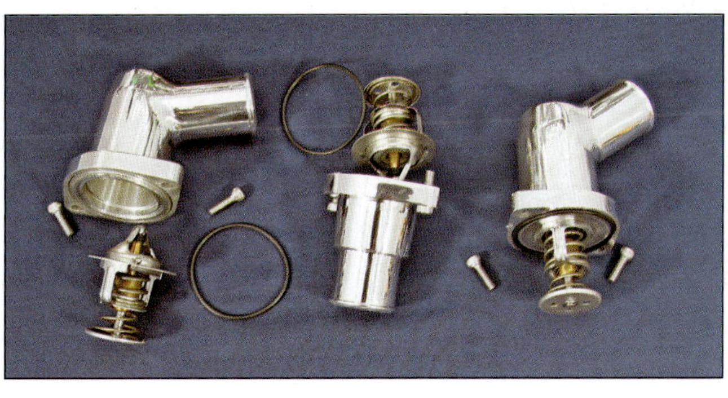

These water necks make swaps a little easier. The 45-degree and 15-degree necks swivel 360 degrees. (Photo Courtesy Street & Performance)

Steam Line Installation

Steam lines are part of the Gen III/IV cooling system and cannot simply be removed. The steam line must be properly fitted to the cooling system to remove air from it. This requires tapping the water pump, installing the proper fittings, and routing it to the radiator. ■

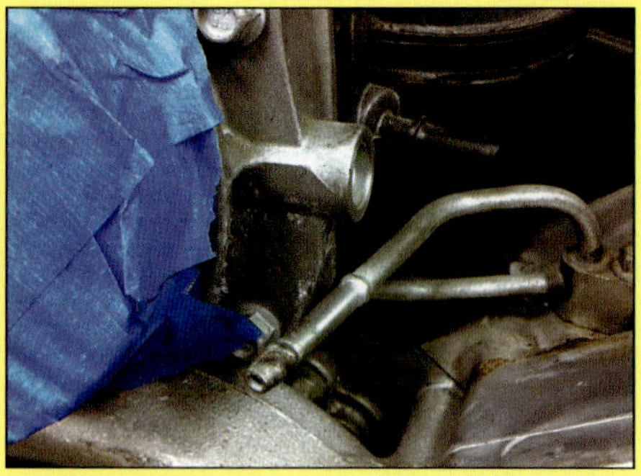

1 *LS engines have an interesting component called steam lines. These lines purge air from the system and feed warm air to the throttle body. This line must be connected to the radiator. (Photo Courtesy Blane Burnett)*

2 *This kit from Summit Racing converts factory steam fittings to AN style. (Photo Courtesy Summit Racing)*

3 *If your radiator does not have an extra input for the steam line, you can add the steam line to the water pump, which also cleans up the engine bay. With the pump off the engine, drill a pilot hole in the flat spot. (Photo Courtesy Street & Performance)*

4 *Drill the full-size hole to install the hose fitting. Here, I am installing a 3/8-inch NPT fitting. (Photo Courtesy Street & Performance)*

5 *The hole must be tapped to match the fitting's threads. Make sure that you use the correct thread pitch; 3/8-inch NPT (pipe thread) is different from 3/8-inch coarse or fine thread. (Photo Courtesy Street & Performance)*

6 *Install the fitting. Use some Teflon thread tape to keep the fitting from leaking. (Photo Courtesy Street & Performance)*

7 *Adjust the fitting for the correct positioning. The pump is ready to be reinstalled. If your pump does not have the flat area, install the fitting near the back of the outlet fitting. (Photo Courtesy Street & Performance)*

8 *Install the steam line hose on the 3/8-inch NPT fitting. (Photo Courtesy Street & Performance)*

9 *Hook the hose to the steam line outlet. The length and routing of the hose depends on the pump and fittings used. Length is not much of a factor, but the connections need to be sturdy so leaks do not develop. (Photo Courtesy Street & Performance)*

10 *The final result is a cleaner engine bay. An alternative solution is to use AN-style fittings and braided line from Summit Racing. (Photo Courtesy Street & Performance)*

11 *Companies such as Griffin can add the extra inlet to their custom radiators, for a price. A local radiator shop can handle this task on a stock radiator as well. (Photo Courtesy Street & Performance)*

AN conversion mounts like these from Trick Flow allow you to run braided hose to the radiator or water pump for a clean look. (Photo Courtesy Summit Racing)

These fittings (in satin aluminum) are a perfect fit for the LS engine. (Photo Courtesy Blane Burnett)

Using a couple of 90-degree fittings, the driver-side steam line runs under the throttle body to the passenger's side via braided Earl's line. (Photo Courtesy Blane Burnett)

radiator or chassis. There are several aftermarket alternatives to the stock cast water neck. Two such options are a straight unit (which is the best one for the early Corvettes), and a 360-degree swivel with either a 45- or 15-degree outlet.

Each water neck must match the water pump design, 1998–2003 and 2004–up. Since there is no mechanical fan to get in the way, you can easily run a lower radiator hose to the driver-side outlet on the radiator to prevent having to buy a new radiator.

Steam Lines

A unique design feature on LS engines is a pair of steam lines that route from the cylinder heads through the throttle body and onto the radiator. These lines circulate warm coolant through the throttle body to warm the intake charge on cold days and ensure that no air is in the cooling system. They must also be routed to the return tank on the radiator. There are three ways to accomplish this.

The first is to use a traditional routing pattern and run a line from the driver-side cylinder head to the return tank on the radiator.

The second option is to drill and tap the top of the water pump with a 1/4-inch tap, install a 90-degree pipe fitting, and route the steam lines to the top of the water pump. This option certainly results in a cleaner look, but requires some additional work. As a bonus, if aluminum or stainless-steel hard line is used, the lines can be polished, adding some flash to a very utilitarian function.

The final option is to splice a "T" fitting into the heater hose, routing the steam line to it instead of to the radiator.

Steam Line Fittings

Steam lines are a necessary component of an LS engine swap. The problem is that they often look less than stellar with barbed fittings and rubber lines. A great alternative to the stock setup is to convert to AN-style lines. Aftermarket plumbing involves AN fittings, which were developed by the aerospace industry. Each AN size directly correlates to a specific outside diameter of metal tubing. Each size is listed as -X with the number after the "-" indicating a 1/16-inch increase in size. Therefore, a -3 fitting is 3/16 inch, -4 is 1/4 inch, and so on.

Choosing which components to use depends on your budget and the

The passenger-side line connects with a T fitting, allowing the lines to be connected side to side and then to the radiator. (Photo Courtesy Blane Burnett)

The AN conversion was performed on a Nissan 240SX LS3 swap. The Hinson conversion radiator in the Nissan 240 SX comes with steam line inlets welded to the tank and barbed hose fittings. The barbed fittings (left) were swapped out with the -6 AN replacement fitting (right). (Photo Courtesy Blane Burnett)

With the fitting threaded into the radiator, a straight Earl's AN fitting was connected. All that is left is to cut a piece of braided hose and the steam lines are done. (Photo Courtesy Blane Burnett)

Some 1999–2005 Vortec 5300 5.3-liter engines used mechanical fans like this. They can be used as is or converted to electric. If you convert them to electric fans, a traditional fan controller, such as the Flex-a-lite or rheostat device, must be used to turn them on as the ECM doesn't have the wiring or the programming (which could also be added and an aftermarket harness used). (Photo Courtesy Street & Performance)

level of performance desired. Earl's Performance Plumbing offers several different types of fittings and hoses to suit each system's needs. The Ano-Tuff hard-anodized fittings resist corrosion and wear better than the more common red and blue anodizing. Swivel-Seal hose ends keep the hose from twisting and collapsing when assembling the lines in the car. The steam line adapters are from Trick Flow and have -6 male ends for the hose connections.

Electric Fans

An electric fan must be used because Gen III/IV (except for 5.3 1999–2005 Vortec) engines do not have provisions for a mechanical fan. There are many options for electric fans, both stock and aftermarket, and each requires custom fitting to the radiator.

For the budget-minded builder, reusing stock radiator fans is an inexpensive option. Most salvage yards include the stock fans (and maybe the radiator) when you buy a complete engine. Because the Gen III/IV platform is relatively new, there is plenty of life left in the fan motors. Of course, new fans have guarantees and can be configured exactly how they are needed.

Electric fans have many benefits over mechanical fans. Electric fans are set to run at a predetermined temperature, allowing the engine to reach operating temperature much faster. This improves fuel economy and reduces engine wear and oil contamination.

The electric fan can also operate when the engine is off, so the coolant in the radiator cools while the car is sitting. This helps keep the engine in its optimum temperature range during all driving conditions. However, correct installation is essential. If electric fans are not installed correctly (with an electric fan shroud), they are not able to draw air through the entire radiator, and efficiency suffers.

When shopping for an electric fan, make sure to purchase

Electric fans are a must for most LS engines. Saving the original radiator and fans from the donor car is a suitable option. This aftermarket fan from Flex-a-lite has the necessary shroud built in. (Photo Courtesy Flex-a-lite)

This staggered fan and shroud setup is an excellent choice for older cars, such as the Tri-Five GM cars. Older cars and trucks typically have square radiators, but adding two fans side-by-side can be tough. One fan might be sufficient, but the dual-speed fan control in the LS ECM allows for two fans to operate at different temperatures, yielding better cooling. (Photo Courtesy Flex-a-lite)

Electric fans require temperature sensors. This one simply snuggles between the tubes and fins. (Photo Courtesy Street & Performance)

The rheostat control can go anywhere, although close to the radiator is best. Once it is set, you don't need to touch it again. (Photo Courtesy Street & Performance)

A more accurate thermostat installs directly in place of the petcock. This unit came from Street & Performance. (Photo Courtesy Street & Performance)

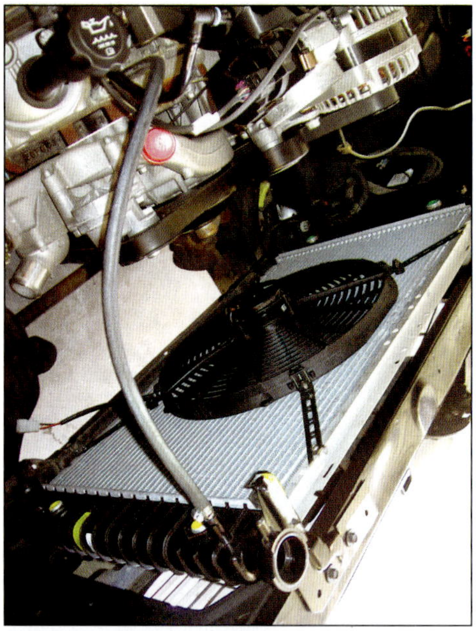

This is an example of a fan that does not use a shroud. Due to its design, air from the fan does not reach much of the radiator. The only time air passes through the radiator is when the car is moving. A shroud ensures more air passes the radiator when idling, an important feature for city drivers. (Photo Courtesy Street & Performance)

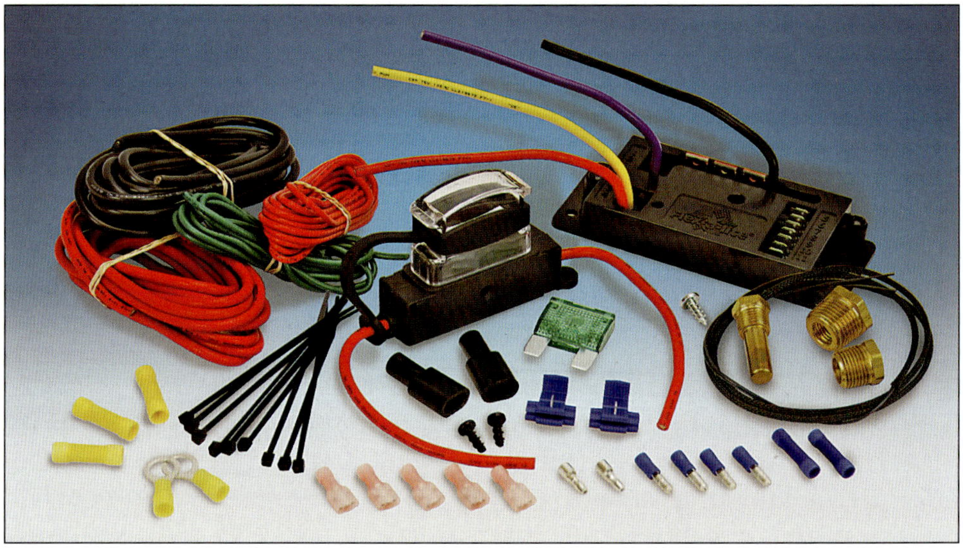

Flex-a-lite offers this electronic fan controller, which might be beneficial for engines running aftermarket controllers. This gives the driver control of the fan, rather than the ECM, so you can regulate operation and engine temperature. (Photo Courtesy Flex-a-lite)

one designed for high-performance engines and one that has a fan shroud for maximum efficiency. Some of the leading electric fans for LS engines are from Flex-a-lite, Griffin, AutoLoc-Zirgo, and Perma-Cool.

Water Pumps

Factory water pumps are suitable for most performance applications with mechanical pumps, being the staple for high-performance street cars. However, electric water pumps have broken free of the stigma of being strictly for drag racing and can update the functionality of an LS swap.

One of the biggest benefits to an electric pump, beyond the horsepower savings, is the ability to wire a timer that circulates coolant through the engine after the engine is shut off, providing a consistent cooling rate. Meziere Enterprises' LS engine pump is available with an idler puller, so the serpentine belt system can be retained, or without an idler pulley for race engines.

There are several flow ratings for electric pumps: from 20 to about 60 gallons per minute (gpm). For street applications, you want an extreme-duty motor that delivers as much GPM as possible, in the 45 to 55 range. The Meziere LS pump provides 55 gpm, as does the CVR electric LS pump.

There are even options for a remote-mount electric pump, using a conversion kit from Moroso, which allows you to put an electric pump anywhere under the hood. The keys to an electric water pump installation are the heater hose fittings. Not all electric pumps come with all the ports required for hooking up heater hoses, so you have to work around that. Stainless-steel mounting hardware is included with this lightweight pump.

Electric pumps clear camshaft belt drives, Jesel belt drives, and most blower drives, but spacers are necessary to clear distributor belt drives without the inlet fitting. The fitting must match the size of the lower radiator hose. The average amperage draw is 6 to 7 amps.

The biggest gain with an electric water pump is through elimination of drag. Just by dropping the drag of the pump's operation from the engine, you can gain 15 hp, plus the cool factor goes way up.

1 *The stock heater line fitting might not clear the suspension or frame in some installations. This can be rectified. (Photo Courtesy Street & Performance)*

2 *Using Vise-Grips and a hammer, tap the fittings out. You could also drill the fitting and use a bolt, along with a slide hammer, if the engine is out of the vehicle. (Photo Courtesy Street & Performance)*

3 *Remove the water pump and tap the fittings holes. The small fitting is the feed to the heater core; the larger one is the return. The small side is 3/8-inch and the larger is 1/2-inch thread. (Photo Courtesy Street & Performance)*

4 *You can then reinstall the pump. Don't forget to clean it out; metal shavings are bad. (Photo Courtesy Street & Performance)*

Gauges

If you plan to run aftermarket gauges, you need to install an adapter into the block to convert the sending unit to SAE threads. The engine has a 12-mm plug on the rear passenger-side head that can be removed to provide the coolant temperature sender location.

Drill and tap for the pipe thread or fit a simple adapter to the head for converting from 12-mm to 1/8-, 1/4-, 3/8-, or 1/2-inch pipe thread. This needs to be done *before* installing the engine in the vehicle; otherwise it is extremely difficult to install the adapter.

Should it be too late to install the adapter, Flex-a-lite offers an in-line adapter to be installed in the upper radiator hose. The adapter, designed to fit 1½-inch and 1¾-inch hoses, has two 1/4-inch NPT threaded holes and a brass plug. This makes it easy to keep tabs on the coolant temperature.

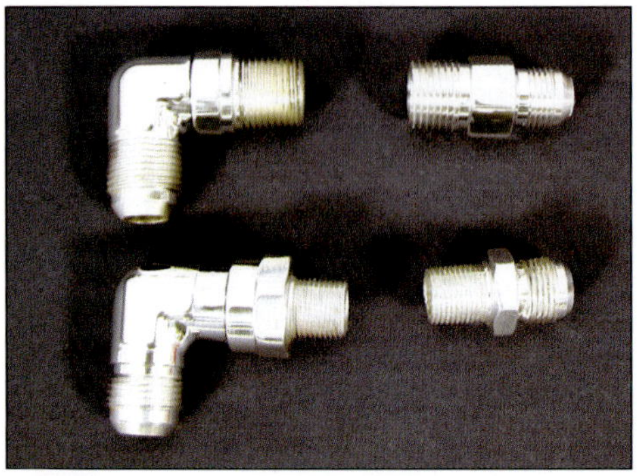

1 *These fittings accept AN -8 or -10 lines, depending on the size needed. AN fittings look nice on heater hoses. (Photo Courtesy Street & Performance)*

2 *In order to accurately measure the temperature of the coolant, you need to install a temperature-sending unit. This location at the back of the passenger-side head is the best place. This hole is threaded with a 12-mm plug. You need an adapter to match the sending unit. (Photo Courtesy Street & Performance)*

3 *This is what a 12-mm sending unit looks like. Most aftermarket gauges use NPT thread, thus the required adapter. (Photo Courtesy Street & Performance)*

4 *If you don't install the sending unit before the engine, there may be a clearance problem. The only reason it could be done afterward on this 1969 Camaro was because the A/C box had been shaved. (Photo Courtesy Street & Performance)*

5 *Another alternative is to use a heater hose coupler. This puts the sending unit in the upper radiator hose. This also serves as a good purge valve for getting any trapped air out the system. (Photo Courtesy Flex-a-lite)*

Feature Vehicle

Gen III Jeep YJ

Photos courtesy Ken Wolkens

The Jeep Wrangler YJ is a venerable off-road vehicle, and most agree that through the years the Jeep Wrangler has delivered better off-road performance than any of its competitors. Whether it's rock crawling, trail riding, or just going where most other 4x4s can't, the Jeep has them all beat. Take it to the street, however, and the small, inline 4.0 6-cylinder engine does not deliver inspiring performance.

Engine swaps for the Jeep platforms have always been popular. The Buick V-6 is a classic Jeep swap, as is the traditional small-block Chevy 350. The most popular is the LS swap. Ken Wolkens is one of those Jeep owners who definitely needed a bit more power. Jeep enthusiasts tend to be of the "built not bought" mindset, using parts from other vehicles to make their Jeep better.

Built as a daily driver with the ability to go anywhere, Ken's 1992 Jeep YJ uses many stock parts taken from salvage yards. The 5.3 4L60E transmission, power control module (PCM), wire harness, and drive-by-wire throttle pedal came from a 2005 Silverado with 24,000 miles on the odometer. To make the Gen II work with the Jeep, an NP231C transfer case with manual shifter and adapter from the transfer case to the transmission were sourced from a late-1980s to a mid-1990s Chevy S10 4x4. Rounding out the drivetrain is a D2 8.8 traction-lock rear axle with disc brakes from a 1995–2002 Ford Explorer.

The NP231 case was split, using the GM front half and the Jeep rear half and output shaft. This allowed Ken to use the Jeep speedometer output from the transfer case to drive the factory speedometer. The rest of the gauges were reused, keeping the Jeep oil and temperature sensors in the Vortec block.

The engine was mounted using a set of motor mounts from Advance Adapters, along with the factory transmission crossmember with a new hole for the 4L60E transmission. To make things easy, Ken cut a hole in the side of the transmission adapter for a vehicle speed sensor that tracks the vehicle speed through a reluctor wheel. This eliminates the need to program shift tables to the two-wheel-drive PCM.

Above: *Under the hood of this classic Jeep YJ is an LS engine. The stock 4-cylinder found in most Jeeps is good for rock crawling but they do not provide outstanding performance on the street. With eight cylinders, a common reaction from other highway drivers is, "Wait, did I just get smoked by a Jeep?"*

Several exhaust manifolds fit the Jeep chassis. F-Body and C5–C6 Corvette LS manifolds work great, but truck manifolds do not. Ken used the C6 factory manifolds, which cleared the chassis perfectly.

The fuel system uses a Walbro GSS 310 255-liter-per-hour in-tank pump feeding a Corvette filter/regulator combo through a new 3/8-inch hard line to the engine. The Jeep fuel system line is a diminutive 5/16 inch, and is not capable of feeding an LS-series engine.

Even though the Jeep chassis is small, there were very few clearance issues. The main challenge with a Gen III/IV engine is clearance from the power steering pump to the lower steering shaft. There is only 3/4 inch, which is fairly tight. Ken used the stock Jeep hose, and adjusted the bends to fit. They worked, so nothing major needed to be done.

Another key issue was the radiator. Ken tried to adapt three radiators until he found one that worked. That one was a "custom-fit Jeep LS swap radiator" he found on eBay. It features a crossflow design with both inlet and outlet on the passenger's side. The hoses were purchased at the local parts store using wire shapes as a guide.

With the details handled, the freshly assembled Jeep YJ has ample power. Passing on the highway requires a deft foot on the pedal to keep it from breaking the tires loose. With V-8 power and fuel economy that rivals the original 4-cylinder, Ken has a great-looking Jeep that can go anywhere and pass anything, including the gas pump.

Photo 1: *The weak 4-cylinder is fine for mail trucks and rock crawlers, but for real highway use, an LS V-8 is much better. Sourced from a 2005 Chevy Silverado truck, the 5.3-liter Gen III more than doubles the Jeep's available horsepower.* ***2.*** *The Advance Adapters motor mounts keep the engine between the frame rails and are an off-the-shelf item, available through many performance parts catalogs.* ***3.*** *The best-fitting manifolds for the YJ chassis are from the C6 Corvette. There is plenty of clearance for all of the important stuff such as steering links.* ***4.*** *The passenger-side manifolds have plenty of clearance for engine twist under acceleration or on the trails.* ***5.*** *The power steering pump is fairly tight to the lower steering rod. Polyurethane motor mounts are suitable because they are stiffer than rubber and limit engine roll more than rubber mounts.* ***6.*** *Ken used the stock Jeep power steering hose and tweaked the metal tubing to reach the GM type-II pump.*

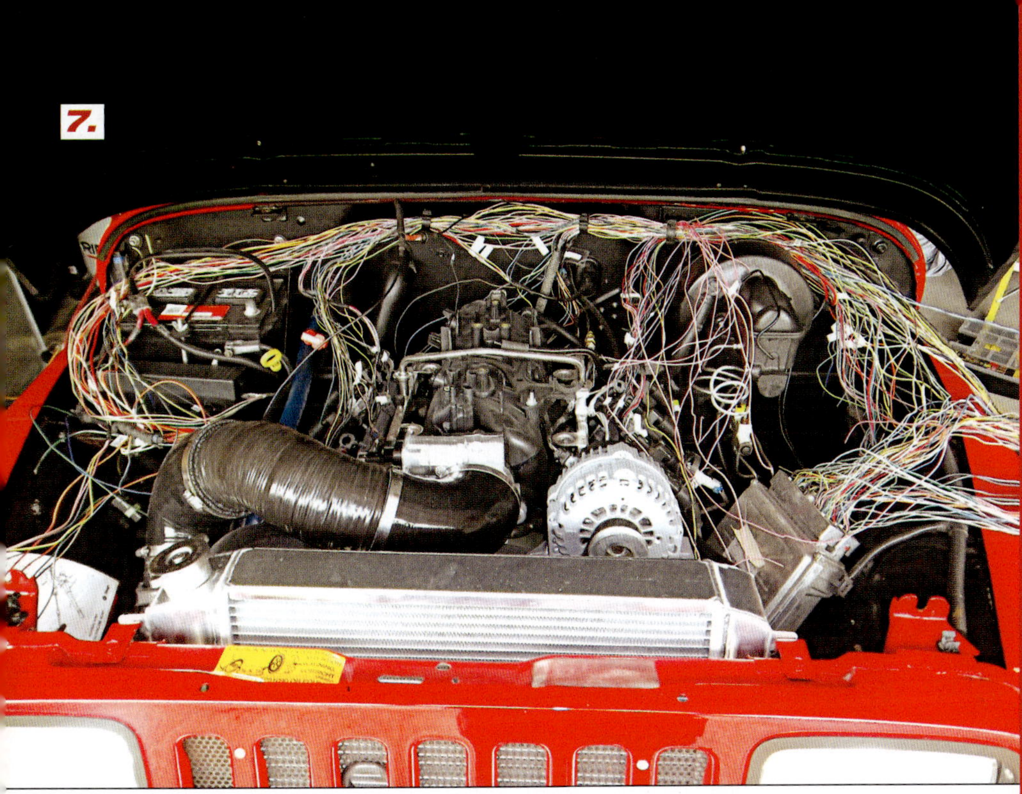

__7.__ Wiring a Gen III with the factory harness can be intimidating if you are not familiar with vehicle wiring. Using the "wire diet" method, Ken removed all of the unnecessary wires. __8.__ When he was done, the engine bay looked like this. The factory PCM was mounted under the hood on the driver-side inner fender. __9.__ The transmission was set to 3 degrees of downward angle to match the rear pinion. The output shaft of the two-wheel-drive 4L60E transmission was swapped out for a four-wheel-drive shaft. __10.__ Ken used a Lokar floor shifter (PN ATS64L60ECM), which fit through the shifter cutout in the Jeep floor perfectly. No mods required. __11.__ The lower radiator hose was also readily available. Ken used bailing wire formed to the shapes needed and matched up a hose at a local parts store. __12.__ The radiator came from a seller on eBay. It features a crossflow design with both inlet and outlet on the passenger's side. Custom-fit radiators are available from numerous manufacturers.

TRANSMISSION AND CLUTCH

When it comes to bolting a transmission to the back of a Gen III/IV engine, there are countless options. From automatics to manuals, stock to modified, there are literally more transmission options available than there are versions of the Gen III/IV engine. The LS-series engines share the same basic bellhousing pattern as the original small-block Chevy, so LS engines can be bolted to anything from a 2-speed Powerglide to a 4L80E.

Automatic Transmissions

Bolting an older transmission to an LS engine requires specialized spacers and flexplates because the Gen III/IV engines are shorter. If you simply bolt an old-style converter to an LS engine without a spacer, you will have major problems after only a few miles of driving. The pump seal will be ruined and will start to leak, causing the pump to fail. The converter doesn't fit and will not center on the back of the crank. To make up for the difference, special conversion flexplates are required.

Flexplate

The 6.0-liter Vortec with a 4l80E transmission is the only Gen III/IV engine that accepts an early GM transmission without a flexplate adapter or spacer. These vehicles came with the GM spacer and bolts and the flat factory flexplate. These are basically the same components needed for the older transmission swap, just performed at the factory.

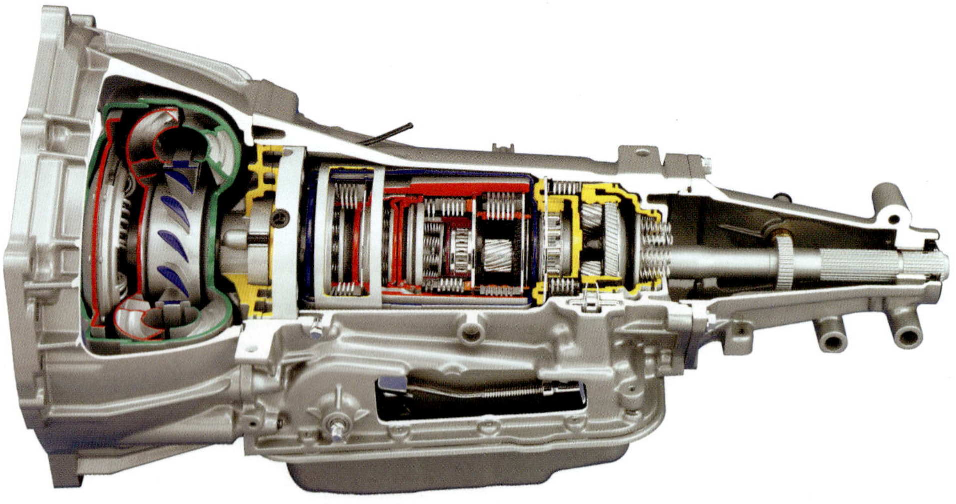

The GM 4L60E is the most popular and most common automatic transmission coupled to a Gen III/IV engine because it efficiently transmits power to the driveline, it's strong, and it's reliable. The overdrive is electronically controlled for precise performance. An evolution of the popular 700R4, the 4L60E, is a popular swap transmission. (Photo Courtesy General Motors)

If you are going to run any automatic transmission other than the correct late-model automatic, you need an adapter ring like this one from General Motors. It adds the required space so the nose of the torque converter fits with the crank. (Photo Courtesy Street & Performance)

The flexplate on the right is the adapter plate, which allows an early-style torque converter to bolt up. The unit on the left is the stock unit. Note the dish on the stock flexplate; this is another reason you must use an adapter flexplate for older transmissions. (Photo Courtesy Street & Performance)

This flexplate adapter from TCI allows you to use an older GM automatic transmission with a Gen III/IV engine, and it's also SFI certified for racing. (Photo Courtesy TCI)

Here, the dish is in the center of the stock flexplate. Because the flexplate is not flat like previous GM units, a special adapter is required when combining the LS with older GM transmissions. (Photo Courtesy Street & Performance)

Flywheels are more than just a connector between the transmission and the engine; they are an integral component to the clutch. The flywheel can also affect the driving characteristics of the engine. A heavy flywheel holds more inertia for smoother shifts and easier street driving. A lighter flywheel allows for quicker revs and shifts; they are great for road racing. This is a RAM 19.2-pound LS7 flywheel bolted to an LS3. (Photo Courtesy Blane Burnett)

The clutch mounts between the flywheel and pressure plate. This is a single-disc LS7 system. If you require more power, twin-disc clutch kits are available for the LS-series engine. (Photo Courtesy Blane Burnett)

General Motors offers the spacer plate and longer bolts over-the-counter. TCI has conversion flexplates for automatic transmissions and kits that include the spacer and longer bolts. You must use a crankshaft spacer, such as the Hughes Performance, TCI, or GM spacer and bolts, or a custom converter must be made with a longer-crank hub. The Bowtie Overdrives LS swap torque converter eliminates the need to use a spacer; it bolts directly to the stock flexplate.

If you're installing a used engine, the best solution for the transmission fit issues is to use the transmission that came with the engine. Then all you have to do is fit the transmission to the car.

TV Cable

Adapting the non-electronically-controlled 700-R4 and 200-4R requires a little more work. The most important component of these two overdrive transmissions is the throttle-valve cable, or TV cable. This crucial system tells the transmission when to shift and determines the amount of pressure sent to the clutches. If this cable is off by even the slightest amount, the clutches do not fully engage, causing the transmission to burn up and eventually fail.

Adapting the TV cable to the throttle body on an LS engine is challenging, and you need to maintain the right geometry. Doing this requires in-depth knowledge of the TV cable system, and is not suggested for novices. Aftermarket manufacturers,

It looks a little odd compared to the earlier Gen I engines, but General Motors left off one of the boltholes on the back of the block. Other than looks, there is no difference in the bolt pattern. Any older GM bellhousing bolts up. (Photo Courtesy Street & Performance)

On older overdrive transmissions, such as this 200-4R, the TV cable is a crucial component. If it is not set right, the transmission may burn out within a few miles, so take the time to ensure it's properly adjusted.

Valve Body Replacement

An alternative to solve the complicated problem of transmission shifting is the TCI transmission valve body that removes the pressure regulation from the TV system. This valve body keeps the transmission at full-line pressure all the time, ensuring the clutches don't burn up from slipping. The TV cable is then relegated to serve as a speed control for shift points only. Fabricating a mount for the TV cable with the precision of the original style is no longer needed, making these transmissions much easier to use. ■

To remove the dangers of the TV cable system, TCI created the Constant Pressure Valve Body. This unit gives the transmission full pressure at all times, so the shifts are firm and solid, but can be dialed down a bit if needed. The best thing about these valve bodies is that the TV cable is reduced to a shift-detent cable, only controlling shift timing. The pressure is out of the equation, which is where the danger is.

1 *The transmission oil pan must be removed in order to replace the valve body. The entire process can easily be done while the transmission is in the car; just drop the pan. If the pan has a drain plug, drain the fluid first.*

2 *The check balls from the old valve body must be retained and reused in the new valve body, but not all of them. Place them in the correct passages according to the instructions and the desired shift characteristics. This part is done on the bench.*

Valve Body Replacement CONTINUED

3 *If you must install the check balls under the car, a little moly grease keeps them in place. Have everything ready to go back into the transmission. If the check balls fall out, they can bounce quite far. If you lose one, your local transmission shop should have extras for sale.*

4 *This kit comes with a new backing plate and gaskets. Use them, as the old ones don't work with this valve body. The accumulator spring sits on the plate as shown here.*

5 *Carefully align the plate to the transmission. Bolt the spring and accumulator bolt back on. This holds the plate in place.*

6 *Install the valve body and hook up the shifter lever. Install the filter, bolt on the pan, and fill the transmission with fluid. Now the TV cable can be adapted to the throttle body without fear of destroying the transmission.*

such as Bowtie Overdrives, offer bolt-on solutions for conversion from TV cable to throttle body.

Computer Controls

Almost all Gen III/IV engines in salvage yards, at swap meets, and on Internet sites already have a transmission attached, and the transmission is generally an automatic. The most common GM automatic is the 4L60E or the 4L65E variant (they are the same dimensionally, but the -65 version has an extra pinion gear internally), depending on whether the engine came from a car or a truck. The larger Vortec engines were typically mated to the 4L80E (and 4L85E variant) automatic transmission. These transmissions require computer controls that are contained in the factory ECM. However, these transmissions can be purchased separately through the aftermarket for carbureted LS conversions or when an aftermarket electronic fuel injection (EFI) controller is used.

In 2006, General Motors released a couple of 6-speed automatics for their vehicles. The 6L80 and 6L90 transmissions are used in heavy-duty GM trucks and most of the performance cars. The Sigma

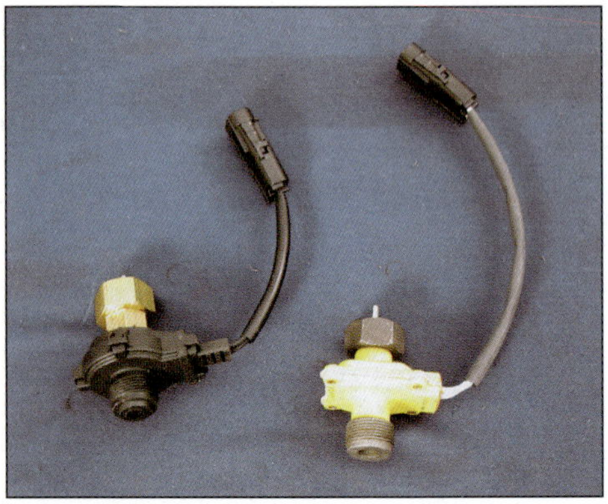

Mechanical/electronic adapters bolt onto the transmission and feed the electronic signal to the computer. A cable then connects to the other side. These are available from Street & Performance, AutoMeter, and most gauge suppliers. (Photo Courtesy Street & Performance)

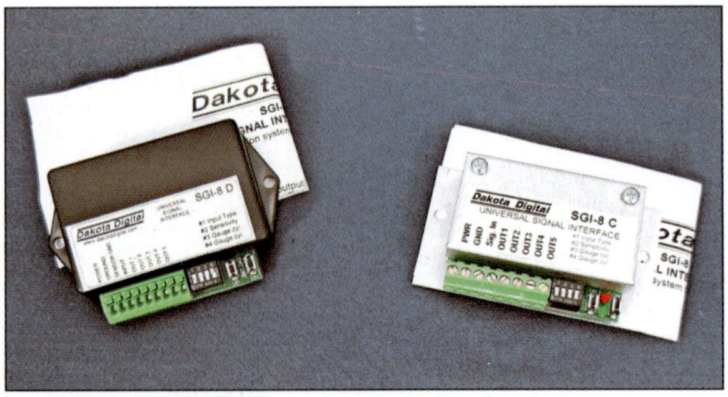

These units from Dakota Digital help convert the transmission's VSS signal to non-programmable electronic speedometers if yours is not compatible with the stock VSS signal. (Photo Courtesy Street & Performance)

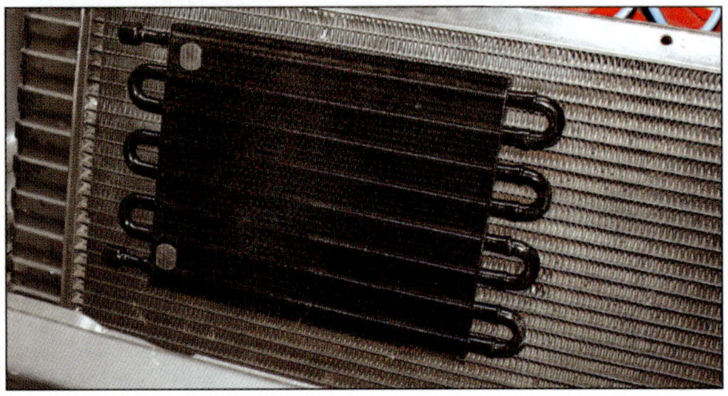

If the radiator does not have a built-in transmission cooler, it's necessary to add an external cooler when running an automatic. This unit from TCI keeps just about any GM high-performance transmission cool. It is placed in front of the radiator.

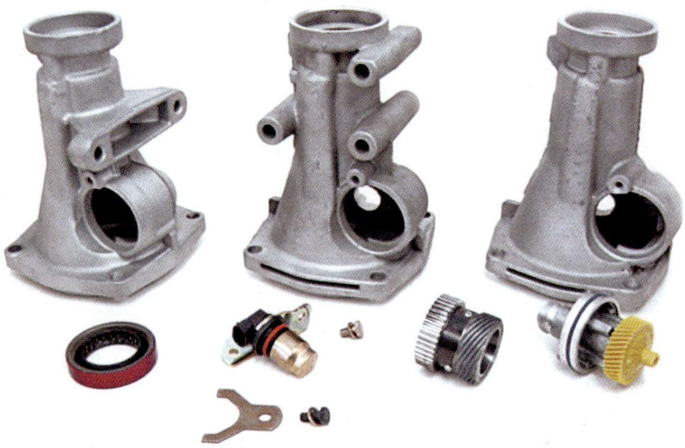

For the newer transmissions, you need to adapt the speedometer output to mechanical output in order to use a mechanical speedometer. These mechanical speedometer tailshafts are for the 4L60E and 4L65E transmissions. (Photo Courtesy Street & Performance)

This tailshaft is for the 4L80E transmission commonly found in larger trucks. The 4L80E can handle a lot of torque; it is quickly becoming the go-to automatic for high-performance LS swaps. (Photo Courtesy Street & Performance)

The tailshaft gear drives the speedometer gear, which in turn, drives the speedometer cable to the speedometer. Adapters are available for electronic speedometers, as well as different gears for tuning mechanical speedometers. (Photo Courtesy Street & Performance)

platform, which covers the Cadillac CTS line, uses either the 5L40/5L50 5-speed or the 6L45/6L50 6-speed automatics.

Custom Swaps

The aftermarket has a vast number of custom-application GM transmissions that work great for LS swaps. One in particular is the TCI 6X 6-speed automatic. It is based on the 4L80E but with new guts to provide six forward gears capable of handling 850 hp. These can be configured in several ways and come with a TCI transmission controller. They can even be set up for a paddle shifter.

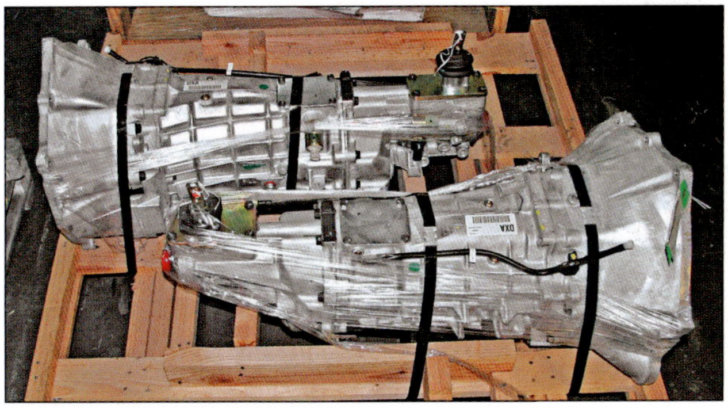

The Tremec T-56 6-speed manual is the most popular transmission for LS swaps. It bolts right up and requires only slight trimming or denting of the transmission tunnel to fit most GM cars and trucks. (Photo Courtesy Street & Performance)

Late-model transmissions and LS engines do not make installing a mechanical clutch simple. Although it can be done, it may not be worth the effort. A hydraulic throw-out bearing setup is the simplest solution. (Photo Courtesy Blane Burnett)

T56 Manual Transmission

The 6-speed T56 manual is the most popular transmission used in LS engine swaps. Formerly offered on the 1998–2002 F-Body and GTO, the T56 bellhousing, flywheel, and clutch pack are readily available. The T56 transmission fits into most GM muscle cars, requiring only minor modifications, if any, to the transmission tunnel. Swap kits help make the install easier. Classic Motorsports Group offers a kit for first-generation Camaros, Firebirds, and Novas

The 1968–1974 Nova requires that the transmission tunnel be enlarged. The clutch mechanism, however, definitely requires some modifications. There are several ways to get around the clutch mechanism, such as using an older-style manual clutch or a modern hydraulic clutch.

As a side note, the 1993–1997 T56s use an external clutch slave cylinder, while the later 1998-up units use an internal slave cylinder. The 1998-up T56 transmission is better suited for the Gen III/IV engines with the correct bolt pattern and input shaft, but McLeod offers components that adapt older T56 transmissions to the Gen III/IV engines.

Mounting Plate

Street & Performance offers a few components that assist in adapting the hydraulic clutch to most GM vehicles, and they can be modified to work with other vehicles as well. The first component is the slave cylinder mounting plate. Available in two versions, 1958–1964 and 1967-up, this plate mounts between the vacuum booster (or master cylinder) and the firewall. The mount holds the master cylinder (GM PN 12570277) to the hydraulic clutch. The clutch fluid reservoir is mounted on the firewall.

Clutch Pedal Adapter Tab

To bolt the original clutch pedal to the master cylinder pushrod, an adapter tab must be installed on the original pedal. This tab must be fabricated and welded to the clutch pedal. The placement of this tab is absolutely critical. If the tab is too high, the pushrod does not fully engage. If it is placed too low, the pedal is hard to push.

Using a piece of 3/16-inch-thick mild plate steel cut to 1 x 3 1/16 inches, the tab should be bent into a Z shape, .300 inch wide, starting at the

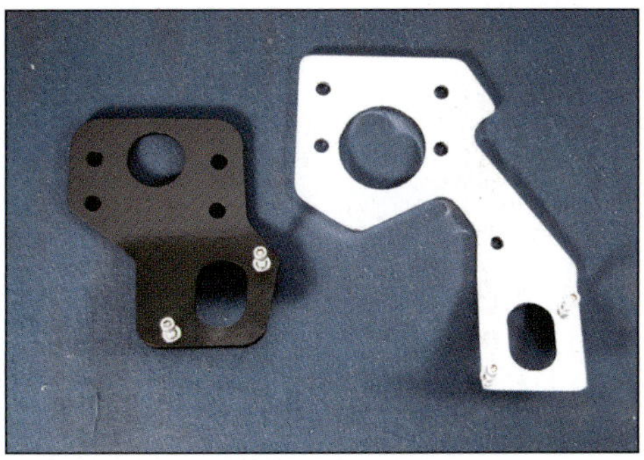

Adapter brackets are available for mounting the hydraulic clutch unit to the firewall based on the brake booster mounts. Brackets are available from Street & Performance (shown), Detroit Speed & Engineering, and several others; or you can make your own. (Photo Courtesy Street & Performance)

The plate bolts in directly behind the brake booster, then the clutch master cylinder bolts on. This is a finished installation. The second line coming off the master cylinder leads to the remote-mount fluid reservoir. (Photo Courtesy Street & Performance)

4L60E Transmission Upgrade

The 4L60E transmission is a worthy unit, capable of withstanding the tortures of street/strip abuse as long as it has been outfitted with a few high-performance goodies like a billet servo, bigger sunshell gear, and red-oxide clutches.

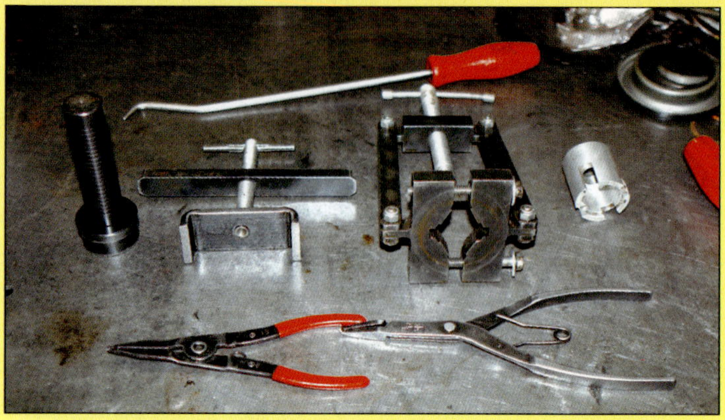

Transmission rebuilding requires specialized tools not found in the average toolbox. Shown here are just a few of the tools needed to work on the 4L60E. Pictured from the top, left to right: cotter key pick, Teflon shaft installer, rear clutch spring compressor, universal pump remover, electrical connection removal tool (a large socket works, but usually breaks a tab), and two snap-ring pliers.

The 4L60E transmission has long been a mainstay in GM's transmission arsenal, and it has a long history of backing up some potent engines. General Motors used it in all rear-wheel-drive cars from 1994 until 2001, when performance demands had increased beyond its current capacity and it was replaced with the 4L65E. The 4L65E was built on the same platform as the 4L60E, but with a few differences.

The 4L60E uses four-pinion planetary carriers rated to 360 ft-lbs of torque. The 4L65E utilizes five-pinion planetary carriers along with a hardened input shaft that boosts torque capacity to 380 ft-lbs. The nice thing about all of this is that the parts from the five-pinion are easily swapped into the 4L60E, allowing you to upgrade your existing transmission without having to buy a new unit.

Replacing the planetary carriers requires a full teardown. This is not the most difficult transmission to build, but it certainly isn't the easiest. It requires a few specialized tools to correctly complete the job: a rear clutch spring compressor, universal pump remover, front pump alignment band, turbine shaft installer, and a Teflon stator shaft installer are all needed to properly disassemble and reassemble the 4L60E transmission.

The 4L60E transmission is an electronically controlled unit, notated as such by the "E." In 1993, when the 4L60E was introduced, the 700-R4 was renamed 4L60. Although they share some parts, they are different.

Cleanliness is a virtue, especially when it comes to transmissions. The case for the 4L60E was washed for a few hours in the hot bath. Since caustic soda bath hot tanks have pretty much been outlawed by the EPA, 150-degree water and soap have to do.

In 1995, General Motors changed the 4L60E converter lockup circuit to a pulse width modulated (PWM) circuit. This type of lockup circuit offers a smoother transition because it pulses the signal instead of transmitting all of it at once. A PWM-type transmission is marked with "PWM" on the front of the pump. The important thing to remember here is that the transmission type, PWM (4l60E) or non-PWM (700R4), must match the computer in the car; otherwise it does not function properly.

Since the upgrade requires a complete teardown, a full rebuild with a few extra performance pieces is a good idea. There are a few areas that require special attention and

The front of the pump has the letters "PWM" cast into it if the unit is from a 1995–up model. This is very important if swapping the transmission into a different car. The computer must *match the transmission; a non-PWM computer does not control a PWM transmission, and vice versa.*

This little spring and ball must be thoroughly cleaned or they cause problems. The pump pressure-relief spring is the number-one cause of post-overhaul failure.

are commonly overlooked. The pump pressure relief is the number-one cause of failure after overhaul. It is very easy to forget this little ball and spring, but it tends to get gummy and starts sticking. Even a few miles down the road it can cause a failure because the converter can't release its pressure and it eventually overheats.

Several kits were used for this rebuild: a Trans-Go reprogramming kit, a Sonnax billet fourth-gear Super Hold servo, a Raybestos Z-pack clutch kit, and Red Eagle red-oxide clutches. We cherry-picked the clutch kit, using the Z-pack for the 3-4 gear clutches. These have superior holding power and are specifically designed to not bow. The red-oxide clutches have better hold for 1-2.

Another must in any high-performance transmission is a beefy sunshell gear for second and reverse applications. The stock parts have a tendency to shear off the gear at the neck (in high-performance applications). The aftermarket responded with the Beast sunshell. This unit is made of thicker material overall and includes a new thrust washer.

These are the required goodies to rebuild the transmission. I chose to use the Z-pack 3-4 clutches over the red-oxide Red Eagle clutches as they don't "cone" or bow under high heat and pressure.

The clutches were soaked in a bucket of Dexron III before being installed in the transmission. Forget this step and you may as well throw it all away.

The sunshell gear is a big liability, especially for a performance transmission. The stock sunshell gear is on the left. The Beast sunshell gear on the right is made of thicker material and is particularly beefy around the neck, where it is prone to sheering. The Beast also comes with a new Torrington thrust bearing. The 2001-up model 4L65E features a completely new design, eliminating the failure-prone features.

4L60E Transmission Upgrade *CONTINUE*

The five-pinion planetary carrier (right) is better built and houses an additional gear. Stock-rated capacity is substantially increased to 380 ft-lbs over the 360 capacity of the four-pinion carrier (left).

The carrier was assembled with the matching top carrier and installed in the transmission.

With the first and reverse clutches installed, a "block saver" was used, which is a $6 clip that keeps the low/reverse sprag from rotating and eventually breaking the case.

The Z-pack clutches were installed in the drum and checked for clearance. You don't want the clutches too tight or too loose. A visual check ensures the top clutch is even with the snap-ring groove. The anti-centrifugal rev springs keep the clutch pack tight.

The drum was in good condition, so it didn't need to be replaced; instead, it needed cleaning with a coarse 3M Roloc pad. If the drum is pitted or severely burned, replacement is required.

The meat of the conversion is the five-pinion rear planetary. In high-performance applications, the rear planetary carrier takes all the stress. Upgrading to the five-pinion unit offers the ability to hold much higher torque values. The 4L60E also uses a four-pinion front planetary carrier, which is more expensive than the rear unit. Upgrading to the five-pinion front carrier is advisable in towing applications and where horsepower numbers reach 500 or more.

The 3-4 gear clutches reside in the drum, which is where the Z-pack comes in. The clutches are stacked in the following order: finger clutch, inside clutch, finger clutch, etc. The final clutch is the brown clutch. The clutches have been correctly stacked when the brown clutch is even with the snap-ring groove. The five anti-centrifugal rev springs are installed next, then the pressure plate and another snap ring.

With the drum assembled, the outer surface needs to be cleaned. Using a 3M coarse surfacing pad, the entire outer surface is cleaned of any glazing. The drum must be flat and smooth. If the drum surface is concave, it should be replaced. For the drum band, a late-model high-intensity band is preferred over a wide band. The wide band has a little more hold, but the high-intensity band grabs and releases faster, which is more important in a high-performance application. The wide band is better suited for towing or in cases where the drum is worn in the center and replacement is cost prohibitive.

The Sonnax Super Hold billet servo offers 40 percent more surface area for better holding power in fourth gear and can be installed with the transmission in the car. This helps eliminate band failure in high-performance

The high-intensity band was installed after the drum was dropped in place. It took a little massaging to get the band to snap in place.

The servo pin was checked for clearance and was in spec, so the washer was installed. Always add a little transmission lube to internal moving parts.

Then the Sonnax Super Hold servo was installed. A snap ring holds it in place. This servo provides additional holding power, increasing the horsepower rating of the transmission.

applications. It is simple to install; only a set of snap-ring pliers is required. Just be sure to use the supplied steel washer. There is some adjustment to be made here, though. The typical servo pin travel is 1/8 inch. If it is greater than that, the pin should be changed or carefully ground down to achieve the desired travel.

Properly modifying the valve body is an important step in 4L60E performance applications. The Trans-Go reprogramming kit comes with everything needed to fix the valve body and make it suitable for high horsepower. The separator plate needs to be modified before the valve body can be bolted on.

The separator plate rests between the transmission case and the valve body. It is a thin piece of die-cut sheet metal with 50 or 60 holes in it. Using the illustration in the re-programming kit's instruction, 10 holes require drilling: the pressure apply and relief ports. Opening these up to .093 inch increases shift firmness and adjusts the timing of each shift. Drilling out the solenoid A and B ports to .040 inch slightly increases shift time, which makes for a nice shift pattern on the street.

The second accumulator body is modified with the springs supplied in the Trans-Go kit. Using two springs

The pump assembly received a new main pressure regulator and boost valve that came with the Trans-Go reprogramming kit. This is not a shift kit; this kit actually creates a new shift pattern.

The kit also came with instructions to modify the separator plate. If you're a veteran builder you can drill out the holes using a .093-inch bit. If not, the drilling should be performed on a workbench with a wood board as a backup.

The second accumulator makes the biggest difference in shift feel, so two springs were installed. The third spring should only be used for race units.

4L60E Transmission Upgrade *CONTINUED*

The valve body cannot be cleaned with soap and water; using a solvent tank is the best way to clean it. Don't be concerned about the electrical components. The solvent doesn't damage them.

gives the transmission a very firm shift; using all three is for full-race applications.

The valve body itself gets a new spring and valve, which modifies the isolator and converter regulator to allow the use of any type of torque converter lockup plate. ■

The valve body received a few springs to tighten the shift points and increase pressures, all part of the performance package.

This little spreader spring keeps the electronic pressure control (EPC) filter screen from collapsing under high suction. Without the spring, the screen just floats around and it can get crushed when the pump is building full pressure.

The valve body was then bolted down to the case and the electrical connections were once again connected. Don't over-torque the bolts.

A new filter and cork gasket finish off the internals of this build. Never use silicone sealant on a transmission pan because there are several small ports on the gasket rail that get plugged if silicone is used, causing the transmission to eventually burn up.

The final step was installing the new rear seal. Brass hammers are a must to prevent breakage when dealing with a transmission.

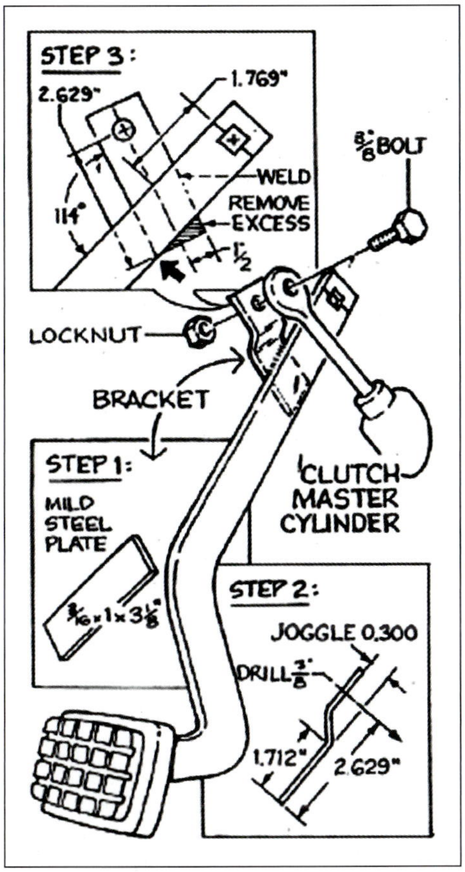

Adapting the hydraulic clutch requires some modification of the stock clutch pedal. This diagram works for all GM muscle cars and early F-Bodies, but double-check your particular application before welding anything. (Illustration Courtesy Street & Performance)

1.712-inch mark. Once bent, the tab is drilled with a 3/8-inch hole, measured from the long side of the tab at 2.629 inches on center. The placement of the tab on the pedal is 1.769 inches from the center of the square hole at the top of the pedal, and it sits at 114 degrees from the pedal side to the top of the tab.

The tab should then be fully welded to the pedal arm. The small, triangular-shaped section of the tab that overhangs the pedal on the underside is trimmed off. The clutch pushrod bolts to the tab via a 3/8-inch bolt and locknut. It is pos-

Here is the tab in place just before welding it on. It must be correctly positioned. Remember, this is only necessary when using a hydraulic clutch. (Photo Courtesy Street & Performance)

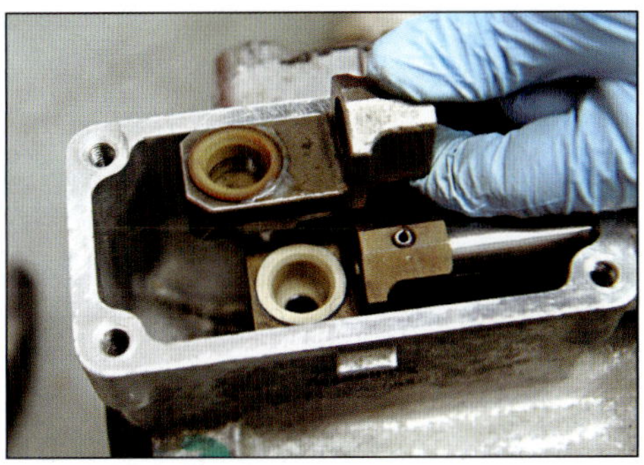

Shifters are interchangeable as long as you swap the receiver (the part that the shifter lever ball operates) bolted inside the transmission. It is retained by a roll pin. (Photo Courtesy Street & Performance)

sible to adapt the LS engine to use a manual clutch linkage. If you are installing an LS and manual transmission in a GM vehicle originally available with a manual clutch setup, you need linkage, clutch, Z-bar, and related components. The Gen III/IV blocks are not drilled for the Z-bar, which makes it difficult to adapt the LS engine to a manual linkage. Fabricating a simple bracket that locates using the bellhousing bolts and attaches to the Z-bar is the best solution.

If the car did not have a manual transmission before, cut the hole in the ideal location, similar to this 1969 Camaro. (Photo Courtesy Street & Performance)

If your car had a manual transmission and you want to retain the stock console, you need an adjustable shifter, such as this one from Driveline Components Company. This shifter allows for clearance of some floorpans, where a stock-style shifter doesn't. (Photo Courtesy Street & Performance)

Shifter

The T56 uses a top-mounted shifter at the rear of the transmission, which creates a compatibility issue for the stock console or shifter location in GM vehicles. This is easily rectified using the Street & Performance shifter relocator kit. As engine and transmission mounts differ, each shifter must be ordered individually.

Upgrading to a High-Peformance Clutch

When swapping an LS engine, you need to determine the best transmission for your combination and application. Many people opt for a manual transmission, such as a Tremec T56 or TKO. If your LS engine produces 400 hp or more, a stock clutch may not hold up, especially under extreme use. A high-performance aftermarket clutch from a reputable manufacturer provides a significant step up in performance and durability. There are many different clutch designs and disc materials used, including Kevlar, ceramic, and organic.

Clutches are made for high-performance street, drag race, circle track, road racing, and other applications. ACT, McLeod, and other manufacturers offer clutches for a variety of applications. The ACT Twin Disc Kit, for example, has double the number of discs as many other clutches and it delivers excellent engagement and quiet operation. The clutch also dissipates heat well for longer life.

The Performance Street Rigid-Hub discs feature organic/copper composition for superior heat-transfer properties. It includes a flywheel, alignment tool, pressure plate, floater, and two discs.

The following is sample of the current clutches available for the LS engine. ■

A complete kit, like this one from ACT, includes a matched flywheel. This ensures everything is balanced and functions properly together. The ACT single disc holds 770 ft-lbs with a sintered-metallic clutch disc. (Photo Courtesy ACT)

A strap-drive twin-disc secures the center disc with a strap that bolts to the flywheel. You can see the tab on the center plate (between the clutches) and the strap on the flywheel. These are quiet and effective. A pin drive is noisy for street use. (Photo Courtesy ACT)

Pressure plate design has a lot to do with the holding power and pedal pressure for the clutch. This is the traditional diaphragm design. These are the most popular street units and they work well for most street applications. (Photo Courtesy ACT)

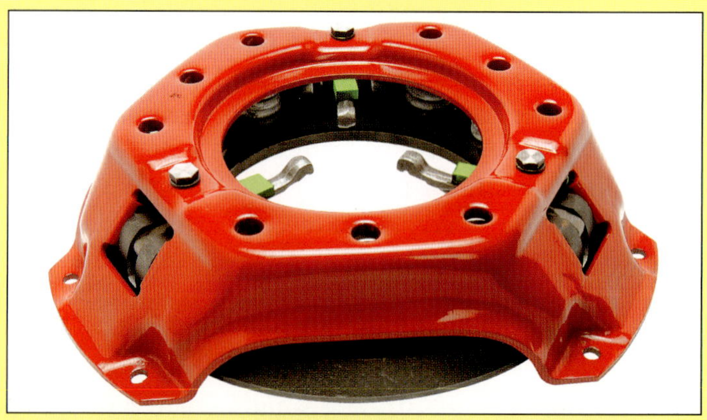

The Ford long-style uses three fingers instead of the multiple spring bars to operate the pressure plate. Nine springs must be compressed to release the clutch. (Photo Courtesy McLeod Racing)

Clutch material is an important choice, especially for a street-driven car. These Exedy Mach-series discs are for street and mild race cars. The Mach 500 is an organic material with a sprung center hub. The Mach 600 uses ceramic/metallic hybrid pads on Marcel springs rated for 600 ft-lbs. Mach 700 discs are five-puck ceramics with a sprung center hub. All of these discs can be used with the same pressure plate. (Photo Courtesy Exedy Globalparts)

Here are a GTO shifter (left) and a new Hurst F-Body-style shifter (right). The placement of the handle is critical. The Hurst shifter is more accurate through precision machining. (Photo Courtesy Blane Burnett)

The T56 relocator shifter can move the shifter 1 to 4.1 inches forward. In addition, the shifter can be centered or offset to the left or right. If you choose to use the stock T56 shifter, it is placed approximately 4 to 5 inches rearward from the stock location, 1 to 2 inches rearward for 1970–1974 F-Bodies, and 4 to 5 inches rearward in the 1968–1974 Nova.

Tremec TKO Manual Transmission

Another popular manual swap is the Tremec TKO 500 or TKO 600. These 5-speed manual transmissions are very popular among GM muscle builders and offer excellent performance. Classic Motorsports Group offers complete kits for installing the TKO into almost any GM muscle car and 1960–1972 Chevy trucks. These kits feature hydraulic clutches, bellhousing, and all the components to make the installation simple and easy.

TKO transmissions use a top-mounted shifter. To adapt these shifters to match the stock location, a Hurst Blackjack shifter can reposition the shifter to the ideal location.

The TKO transmission does not fit quite as neatly under the body as the T56 does. This transmission fits some GM vehicles without modifications, while others require serious cutting. The Tri-Five Chevy and similar-era GM cars, 1967–1981 F-Body (Camaro and Firebird), and C1–C3 (1956–1981) Corvettes do not require any floorpan modifications. The C4 Corvettes fit the TKO, but the stock shifter box must be removed and patched.

The 1964–1972 GM A-Body (Chevy Chevelle, Buick GS, Olds 442, etc.), 1960–1969 B-Body (Impala), and 1962 Novas all require a large section of the transmission tunnel to be removed and replaced with a reshaped panel. The Classic Motorsports kits come with the requisite patch panel, cut guide, and instructions, taking the guesswork out of the swap.

For reasons that may include nostalgia, economy, personal taste, simplicity, or originality, some builders prefer to keep the stock manual gearbox in their muscle car or truck when swapping in a Gen III/IV engine. These swaps bolt up similarly to the automatic transmissions, but require a few specialized parts.

Bellhousing

The input shaft is too far from the crank with a stock bellhousing (the same situation as with the automatic transmission). There are two ways to remedy this problem. The first and best way is to use a retrofit bellhousing and flywheel package. General Motors sells these components individually through its Chevrolet Performance dealers.

The Chevrolet Performance retrofit bellhousing features thick-wall titanium and aluminum alloy construction; CNC machining, including spot-faced mounting holes; precision dowel pin holes; and bores that yield a precise fit. This bellhousing bolts to all GM Gen III/IV V-8 engines for the installation of the Muncie, T-10, Saginaw, Richmond, Tremec TKO, Tremec T56-011, and other specially built transmissions.

This bellhousing works with stock clutch linkage and hydraulic clutch actuators, and includes steel inspection cover and mounting hardware. It is also designed to use a 168-tooth flywheel and standard GM starter. This bellhousing is lightweight (15 pounds) and uses all factory linkage parts, including clutch forks, Z-bar, rubber dust boot, etc.

According to Chevrolet Performance, the LS Truck flywheel (PN 12561680), 12-inch clutch and pressure plate (PN RAM88744), and six metric pressure plate bolts (PN 12561465) must be used.

Aftermarket Kits

Clutch kits are available from aftermarket sources such as McLeod and Advance Adapters. They are designed to adapt the Gen III/IV engines to early-style GM manual transmissions, such as the M21/M22, SM420, SM465, and NV4500. Additionally, these kits allow the installation of Richmond Gear manual transmissions, such as the Richmond Overdrive 6-speed.

This kit from Advance Adapters allows any older GM manual transmission to bolt up to a Gen III/IV engine. It includes the adapter flywheel, spacers, clutch, and everything else needed to make an older transmission, such as the M22, fit an LS engine. (Photo Courtesy Advance Adapters Inc.)

The T56 needs a different tailhousing for a mechanical speedometer. Most stock units have electronic sensors for electronic speedos. (Photo Courtesy Street & Performance)

The Advance Adapters clutch kits typically include a custom flywheel, 11-mm flywheel bolts, 11-inch centerforce pressure plate and disc, pilot bushing spacer, throw-out bearing, collector gasket, 10-mm bellhousing bolts, 10-mm lock washers, and XRP dowel bolts. If you want to assemble your own parts, the key is to match the flywheel and clutch to the engine, while making sure the splines on the clutch disc match the transmission.

GM transmissions use 10- and 26-spline input shafts; early manuals (before 1971) typically have 10 splines, and later units have 26 splines. That being said, some other aftermarket manual transmissions have either 10 or 26 splines. A 26-spline shaft is more durable than a 10-spline shaft because it distributes the input load better.

As a side note, the Advance Adapters kit can be used with Gen III engines mounted to Jeep manual transmissions (PN AX15/NV3550) and Ford manual transmissions (PN NP435/T-18). The throw-out bearing retainer must be machined to accept the adapter bearing, and a different clutch disc is likely needed.

The other option is to use an extended bearing. This retains the original old-style bellhousing, matches the clutch to the engine, and uses a longer bearing to make up the difference for the shorter crank flange. There are several manufacturers of these bearings, including McLeod (PN 8617) and General Motors (PN 12557583). By using the old-style bellhousing, you should have a provision for the Z-bar and be able to run a manual clutch setup.

Feature Vehicle

Tri-Five Chevy

Photos courtesy General Motors

The 1955–1957 Chevrolet Tri-Five, or Shoebox, as these are often called, is likely the single most iconic model ever created. The base 110, mid-range 210, and the ubiquitous Bel Air had many options. As the first Chevy to receive the new-for-1955 small-block V-8, it's the perfect candidate to swap in an LS-based power plant. The guys at Chevrolet Performance Parts certainly agree, considering they chose a 1955 Bel Air to showcase the Chevrolet Performance 50-state-legal E-Rod LS3-based engine package. Since its completion, the E-Rod has been to many shows across the country.

Here, Mike Copeland, Project Manager of the E-Rod build for Chevrolet Division, shares the details about this build of a 1955 Chevy. He explains how they shoehorned the LS3 into the stock chassis and the problems they faced. One of the goals for this project was to use as many factory components as possible, and most of the build came straight from the Chevrolet Performance Parts catalog.

Adapter Plates

"We used a set of off-the-shelf LS-to-small-block-Chevy adapter plates with traditional Chevy motor mounts from Chevrolet Performance," Copeland said. "Because we wanted to take advantage of engine placement for steering clearance, we made our own frame towers."

That turned out to be a key issue for the build, and is an issue for most Tri-Five Chevy cars, as well as the other Tri-Five GM platforms, such as Buick and Oldsmobile. The

Above: *The Tri-Five Chevy is considered by many to be the ultimate classic car. It can be a restored beauty, a hot rod, or a pro-streeter; it fits just about any mold you want to put it in. Being the first car to get the legendary small-block V-8, it is the perfect choice for an LS-based swap.*

standard Tri-Five motor mount is a biscuit-style mount that uses replaceable rubber bushings.

Crossmembers

The transmission crossmember for Tri-Five cars must be fabricated or purchased from a specialty dealer. The issue here is that the later-model transmission designs (3-speed automatics) are quite different from the early non-corporate designs. The factory crossmembers share nothing with the later designs and are in the way of most of the later transmissions.

Several aftermarket swap versions are available from various manufacturers, such as Street & Performance, Southern Performance Systems, and Hedman Hedders. All of these offer swap kits with motor mounts and transmission crossmembers.

Steering Linkage

The steering linkage is the biggest challenge facing Tri-Five swappers. Using the stock steering linkage, the factory frame tower placement puts the oil pan directly in the way. One option is to modify the oil pan or modify the frame towers. The crew at General Motors actually did a little of both. One trick that they employed was to set the engine as far back as possible, just before the engine hit the firewall, with a 3-degree down-angle, to get the best possible positioning.

The E-Rod LS3 was packaged with a truck oil pan that was modified with a cutout on either side to clear the steering linkage. Once the pan was modified, the steering cleared with ease, lock to lock.

__Photo 1:__ The stock chassis takes an LS engine without any major adjustments. The team at GM's Performance Division used the Chevrolet Performance E-Rod engine package to make this happen. The transmission crossmember was a simple bolt-in proposition. __2.__ Although stock engine stands work for the E-Rod, Copeland opted to build custom frame towers in order to assist in clearing the stock steering linkage. The LS3 was mounted with a 3-degree down-angle using off-the-shelf Chevrolet Performance LS-to-small-block-Chevy motor mount adapters. __3.__ Instead of headers, the E-Rod used Chevy Colorado exhaust manifolds, which worked well in the Tri-Five chassis. They made custom adapter flanges to connect the E-Rod mini-catalytic convertors to the engine.

Some aftermarket swap kits use the LH8 oil pan; others use a modified F-Body oil pan. There are also aftermarket pans designed specifically to fit the 1955–1957 chassis, such as the Milodon LS swap oil pan (PN 30916K) specifically for the Tri-Five to eliminate the steering clearance issue.

The Tri-Five Chevy works well with the Corvette accessory drive, which was taken directly from the Chevrolet Performance catalog.

Exhaust System

Another trick the engineers put to use was in the exhaust department. Instead of using headers, Copeland showcased some GM production parts with a set of Chevy Colorado (GM's mid-size truck) LS manifolds. The team fabricated new flanges and lead pipes to connect to the E-Rod mini-catalytic converters and mufflers. The rest of the exhaust was made from 2.5-inch stainless-steel tubing.

Fuel System

The LS-series engines require 60 psi of fuel pressure, and there are several ways of getting the fuel to the engine. All EFI engines require a return-style fuel system, but this does not always mean two full-length fuel lines must be run. The C5 Corvette came up with a special rear-mount filter/regulator that provides the necessary 60 psi of fuel pressure to the engine, but vents the excess fuel directly back to the tank.

Copeland took advantage of this, installing a C5 Corvette in-tank pump assembly in a stock-style 1955 Chevy fuel tank and used the C5 filter/regulator under the car. This keeps the engine bay clean, with just the one fuel supply line.

Wiring

Because the E-Rod is a complete engine package, the wiring and ECM are included. This makes the installation a plug-and-play operation—it literally cannot be any easier to install. The ECM, fuse, and relay center were mounted to a fabricated bracket on the driver-side inner fender under the hood.

Finished Project

The end result is a seriously clean custom ride that has in excess of 160 percent more horsepower than the 265 V-8 that originally powered it. When I asked Copeland what he would change if he had to build the car over again, he told me, "If I were going to build the car today, I would not change a single thing. The car has made a number of trips across the country and never misses a beat."

Above: *Under the hood, the E-Rod wiring leaves a super-clean installation. The ECM, fuse, and relay center are mounted to the driver-side inner fender, next to the power brake master cylinder. It doesn't get much cleaner than this.*

WIRING HARNESS AND WIRING

The wiring aspect of any LS swap is undoubtedly the most difficult. Most builders are familiar with fabrication techniques, trouble shooting, and parts swapping to make things work, but electronics rise to a much higher level of complexity. Wiring has carried an aura of mystery that can send a shiver down the spine of even the most seasoned builder, making them wish for a simple carburetor and distributor. If you fall into this group, don't lose hope. This chapter has the answers you seek with easy-to-understand instructions for tackling the wiring of an LS swap.

Gen III/IV engines feature complex computers that control everything from timing and ignition to fuel and air intake. On many LS engines, even the throttle is computer controlled; the pedal is connected to a sensor box that tells the throttle how much to open. These systems can be overwhelming, but the key is to tackle one circuit at a time. Although the factory systems are certainly adequate, the aftermarket has fully embraced the LS platform and there is definitely more than one way to do it right.

Wiring Harness Basics

If you picked up an engine from a salvage yard or other used vehicle, you need all the electrical components to go with it. Let me repeat: it is imperative to get everything. This includes the computer, wiring harness, mass airflow sensor (MAF), oxygen sensors, and if

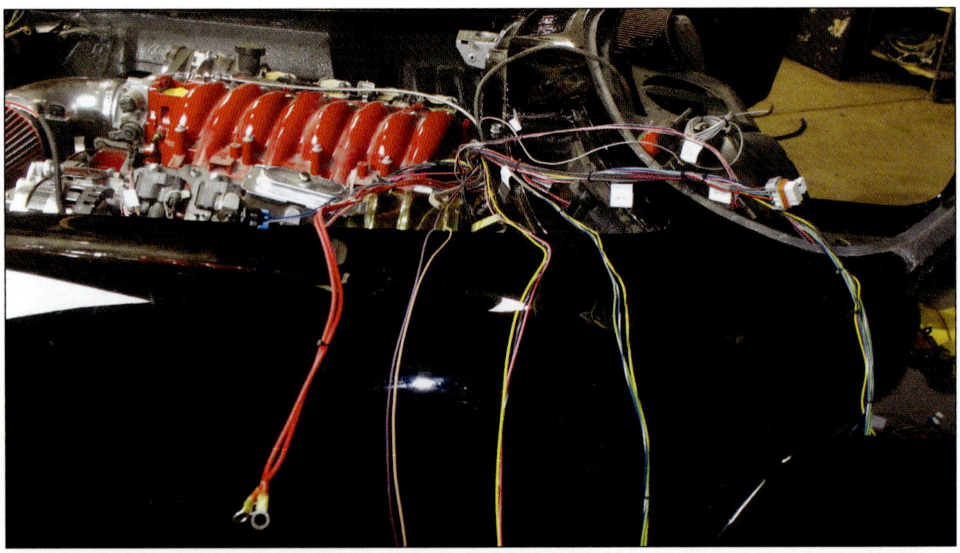

Retrofitting the stock harness requires knowledge of electrical circuits, soldering skills, and attention to detail. It is not a simple plug-and-play procedure, so make sure you are up to the task before hacking into the wiring harness.

A stock harness can be used as-is in the swap, or can be given the "wire diet" by cutting off the loom and removing the wires that are not needed. This is a great way to get to know the engine's wiring in detail. Keeping track of each wire can be a bit of a headache, though.

the engine is drive-by-wire, the gas pedal and throttle actuator control (TAC) module. Each engine requires the use of its own specific computer and harness, and keep in mind that there were changes made to each system year by year. In order to reuse as many of the factory components as possible, you need to get all of them with the engine. Matching key components such as a TAC module with the ECM can be tricky without all vehicle/engine-specific details such as year, make, and model.

Retrofitting a stock wiring harness is seemingly complex and perhaps overwhelming. In fact, it is really not that difficult. With the proper diagrams and instructions, it can be modified to greatly simplify the process of wiring the engine. The majority of the wires in the stock harness are not needed in a retrofit application. Seriously, what 1969 Camaro needs an evaporative canister purge solenoid control? There are differing opinions on what to remove from the stock wiring harness, however.

Wiring a Classic Corvette

Rat's nest, spaghetti, copper conjunctivitis; call it what you want, but wiring is the single most feared aspect of all automotive projects. Whether you are chasing gremlins through a 50-year-old survivor or re-wiring a muscle car, most gearheads just don't enjoy wiring. It doesn't have to be this way, though, as there are tricks and tips that can turn a nightmare into a job well done. And it doesn't require a degree in electrical engineering either.

Whether using a stock or an aftermarket harness, the cleaner the install, the better. This Painless Performance PowerBraid protects the wires from abrasions and heat while keeping a stock look.

Each Painless Performance kit comes with all the basics: terminal pack, relays, and zip ties. You often need more terminals than what is included, so be sure to have plenty of assorted terminals on hand. Bulk terminals can be ordered directly from Painless.

Friction tape at the ends secures the braid. Regular electrical tape works, but make sure it is good-quality stuff such as 3M Super 33. The cheap stuff falls off.

Here is the completed wire-diet LS1 harness install with the full loom. This takes some time to complete, but the results are worth it.

There are two main types of wiring projects: fixing an existing system or replacing it. With 40-plus-year-old wires, often the best solution is total replacement, especially if the car is apart already.

The crew at Red Dirt Rodz handled all of the wiring details for this 1967 Corvette roadster. This car came into the shop as many do, fully disassembled, as one person's failed build sold off to another. Although the original harness was still there, most of the terminals were broken, the wires were cracked and corroded, and it simply was not worth trying to fix, especially considering the car was being fully rebuilt. Starting with a clean slate is always nice. One call to Painless Performance and the harness was on its way.

They could have ordered a factory replacement harness, which is already terminated and bundled, just like the factory harness, and everything is where it should be for the stock components. But that wouldn't work for this project as the roadster has an LS1, electronic transmission, aftermarket gauges, and all the newfangled goodies found on a new car. This situation called for a new plan with new routing for this complicated wiring system.

To do that, a 12-circuit universal harness, LS1 engine harness, and a really cool system called Phantom Key were ordered. The Phantom Key is a transponder-based push-to-start module that eliminates the need for a key. Just hit the button to unlock the doors, get in, and hit the button to start, just like the newest cars coming out of Detroit. This provides the ultimate in cool factor.

The tools for wiring are critical. Using junky terminal crimps and dull cutters don't make it any

1999–2000 LS1 PCM Plug 1

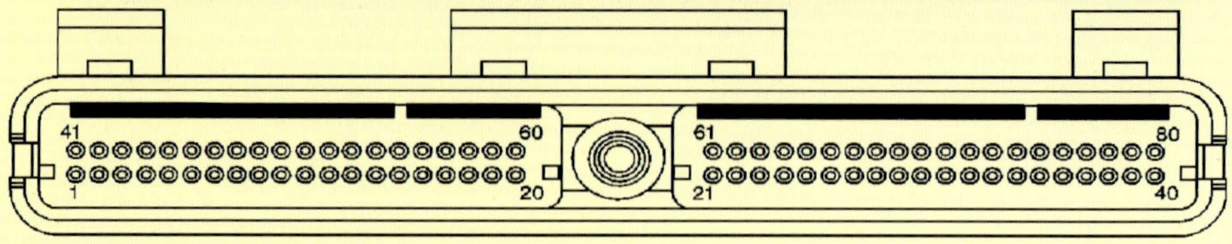

(Street & Performance)

Connector Part Information		PCM Connector C1 Assembly 12191489	
		TPA (BLU) 12176408	
		Connector Cover 12191108	
Pin	**Wire Color**	**Circuit No.**	**Function**
1	BLK	451	PCM Ground
2	LT GRN	1867	Crankshaft Position Sensor B+ Supply
3	PNK/BLK	1746	Injector 3 Control
4	LT GRN/BLK	1745	Injector 2 Control
7	--	--	Not Used
8	GRA	596	TP Sensor 5V Reference
10	--	--	Not Used
11	LT BLU	1876	Knock Sensor Signal Rear
12	DK BLU/WHT	1869	Crankshaft Position Sensor Signal
13-16	--	--	Not Used
17	DK BLU	1225	Transmission Range Signal B
18	RED	1226	Transmission Range Signal C
19	PNK	439	Ignition Positive Voltage
20	ORN	340	Battery Positive Voltage
21	YEL/BLK	1868	Crankshaft Position Sensor Reference Low
22	--	--	Not Used
23	GRA	720	Fuel Tank Pressure Sensor/Fuel Tank Sender Ground
24	--	--	Not Used
25	TAN	1671	HO2S Signal Low Bank 2 Sensor 2
26	TAN	1667	HO2S Signal Low Bank 2 Sensor 1
27	--	--	Not Used
28	TAN/WHT	1669	HO2S Signal Low Bank 1 Sensor 2
29	TAN/WHT	1653	HO2S Signal Low Bank 1 Sensor 1
30-31	--	--	Not Used
32	GRY	48	Clutch Pedal Position Switch Signal
33	PPL	420	TCC Brake Switch
34	ORN/BLK	434	PNP Switch Signal
35	--	--	Not Used
36	BLK	1744	Injector 1 Control
37	YEL/BLK	846	Injector 6 Control
38-39	--	--	Not Used
40	BLK	451	PCM Ground
41	BLK	407	EGR Pintle Position Sensor Ground
42	DK GRN	335	Engine Cooling Fan Relay 1 Control
43	RED/BLK	877	Injector 7 Control
44	LT BLU/BLK	844	Injector 4 Control
45	GRA	474	A/C Refrigerant Pressure Sensor 5V Reference
46	GRA	474	Fuel Tank Pressure Sensor 5V Reference
47	GRA	416	EGR Pintle Position Sensor 5V Reference
48	GRA	416	MAP Sensor 5V Reference
49-50	--	--	Not Used
51	DK BLU	496	Knock Sensor Signal Front
52	--	--	Not Used
53	BLK	407	Transmission Temperature Sensor Ground
54	ORN/BLK	407	MAP Sensor Ground

Pin	Wire Color	Circuit No.	Function
55	BRN	1456	EGR Pintle Position Sensor Signal
56	--	--	Not Used
57	ORN	340	Battery Positive Voltage
58	DK GRN	1049	Serial Data
59	--	--	Not Used
60	BLK	452	TP Sensor Ground
61	PNK/BLK	632	Camshaft Position Sensor Reference Low
62-64	--	--	Not Used
65	PPL	1670	HO2S Signal High Bank 2 Sensor 2
66	PPL	1666	HO2S Signal High Bank 2 Sensor 1
67	--	--	Not Used
68	PPL/WHT	1668	HO2S Signal High Bank 1 Sensor 2
69	PPL/WHT	1665	HO2S Signal High Bank 1 Sensor 1

Pin	Wire Color	Circuit No.	Function
70	BRN	1174	Low Oil Level Switch
71-72	--	--	Not Used
73	BRN/WHT	633	Camshaft Position (CMP) Sensor Signal
74	YEL	410	Engine Coolant Temperature (ECT) Sensor Signal
75	--	--	Not Used
76	BLK/WHT	845	Injector 5 Control
77	DK BLU/ WHT	878	Injector 8 Control
78	--	--	Not Used
79	GRA or WHT	587 or 687	Skip Shift Solenoid Control (M/T) or 3-2 Shift Solenoid Control (A/T)
80	BLK	407	Engine Coolant Temperature (ECT) Sensor Ground

1999–2000 LS1 PCM Plug 2

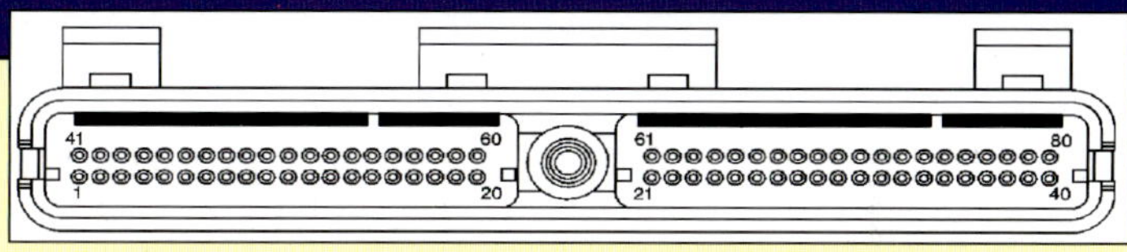

Connector Part Information	PCM Connector C2 Assembly 12191488
	TPA (RED) 12176410
	Connector Cover 12191108

Pin	Wire Color	Circuit No.	Function
1	BLK	451	PCM Ground
2	BRN	418	TCC Control Solenoid
3	--	--	Not Used
4	PPL	421	AIR Solenoid Relay Control
5	--	--	Not Used
6	RED/BLK	1228	Transmission Fluid Pressure Control Solenoid High
7	RED	1676	EGR Control
8	LT BLU/ WHT	1229	Transmission Fluid Pressure Control Solenoid Low
9	DK GRN/ WHT	465	Fuel Pump Relay Control
10	WHT	121	Engine Speed (Tach) Output Signal
12	--	--	Not Used
13	WHT	85	Cruise Control Enable Signal
14	RED/BLK	380	A/C Refrigerant Pressure Sensor Signal
15	RED	225	Alternator L Terminal
16	--	--	Not Used
17	DK GRN/ WHT	762	A/C Request Signal
18	DK GRN	59	A/C Status Signal
19	--	--	Not Used
20	LT GRN/ BLK	822	Vehicle Speed Sensor (VSS) Reference Low
21	PPL/WHT	821	Vehicle Speed Sensor (VSS) Signal
22-23	--	--	Not Used
24	DK BLU	417	TP Sensor Signal
25	TAN	472	IAT Sensor Signal
26	PPL	2121	Ignition Control 1
27	RED	2127	Ignition Control 7
28	LT BLU/ WHT	2126	Ignition Control 6
29	DK GRN/ WHT	2124	Ignition Control 4
30	DK BLU	229	VTD Fuel Enable Signal
31	YEL	492	MAF Sensor Signal
32	LT GRN	432	MAP Sensor Signal
33	DK BLU	473	Engine Cooling Fan Relay 2 and 3 Control
34	DK GRN /WHT	428	EVAP Canister Purge Valve Control
35	--	--	Not Used
36	BRN	436	AIR Pump Relay Control
37	DK GRN	83	Cruise Control Inhibit
38	--	--	Not Used

Pin	Wire Color	Circuit No.	Function
39	RED	631	Camshaft Position Sensor B+ Supply
40	BLK	451	PCM Ground
41	GRA	435	EGR Position Sensor Ground
42	TAN/BLK	422	TCC Enable Circuit
43	DK GRN /WHT	459	A/C Clutch Relay Control
44	LT GRN	1652	Reverse Inhibit Solenoid Control
45	WHT	1310	EVAP Canister Vent Valve Control
46	BRN/WHT	419	Malfunction Indicator Lamp (MIL) Control
47	YEL/BLK	1223	Transmission Shift Solenoid B
48	LT GRN	1222	Transmission Shift Solenoid A
49	--	--	Not Used
50	DK GRN /WHT	817	Vehicle Speed Output Circuit
51	YEL/BLK	1227	Transmission Temperature Sensor Signal
52	--	--	Not Used
53	GRA/BLK	1687	Spark Retard Signal
54	PPL	1589	Fuel Level Sensor Signal
55-56	--	--	Not Used
57	PPL	719	IAT Sensor Ground
58-59	--	--	Not Used
60	BRN	2129	Ignition Control Reference Low Bank 1
61	BRN/WHT	2130	Ignition Control Reference Low Bank 2
62	--	--	Not Used
63	PNK	1224	Transmission Range Signal A
64	DK GRN	890	Fuel Tank Pressure Sensor Signal
65	--	--	Not Used
66	PPL/WHT	2128	Ignition Control 8
67	RED/WHT	2122	Ignition Control 2
68	DK GRN	2125	Ignition Control 5
69	LT BLU	2123	Ignition Control 3
70-75	--	--	Not Used
76	LT GRN/WHT	1749	IAC Coil B High
77	LT GRN/BLK	444	IAC Coil B Low
78	LT BLU/BLK	1748	IAC Coil A Low
79	LT BLU/WHT	1747	IAC Coil A High
80	--	--	Not Used

The first step is to break down the harness and split up the groups of wires.

Plan the layout of the harness before getting to the car.

Solder Connections

Crimps are okay for most connections; however, when working with important engine management connections the best option is soldering. The problem here is that most people don't do it correctly. ■

1 *Start by crossing the wires to be soldered. If you are using shrink tubing, slide it on before soldering.*

2 *Next, wrap both wires around each other. You do not want a "pig tail" (a short section of wire coming off the side of the wire). The joint should resemble a single length of continuous wire.*

3 *Heat the wires from the bottom of the joint and apply the solder from the top. This draws the solder through the wire, yielding a proper connection and not a cold solder joint. You should be able to see individual strands of wire through the solder.*

4 *The last step is to cover the connection with either shrink tubing or electrical tape. Tubing is better, but you must slide it over the wires (past the joint) before soldering.*

It's very important to properly install wire terminals. A speed stripper really speeds up the process and is a worthwhile investment.

The key to a good crimp is quality crimpers. This pair works great for insulated terminals, the kind used on this car. They also work for non-insulated terminals.

Next, locate where the engine side of the harness goes through the firewall. On the Corvette, we used the stock location. Be careful, as sometimes the chosen hole has another function.

easier. The most important tool in a wiring job is the crimpers. Crimp connections often get a bad reputation because of poor installation. A properly made crimp is just as good as a solder joint. The key is correctly sized terminals and quality crimpers. Those cheap combo crimp-n-strip tools are no good; throw them away. They are only good for emergency repairs. You need a set of good crimpers designed for insulated terminals. Klein Tools and KD Tools make excellent crimpers.

Select the correct size of terminal for the wire and insert it into the corresponding set of jaws in the tool. Using the wrong jaws can result in over-crimping (which breaks the terminal) or under-crimping (which results in a loose connection).

The fuse box mounts to the firewall with two bolts. It can be a real pain to install the fuse box; having a helper alleviates a lot of frustration here.

Selecting the correct wire size for the terminal is critical. Using a terminal that's too large results in a weak connection. Most terminals are color coded for size. Red is the smallest, fitting 22- to 18-gauge wire; blue is for 16- to 14-gauge wire, and yellow is for 12- to 10-gauge wire. Anything bigger is sold by the size, not color.

Primary wire is typically an 18-gauge wire and is the most common wire found in wiring harnesses. The larger wires that feed heavy-draw circuits are typically 14- to 12-gauge.

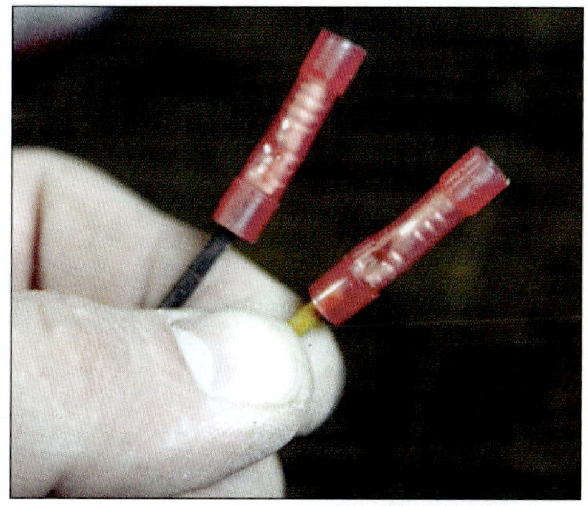

A properly applied crimp should look like this. The insulation is slightly bulged, but not squished. Always tug on the wire and terminal to ensure it is not loose.

The metal backup plate was trimmed to match up with the firewall.

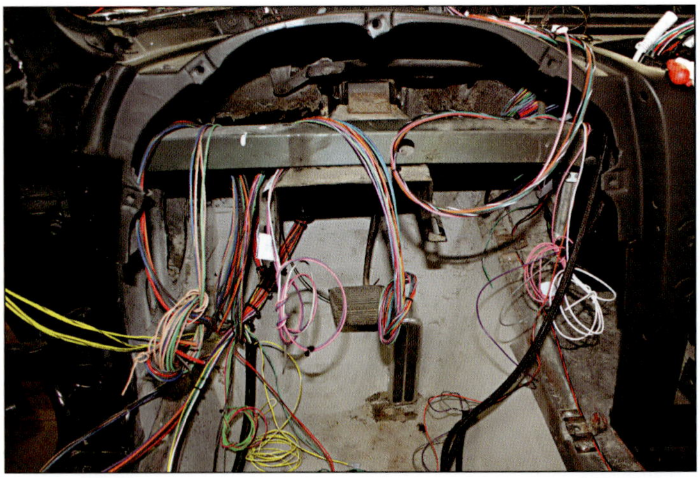

Inside the car, the bundles of wire were split into groups and routed to their locations. Don't cut any wire until the entire harness has been routed.

The neutral safety switch and backup light wires were routed to the shifter and terminated with spade terminals. This makes removing the shifter a no-cut proposition. You may not need to remove it, but if you do, this makes it easier.

This is the Painless Phantom Key push-to-start system, which includes keyless entry. This system replaces the ignition key with a push button and includes all the relays, which were mounted under the center console in the Corvette.

All the main ignition wires are 12-gauge wire. These feed the majority of the electrical system. The key to safe wiring is using the proper-gauge wire for the amperage. The longer the wire, the larger the gauge needs to be.

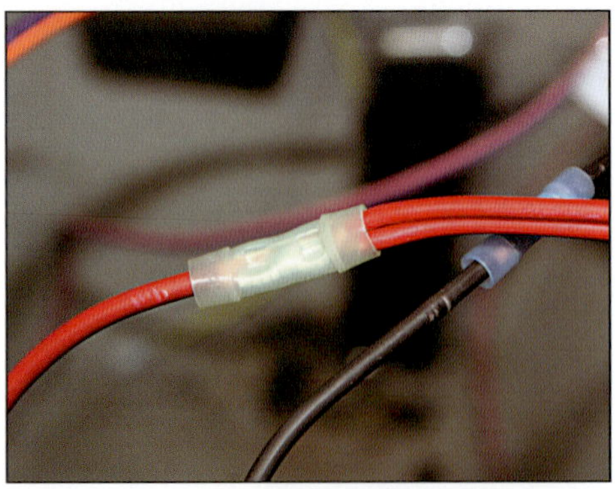

There are two main power feed wires, which are terminated to the large feed wire that connects to the battery. Terminate this with a single large 12-gauge wire terminal. The two wires on one side are smaller than the main feed wire.

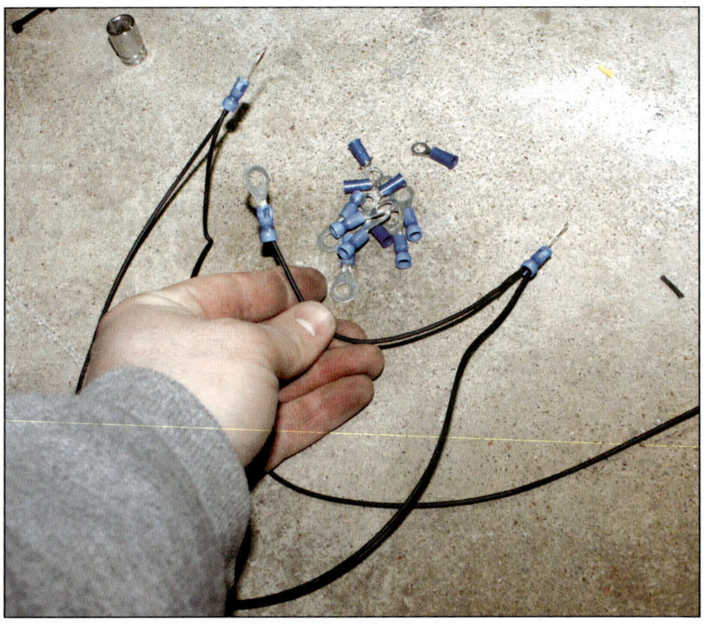

Most Painless kits do not come with any ground circuits. Usually this is not an issue, but with Corvettes, locating a good ground can be a bear. Use a ground harness for the rear taillights; use ring terminals and 14-gauge primary wire to provide grounds for each light.

The key to a good ground is a solid connection. The paint should be removed from the metal surface of the ground location. If you can't remove the paint, a star washer is an alternative, as it cuts into the metal as the bolt/screw is tightened.

Next, bolt the ground feed to the frame using the fuel pump mounting point as the ground point. By using the same bolt, the number of holes in the chassis is limited and it keeps everything neat and clean.

Then route the ground harness to each light. The taillights ground on the mounting stud. When using speed-nuts, you have to be careful not to over-tighten them or they strip.

Under the hood, separate each wire group just as it was inside the car. There are a lot of small groupings of wire here, so it is important to take each one separately.

As each wire group is positioned on the engine, the harness starts to come together. Keeping each circuit group together can be tricky, so be patient. The hardest part of wiring is the planning.

The wire in Painless Performance kits runs a little larger than the standard; the primary wires are 16-gauge, with 12-gauge for heavy-draw items such as the headlights.

Opening the box and seeing several thousand feet of wire can be scary. Fear not. It is not that bad; just be patient. The first step is to take it all out of the box and lay it out on the bench or floor. Separate all the bundles. Painless kits come pre-bundled in all the major groups: engine, dash, and tail. From there, they are divided into sub-categories.

These are good for the typical project, but there may be a few wires that need to be moved to a different section. Now is the time to reroute any wires. Once inside the car, this becomes much more difficult. Go over each wire and its location and check the car. For example, if you are installing an electric fuel pump under the hood, you need to alter that wire's routing as it is normally found in the tail section.

All Painless wiring kits provide only the power side of the circuit. Except for a couple of situations, you must provide all ground connections. Although this is typically a simple thing, Corvettes require some

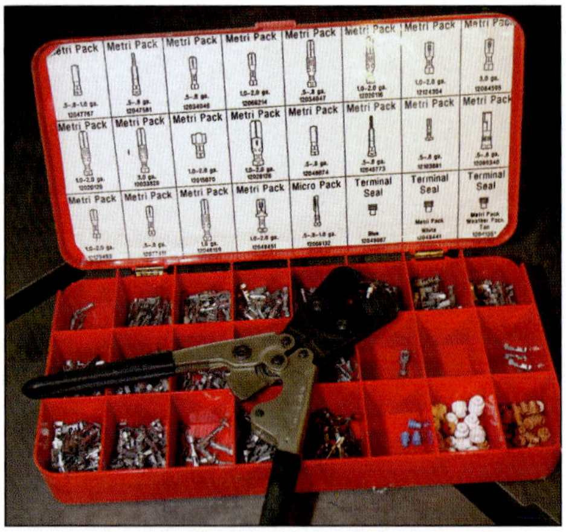

Another component used in Gen III/IV wiring is the Weather Pack and Metri-Pack terminal. These are small pins that require special tools to crimp. They are used in every connector on a late-model engine. Most builders don't have to deal with disassembling and reassembling terminals but if you are retrofitting a stock harness, you do.

The components of Metri-Pack or Weather Pack terminals are a Molex or nylon housing, a silicone wire seal, and the terminals. The housings are shape-specific; you must make sure that you have the correct male and female components. The terminals can sometimes be specific to the housing as well.

These are the crimpers used for the terminals. They are available in many configurations, and most have ratcheting locks for a completed crimp.

additional forethought, as fiberglass does not make a good ground. Painless Performance thought ahead on this one, and they offer a ground kit that comes with wire and several terminal strips to provide multiple ground circuits where you need them.

Wiring an entire car requires planning, time, and lots of patience. If you find yourself getting frustrated with a particular section, get up and walk away for a minute. A novice builder should be able to complete a basic wire harness replacement in three to four days. The more circuits and the more complications, such as EFI, audio systems, etc., the longer it takes. But if you take your time and plan out the locations of all the wires before cutting anything, your wiring project will look and function great.

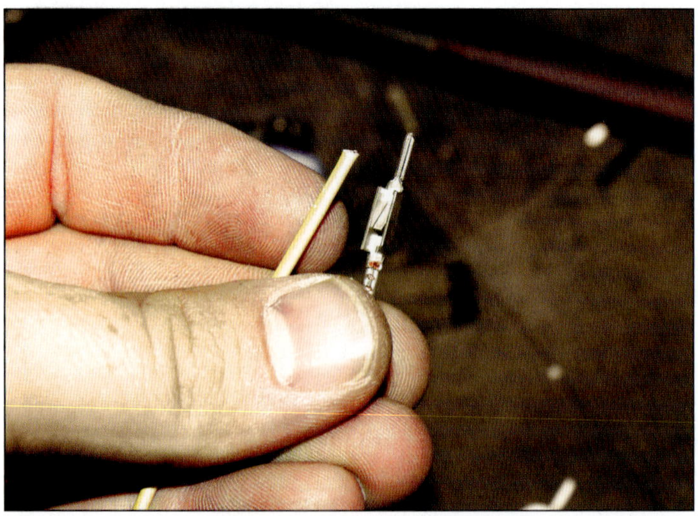

The terminals must be crimped twice, once on the bare wire and once on the silicone insulation. Make sure you slide the wire through the silicone boot before crimping.

Each terminal style has different pin types. All styles lock into the plug housing with spring locks built into the terminal itself. Unlocking these can be a pain; the trick is to use a small pick or unfolded paper clip to unlock it. Every terminal uses a different lock location.

Connectors for 1997–1998 LS1 Engines

The 1997–1998 LS1 wire harness is different from the 1999–2002 models, and the Vortec truck harnesses are different from that. These guidelines do not include wiring for AIR injection, A/C, traction control, or cruise control. (Provided by LS1Tech.com & Daniel Polcyn)

Connector C100

Connector and Description

A. This is the power for the odd fuel injectors; route it to IGN 1 15A fuse
B. Not used
C. Not used
D. Not used
E. Not used
F. Not used
G. Engine control power; route to IGN 3 15A fuse
H. Cooling fan 2/high-speed relay; route to terminal 86 of cooling fan 2 relay
J. Cooling fan 1/low-speed relay; route to terminal 86 of cooling fan 1 relay
K. Not used

Connector C101

Connector and Description

A. Not used
B. Power for even coils; route to IGN 2 15A fuse
C. Not used
D. Output for fuel-pump relay; route to terminal 85 of fuel-pump relay
E. Computer power; route to IGN 4 15A fuse
F. Not used
G. Constant computer power; route to BAT 1 10A fuse
H. Not used
J. Not used
K. Not used

Connector C105

Connector and Description

A. Not used
B. Engine sensor power; route to IGN 5 20A fuse
C. Not used
D. Not used
E. Serial data signal; route into car to Data Link Connector terminal 9 (or OBDII port)
F. Not used
G. Not used
H. Not used

Connector C220

Connector and Description

A. Generator warning light negative (-) side. If your vehicle already has a generator light, it should plug in and work. If your vehicle had an internal regulated alternator, connect this to the wire that connected to terminal 1 on the alternator. If you need to add a generator light, wire this to one side of the light's terminals and the other side of the light's terminals to an ignition 12-volt fuse. The same wire with a 20-amp fuse can power all of the warning lights.
B. Oil-pressure output. If using the LS1 oil-pressure sender with the stock gauge, connect this wire to the oil-pressure gauge. The most common procedure is to use an aftermarket oil-pressure sending unit, and delete this wire. The same wire with a 20-amp fuse can power all warning lights.
C. Low-oil-level warning lamp ("–" output, this is a negative trigger). This one is also an optional accessory. If you want a low-oil light, attach this wire to one terminal of a light and the other to a 12-volt ignition source (fused, of course). The same wire with a 20-amp fuse can power all warning lights.
D. Not used
E. Not used
F. Not used
G. Vehicle speed sensor (VSS) output from computer. This is a 4,000-pulse-per-mile square-wave output: it works for GM electronic speedometers, as well as some aftermarket speedometers.
H. Not needed
J. Not needed
K. Temperature gauge output. This signal may work with older GM electronic temperature gauges, but it might not be as accurate. Most builders opt to install an aftermarket sending unit on the back of the block.

Connectors for 1997–1998 LS1 Engines CONTINUED

Connector C230

Connector and Description

A. Not used

B. This is the fabled "Service Engine Soon" light, and it is a negative trigger output. Route this wire to one terminal of a 12-volt lightbulb and the other terminal of the bulb to an ignition 12-volt fuse. The same wire with a 20-amp fuse can power all warning lights.

C. Not used

D. Tachometer output. This is a 4-cylinder, two-pulse-per-revolution output. The tach must be able to be set to 4-cylinder or be a compatible GM tachometer.

E. VATS (vehicle anti-theft system) fuel enable. This wire is not needed if the VATS has been deleted in the computer, or it could be retained and a VATS bypass box added for the extra security. Most builders remove the VATS system as it is not very user friendly.

F. Not used

G. Not used

H. To brake torque converter clutch switch. A switch that provides 12 volts to this wire must be provided when the car is running. It cuts power when you press the brake pedal. There may be a cruise control switch that does this already, or one may have to be added. Adding a micro-switch (like those used in nitrous kits) from any electronics parts store will work. Build a small bracket to hold the switch behind the brake pedal lever so the switch is depressed when the pedal is at rest but opens when the brake pedal is pushed down. One terminal needs to be connected to 12-volt ignition power, and the other to this wire. This is only for automatics.

J. Park neutral position switch, negative trigger. If this switch is not wired, the car is able to be started in gear, which is bad. The stock shifter may have this already. If not, one needs to be added. The process is the same as the brake converter switch above. The terminals are wired to ground instead of power. This is only for automatic transmission cars.

K. Serial data output to the diagnostic link connector (DLC) or OBDII connector terminal 2. This is for an OBDII port for engine diagnostics and tuning.

Relays for 1997–1998 LS1 Engines

Based on the use of 30-amp Bosch-style automotive relays, relays 1, 2, and 3 can be combined if you use one 80-amp relay. Keeping them separate simplifies any troubleshooting, plus 80-amp relays are expensive. (Provided by LS1Tech.com & Daniel Polcyn)

Relay 1

Terminal No. and Description

85 To conversion car wiring (a wire that is hot in run and start modes). This wire is typically used to power the original coil. The ballast resistor must be removed.

86 To ground

30 Direct to battery voltage

87 To two 15A fuses (IGN 1 and IGN 2); route IGN 1 fuse to pin A of C100 connector, and IGN 2 fuse to pin B of C101 connector

Relay 2

Terminal No. and Description

85 To conversion car wiring (a wire that is hot in run and start modes). This wire typically powers the original coil. The ballast resistor must be removed.

86 To ground

30 Direct to battery voltage

87 To two 15A fuses (IGN 3 and IGN 4); route IGN 3 fuse to pin G of C100 connector, and IGN 4 fuse to pin E of C101 connector

Relay 3

Terminal No. and Description

85 To conversion car wiring (a wire that is hot in run and start modes). This wire is typically used to power the original coil. The ballast resistor must be removed.

86 To ground

30 Direct to battery voltage

Relays for 1997–1998 LS1 Engines CONTINUED

87 To one 20A fuse (IGN 5); route IGN 5 to pin B of connector C105

Relay 4 Fuel-Pump Relay

Terminal No. and Description

85 To pin D of connector C101
86 To ground
30 Direct to battery voltage
87 To one 20A fuse, then to the fuel pump

The cooling fans can use two relays or one, depending on the radiator fan setup. Two fans that run at the same time can be on one circuit, or the two fans can be wired to separate circuits, as with the factory unit. One fan functions as a low-speed fan while the other is a high-speed fan, which comes on in the event the engine is not cooling down. Use the low-speed fan relay if running only one fan.

Relay 5 Cooling Fan 1/Slow-Speed Fan

Terminal No. and Description

85 To conversion car wiring (a wire that is hot in run and start modes). This wire is typically used to power the original coil. You must remove the ballast resistor.
86 To pin J of connector C100
30 Direct to battery voltage
87 To one 20A fuse or larger, depending on the cooling fan requirements

Relay 6 Cooling Fan 2/High-Speed Fan

Terminal No. and Description

85 To conversion car wiring (a wire that is hot in run and start modes). This wire is typically used to power the original coil. The ballast resistor must be removed.
86 To pin H of C100 connector
30 Direct to battery voltage
87 To one 20A fuse or larger, depending on the cooling fan requirements

The last wire to connect is the starter wire. If the conversion car is a GM model, this is a large purple wire. Simply route this to the starter solenoid.

Connectors for 1999–2002 LS1 Engines

The later 1999–2002 LS1 wiring harnesses are a little different because the connections are different and there are more circuits. The following is a basic guide to a later LS1 retrofit harness. Most of the wires are the same, although the placement might be different. This does not include wiring for traction control, cruise, or A/C. (Provided by LS1Tech.com & Daniel Polcyn)

Connector C100

Connector and Description

A. This is the power for the odd fuel injectors; route it to IGN 1 15A fuse
B. Not used
C. Not used
D. Not used
E. Not used
F. Not used
G. Engine control power; route to IGN 3 15A fuse
H. Cooling fan 2/high-speed relay; route to terminal 86 of cooling fan 2 relay
J. Cooling fan 1/low-speed relay; route to terminal 86 of cooling fan 1 relay
K. Not used

Connector C101

Connector and Description

A. Not used
B. Power for even coils; route to IGN 2 15A fuse
C. Not used
D. Output for fuel-pump relay; route to terminal 85 of fuel-pump relay
E. Computer power; route to IGN 4 15A fuse
F. Not used
G. Constant computer power; route to BAT 1 10A fuse
H. Ground this wire
J. Not used
K. Not used

Connectors for 1999–2002 LS1 Engines *CONTINUED*

Connector C105

Connector and Description

A. Not used
B. Engine sensor power; route to IGN 5 20A fuse
C. Not used
D. Not used
E. Not used
F. Not used
G. Tachometer output. This signal is a 4-cylinder, two-pulse-per-revolution output. The tach must be able to be set on 4-cylinder or be a compatible GM electronic tachometer.
H. Not used on a 1999. For a 2002 harness, this is the EGR valve. The EGR is typically bypassed for conversions.

Connector C220

Connector and Description

A. Oil-pressure output. This signal can be used for a GM electronic oil-pressure gauge. If it does not work, install an aftermarket sending unit.
B. Clutch pedal position switch on a 6-speed transmission. This is obviously not used on an automatic.
C. Power supply to torque converter clutch (TCC) stop lamp switch. This is not used in a 6-speed car or if the car already has a TCC stop switch. If the car does not have a stop lamp switch, use this to feed power to the switch.
D. To brake torque converter clutch switch. There must be a switch that provides 12 volts to this wire when the car is running and then cuts power when the brake pedal is depressed. There may be a cruise-control switch that does this already, or one may have to be added. Adding a micro-switch (such as those used in nitrous kits) from any electronics parts store works. Build a small bracket to hold the switch behind the brake pedal lever so the switch is depressed when the pedal is at rest but opens when the brake pedal is pushed down. One terminal needs to be connected to 12-volt ignition power, and the other to this wire. This is only for automatic transmissions
E. This wire must be grounded
F. Not used
G. Reverse light switch for 6-speed transmissions; not used in an auto
H. Park/neutral position switch, negative trigger. If this switch is not wired, the car can be started in gear, which is bad. The stock shifter may have this already. If not, one needs to be added. The process is the same as the brake converter switch above. The terminals are wired to ground instead of power. This is only for automatic transmission cars.
J. Not used
K. VSS output from computer. This is a 4,000-pulse-per-mile square wave output; it works for GM electronic speedometers, as well as some aftermarket speedometers.

Connector C230

Connector and Description

A. Not used
B. This is the fabled "Service Engine Soon" light. This is a negative trigger output. Route this wire to one terminal of a 12-volt lightbulb and the other terminal of the bulb to an ignition 12-volt fuse. The same wire with a 20-amp fuse can power all of the warning lights.
C. Not used
D. Not used
E. VATS fuel enable. This wire is not needed if the VATS has been deleted in the computer, or it could be retained and a VATS bypass box added for the extra security. The best way is to delete VATS altogether.
F. Not used
G. Not used
H. Not used
J. Not used
K. Serial data output to DLC or OBDII connector terminal 2

Relays for 1999–2002 LS1 Engines

Based on the use of 30-amp Bosch-style automotive relays, relays 1, 2, and 3 can be combined with an 80-amp relay. However, keeping them separate simplifies any troubleshooting, and 80-amp relays cost quite a bit. (Provided by LS1Tech.com & Daniel Polcyn)

Relay 1

Terminal No. and Description

85 To conversion car wiring (a wire that is hot in run and start modes). This wire is typically used to power the original coil. The ballast resistor must be removed.
86 To ground
30 Direct to battery voltage
87 To two 15A fuses (IGN 1 and IGN 2); route IGN 1 fuse to pin A of C100 connector, and IGN 2 fuse to pin B of C101 connector

Relay 2

Terminal No. and Description

85 To conversion car wiring (a wire that is hot in run and start modes). This wire is typically used to power the original coil. The ballast resistor must be removed.
86 To ground
30 Direct to battery voltage
87 To two 15A fuses (IGN 3 and IGN 4); route IGN 3 fuse to pin G of C100 connector, and IGN 4 fuse to pin E of C101 connector

Relay 3

Terminal No. and Description

85 To conversion car wiring (a wire that is hot in run and start modes). This wire is typically used to power the original coil. The ballast resistor must be removed.
86 To ground
30 Direct to battery voltage
87 To one 20A fuse (IGN 5); route IGN 5 to pin B of connector C105

Relay 4 Fuel-Pump Relay

Terminal No. and Description

85 To pin D of connector C101
86 To ground
30 Direct to battery voltage
87 To one 20A fuse, then to the fuel pump

The cooling fans can use two relays or one, depending on the radiator fan setup. Two fans that run at the same time can be on one circuit, or the two fans can be wired to separate circuits, as with the factory unit. One fan functions as a low-speed fan while the other is a high-speed fan, which comes on in the event the engine is not cooling down. Use the low-speed fan relay if running only one fan.

Relay 5 Cooling Fan 1/Slow-Speed Fan

Terminal No. and Description

85 To conversion car wiring (a wire that is hot in run and start modes). This wire is typically used to power the original coil. The ballast resistor must be removed.
86 To pin J of connector C100
30 Direct to battery voltage
87 To one 20A fuse or larger, depending on the cooling fan requirements

Relay 6 Cooling Fan 2/High-Speed Fan

Terminal No. and Description

85 To conversion car wiring (a wire that is hot in run and start modes). This wire is typically used to power the original coil. The ballast resistor must be removed.
86 To pin H of C100 connector
30 Direct to battery voltage
87 To one 20A fuse or larger, depending on the cooling fan requirements

In order to tune the computer, you need a DLC or an OBDII port. These can be taken from any DLC- or OBDII-equipped car; the salvage yards are full of them. They can be mounted anywhere inside the vehicle. The pins on the port are typically labeled 1 through 16, starting at the top left with 1, and proceeding sequentially with the bottom right pin being 16. The port should be wired as follows:

Pin 2: Serial Data line (purple)
Pin 4: Ground (black)
Pin 5: Ground (black/white)
Pin 9: DLC Serial Data Line
Pin 16: Constant 12 volts (not ignition) (orange)

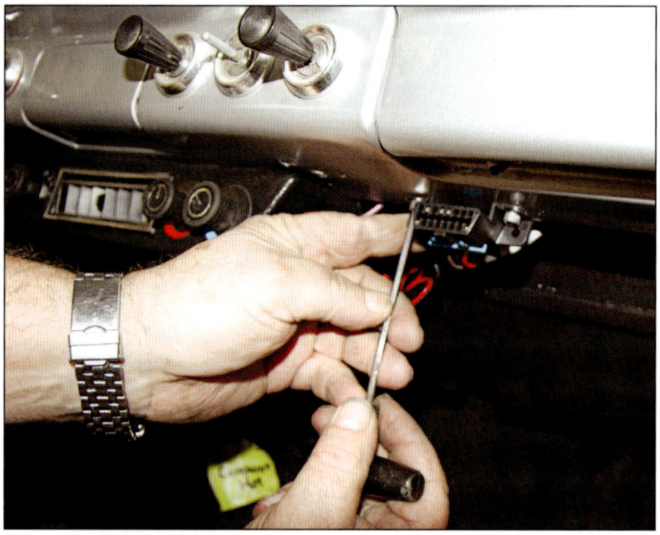

The DLC or OBDII port is a must-have for any LS swap, and it is often overlooked when retrofitting a stock harness. Make sure you grab the wiring harness from the donor car. If you don't, you have to head back to the salvage yard or take your chances on eBay. (Photo Courtesy Street & Performance)

Aftermarket Harnesses

All of the connector and relay data (pages 87–91) represent what can be done with an LS1 wiring harness. The pin-outs for the later models are included on pages 81–82, but each computer and engine has different requirements to make it operational. Drive-by-wire and displacement-on-demand engines make this more complicated.

A pre-made retrofit wiring harness is generally the best solution for any Gen III/IV swap. This puts all of the responsibility in the hands of technicians who have tested each harness and guarantee it is correct. A simple crossed wire can fry the stock computer, rendering it useless. In addition, purchasing an aftermarket wiring harness also affords the luxury of having access to troubleshooting tech assistance. If you get into trouble with an aftermarket harness, simply call the tech line to get it going and save valuable time and money and potentially a dead computer.

The plug-and-play nature of an aftermarket harness combined with its relative affordability makes it the best option, plus it generally looks better than a hacked-up stock harness. Another thing to consider is that many factory harnesses are fairly old. With age, wiring becomes brittle and corroded. An aftermarket harness is all new, so the swap gets more life out of the wires. It's also impossible to know if the computer and harness were removed with care or yanked out, which can damage the wires and connectors.

Ordering a Harness

Most aftermarket harnesses are similar in their connections; it is the finer points of the finish and overall look that separates them. Many aftermarket harnesses are left in loose form, that is, without any loom or wrap on the wires. Certain wires are grouped together for their placement on the engine, such as the fuel injector harnesses, but that is as far as it

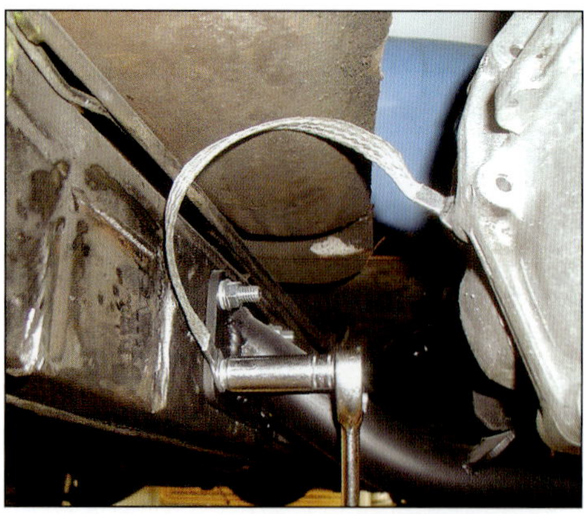

Everything in modern drivetrains is electronic, so proper grounds to the transmission are important. A simple braided ground strap to the frame will do. This also helps reduce electrolysis in the cooling system. (Photo Courtesy Street & Performance)

The body needs to be grounded as well. Scrape the paint away from the metal at the grounding point or use a star washer for solid contact. (Photo Courtesy Street & Performance)

Some LS wiring harnesses include the underhood fuse box. Bolt this down in a convenient location. If you are using an aftermarket harness without a fuse box, make sure that the power wires are properly fused. (Photo Courtesy Street & Performance)

Anytime wiring is run through the body, a grommet is required. This protects the wiring from chaffing on the body, causing grounds and the possibility of fires.

goes. This leaves it up to you to cover the harness for the final finish.

Some aftermarket harnesses group each set of wires together as they are on an engine, and complete the job with wire loom or tape, making it a clean, out-of-the-box installation. If any of the stock components have been changed or moved to another location, the harness may have to be altered, so that is something to think about before ordering.

These wires are the stock ignition connectors for most GM cars. The big purple wires connect the relay to the starter. This is the quickest way to connect the vehicle's ignition switch to the LS starter.

To make sure you get the correct aftermarket harness, there are a few things to consider before placing an order. First, identify the engine and computer, whether it's an automatic or a manual transmission, and if the particular transmission is electronically controlled.

Old-style automatics, such as the TH350, and manuals such as the Muncie M22, are not electronically controlled, but the 4L60E automatic is electronically controlled. That is important because it must be connected to the computer. The MAF sensor is either a three- or five-pin (make sure to get this information from the donor vehicle).

Determining if the throttle body is drive-by-cable or drive-by-wire is also essential.

The type of fuel injector is the last piece of component information you need. There are three types: the old-style STD injector (which has a large metal bale clip), the T-style injector (which uses a Delphi 45 plug), and the Flex Fuel injector (which is also known as the Z-style). LS engines are plug-and-play, so installing the harness is quite simple.

Gauges

Once the engine is wired up there are still those pesky little acces-

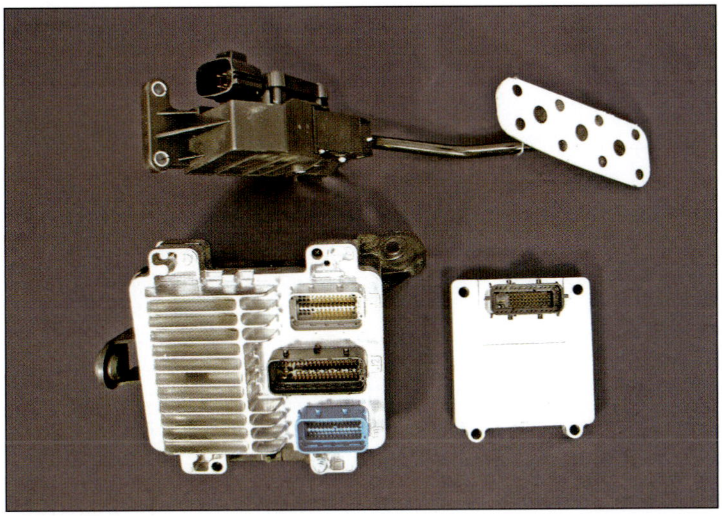

Each drive-by-wire engine requires its own specific pedal, throttle body, and possibly TAC module. This is an LS2 kit for a GTO. The small box on the lower right is the transmission control module (TCM). (Photo Courtesy Street & Performance)

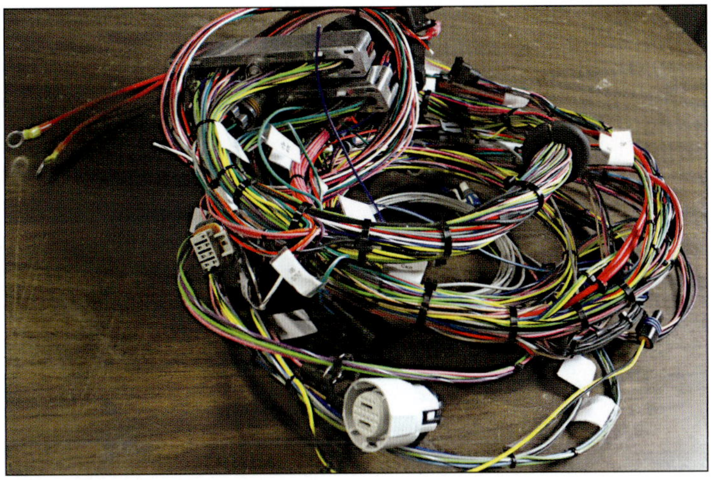

Most aftermarket harnesses are purely plug-and-play: just plug it in, make four wiring connections, and, theoretically, fire up the engine. Know the specifics of your engine and transmission before ordering, however, as there are a lot of options. An un-loomed harness allows rerouting of any wires to components that may have been moved.

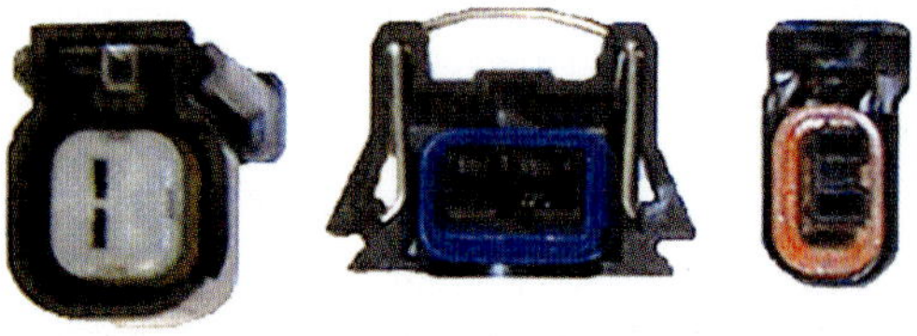

There are three types of fuel injectors. Shown from the left: flex-fuel Z-style, old-style STD, and Delphi 45 T-style. Flex-fuel engines have the Z-style, and the other two were used across years, makes, and models. (Photo Courtesy Street & Performance)

Even throttle-by-cable throttle bodies have wires. The throttle position sensor and MAF sensor must be plugged in. The MAF sensor mounts directly in front of the throttle body. It can be moved with elbows and other induction piping components. There are three types of MAF sensors: three-pin, five-pin, and LS7-style. They are not interchangeable without ECM changes. (Photo Courtesy Street & Performance)

sories, such as gauges, that need to be connected. Since the original vehicles were so heavily dependent on the computer system, all the gauges were routed through the computer. Although this is fine for a 1999 Corvette, most older muscle cars require significant modification in order to retrofit late-model computer-controlled gauges.

A cable-driven speedometer does not do much good with a VSS wire attached to it; neither does a stock 1965 tachometer. Special consider-

Throttle-by-cable is the most compatible with older transmissions because the brackets are already there for the kickdown or TV cables. (Photo Courtesy Street & Performance)

ations that must be made in order to get the information from the engine to the driver.

Tachometer

Tachometers are simple gauges that measure the revolutions per minute of the engine. Although not absolutely necessary they are particularly useful, especially in manual transmission cars. If you're driving a car aggressively, you need to know how hard the engine is being worked.

Getting the tach signal to an old stock tach requires an adapter. The signal is modulated at a different rate from that of a typical V-8 tach. The LS signal must be converted to a standard signal with a module. These modules are available from Dakota Digital. Their SGI-8 module converts the tach signal to different

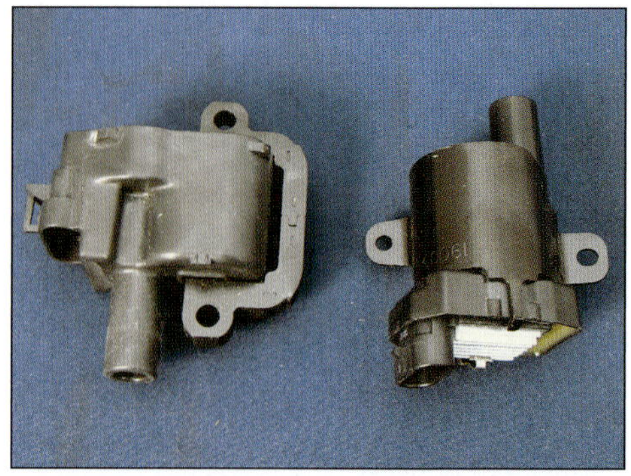

The coil packs for Gen III/IV engines are very good from the factory, so there is no need to replace them at all. Their failure rate is very low. You would be hard pressed to find a dealer that has seen any failed coils. (Photo Courtesy Street & Performance)

settings, such as 4- or 6-cylinder. The tach signal coming from the LS1 is representative of a 4-cylinder signal. Therefore, a factory 6- or 8-cylinder tach must use this module to read the correct signal and display the proper reading.

Programmable tachometers such as an AutoMeter or VDO do not need this module, as they can be set to read a 4-cylinder tach signal.

Speedometer

With an electronically controlled transmission, an electronic speedometer can receive the signal from the VSS system via the computer, or an aftermarket speedometer can receive a direct signal from the VSS system. If the stock cable-driven speedometer is being used with a late-model transmission, the transmission must be adapted to drive the cable.

For 4L60E and T56 OEM transmissions, this is not a huge problem. Street & Performance offers replacement cable-driven tailshafts. Most aftermarket transmissions already have a cable-drive provision.

From left to right: K&N air filter, three-pin MAF, 90-degree elbow with three-pin MAF, and five-pin MAF. (Photo Courtesy Street & Performance)

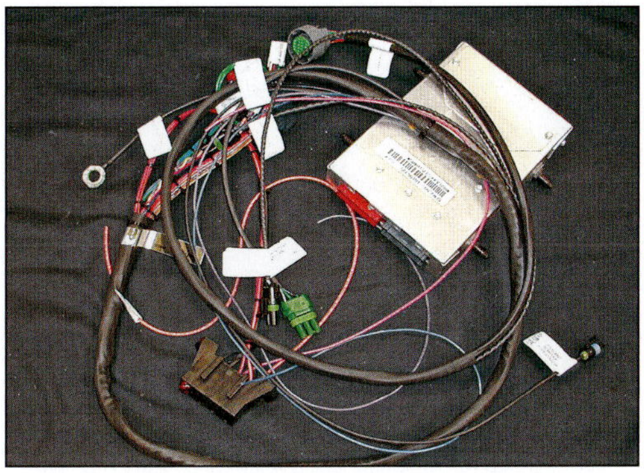

If you're running a carbureted LS engine and a late-model electronic transmission, you need a transmission controller. This 4L60E/4L80E controller from TCI provides precise control and solid shifting of electronic automatic transmissions.

Oil-Sending Unit

The oil-sending unit also requires adapting. The oil cooler bypass fitting on the oil pan just above the oil filter is an ideal place to install an oil-pressure fitting for the sending unit. Depending on the specific engine, select one of three bypass fitting options: a drilled and tapped fitting; a blank boss fitting, which can be drilled and tapped; or a dome top fitting.

The 1997–2004 Corvette engines have a drilled and tapped 1/4-inch pipe thread from the factory, and the 1998–2002 F-Body pans have a boss, but it is not drilled or tapped. The 2005-up engines have a domed cap with no boss. Any of these can be used. If you need to drill and tap the fitting, simply drill it and tap it to the thread size that the oil-sender fitting requires. You can also use the 16-mm threaded hole behind the intake manifold with an adapter that converts to 1/8-, 1/4-, 3/8-, or 1/2-inch NPT threads for the oil-pressure sending unit.

Drive-by-Wire

The drive-by-wire system is a potentially confusing portion of the wiring conversion. Each engine that uses the drive-by-wire system requires a specific pedal, throttle body, and, in some cases, a TAC module. In most cases, the drive-by-wire components are not interchangeable. The pedal, TAC module, and throttle body must remain with the engine in order for it to work properly. The only interchangeable components are the Vortec truck modules, but the programming in the computer must be changed as well. There are several different component packages, which vary by vehicle.

The 1997–2004 Corvette uses a pedal and separate TAC module to operate the specific throttle body. In 2005, General Motors went to a drive-by-wire pedal that incorporated the TAC sensor in the pedal, so only the pedal and throttle body are needed for a swap. The same goes for the 2005–2006 GTO, which uses a specific GTO-pedal-only configuration. Chevy SSR trucks use a dedicated drive-by-wire pedal with a TAC module. The Cadillac CTS-V uses a pedal and TAC module up to 2004, when it switched to a pedal only in 2005-up. The 2007 Trailblazer uses a pedal only and is different from the rest of the trucks.

Vortec-powered trucks with the adjustable pedal system are not suitable and must be adapted for use with conversion engines. These trucks use a drive-by-wire pedal mounted on a moving platform that adjusts to the height of the driver. Of course, you could simply swap to a cable-driven throttle body or a carbureted setup for one of these engines.

The trucks' pedals and TAC modules are very confusing; General Motors seemed to do a lot of different things with the trucks over the years. Drive-by-wire was first available in the trucks in 1999, and there have been many different pedals with and without TAC modules. This is why it is so important to get all of the components from the donor vehicle beforehand. If you didn't grab the pedal (not everybody thinks to grab the gas pedal when doing an engine swap), you can purchase one from any GM dealer, salvage yard, or even a few aftermarket shops, but you need all the details for your particular engine and ECM.

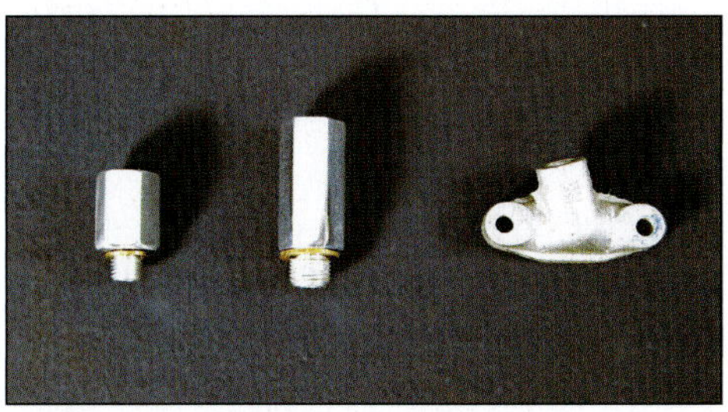

Although not strictly a part of the wiring, you need sensor adapters such as these if you plan to have any kind of engine monitoring that is not wired to the ECM. From left to right: adapters for coolant temperature, oil pressure at the block, and oil bypass. (Photo Courtesy Street & Performance)

Feature Vehicle

Volvette: A Corvette-Engined Volvo

Photos courtesy Doug Strickler

This Volvette started out as a daily driver for Douglas Strickler's dad, Dale Strickler. He spent many years as an avid Volvo enthusiast. When Dale passed away in 1999, the rest of the Strickler family decided to give the 1989 Volvo 740 Turbo Wagon to Doug. Having been around Volvos for years, Doug started playing with the wagon, modifying the stock turbo 4-cylinder.

Eventually, Doug couldn't extract much more performance without sinking a lot of additional money into it, so he decided to change power plants and installed an LS1. The reliability, ease of use, and the obviously larger aftermarket were all a part of his decision. Of course the wagon still had "turbo" badges on it, and Doug figured there was no reason to give them up. The build was on, and Doug certainly had his hands full.

Mounting the LS1 in the Volvo chassis was the most difficult part of the entire swap. The motor mounts were hand fabricated, along with a completely custom crossmember built from 1/8-inch plate steel.

The trick to fabricating custom motor mounts is to suspend the engine over the frame where you want it to be. This can be done with the engine on a hoist and setting blocks under the engine to secure it. The hoist supports the bulk of the weight.

Another option is to use a plastic engine block from Pay-R. These lightweight plastic engines are dimensionally accurate and are a great way to safely lay out motor mounts for custom installs.

The engine needed to sit back as far as possible toward the firewall to allow room for the turbos to clear. The transmission crossmember was built in a similar manner, using 1/8-inch plate steel.

As a turbo enthusiast, Doug figured if one is good, two is better, so he opted for a pair of 60-trim Garret T4 turbos to straddle the LS1. Doug built everything on the Volvo, and Carolina Auto Masters tuned it.

Currently, Doug drives the car daily and enjoys 30 mpg on the highway. The Volvo makes 544 hp at the rear wheels and has no drivability issues. To support the turbos, an Aeromotive A1000 fuel pump feeds the 42-pound fuel injectors.

To eliminate accessory drive issues, Doug built his own system. Part of the turbo brackets double as the accessory drive mounting. This swap is about as custom as they get; very few aftermarket pieces were used and everything was custom made.

The T56 is coupled to a performance-built Ford 8.8 rear end with 9-inch 32-spline Strange axles, bearing girdles, and 4.10:1 gears. Doug says he likes the deep gears because the power output is big enough to move the car as fast as he wants to go, and it lets him shift a little less. The Volvette has traveled the quarter-mile to the 11-second mark. Not bad for the ol' grocery-getter.

Above: *This seemingly normal 1989 Volvo 740 turbo wagon is a good looker. You'd be advised not to get tangled up with it at the next stoplight, though. It is packing heat with an LS1 that has been fitted with a pair of turbos.*

Photo 1: *The twin-turbocharged LS1 is a work of beauty, and the exhaust alone is worthy of an art museum. Owner Doug Strickler built the 544-hp LS-powered Volvo at home. The project took several years to complete.* ***2.*** *The transmission crossmember is a stout unit and actually looks a little over-built, but it was necessary to support the 544 hp.* ***3.*** *The headers started out as simple collectors and progressed piece-by-piece from there. An Aeromotive fuel pressure regulator, eight 42-pound injectors, and a 150-pound fuel pump keep the engine properly supplied.* ***4.*** *The turbo brackets also double as accessory drive brackets. That is good engineering; it eliminates a potential fitment issue for the accessory drive.* ***5.*** *Strickler also built the headers. Once completed, JetHot Coatings coated them to reduce underhood temperatures and increase scavenging.* ***6.*** *The exhaust system is made of stainless-steel pipes and mufflers. It looks as if the pipes Y into one, but there are actually two pipes and two mufflers all the way back for maximum flow.* ***7.*** *Truly a work of art, the equal-length tuned headers couple the Garret T4 turbos to the Tial 38-mm wategates. A GReddy blow-off valve controls the boost levels.*

CHAPTER 7

Engine Management Systems, Tuning Software and Controllers

Each engine requires its own computer, and the programming must match the engine, so computers can't be swapped even if the plugs are the same type. General Motors produces several computer types and each is built for a specific engine group. Some work with many engines, and some only work with one. It is very important to obtain the original computer, harness, and sensors when buying a used engine. This ensures that you have everything needed to make the swap as simple as possible.

Of course, if you are buying a crate engine or can't get all the original components, the aftermarket will come to your rescue. They offer engine management systems for both EFI and carbureted engines (carbureted LS engines are available from Chevrolet Performance as crate or carb-converted Gen III/IV engines). The possibilities are almost endless.

Later ECMs for 1999–2002 LS1s look different and are different than those for a 1997–1998. The wires are in different places, so an early harness cannot be wired to a later ECM; it simply doesn't work. (Photo Courtesy Street & Performance)

It has been said before, but it bears repeating: The ECM can't be changed to operate a different reluctor wheel. The reluctor wheel setup can be changed, but it requires the corresponding computer. Gray sensors are 58x, and black sensors are 24x. (Photo Courtesy Street & Performance)

There are two main types of computers: 24-tooth and 58-tooth reluctor wheel engines. The reluctor wheel is mounted to the crankshaft inside the block to the rear. The crank position sensor is mounted to the rear of the block, behind the starter. As the crankshaft rotates, the teeth on the reluctor wheel interrupt the magnetic field created by the sensor.

The sensor records these interruptions and sends a signal to the computer. These signals are used to detect issues, such as misfires and detonation, with the ignition system.

Reluctor Types

It is important to know which reluctor type you have, 24x or 58x. You can tell by looking at the reluctor wheel sensor: a black sensor is a 24x wheel, a gray sensor is for a 58x engine.

The following engines came with a 24-tooth reluctor wheel:

- 1997–2004 Corvette, LS1 or LS6 (all were drive-by-wire)
- 2005 LS2 Corvette
- 1998–2002 Camaro/Firebird

The 1997–1998 LS1 Y- and F-Body computer is different from the later LS1 ECM. The pin-outs and wiring harnesses are different. This is a 1998 Camaro ECM, front and back side. (Photo Courtesy Street & Performance)

- 2004 LS1 GTO
- 2005–2006 LS2 GTO, 2004–2006 SSR (LS2 and 5.3 liter)
- 1999–2006 4.8-, 5.3-, and 6.0-liter Vortec truck engines

Engines can be drive-by-cable or drive-by-wire, depending on the vehicle. The 58-tooth reluctor wheel is found on drive-by-wire engines only. This reluctor wheel *cannot* be used with a drive-by-cable throttle body without modifications. If you want to run these engines with a traditional throttle cable, they need to be converted to a 24-tooth reluctor wheel, along with a 2005 cam gear on the front of the engine and a 24-tooth reluctor wheel computer.

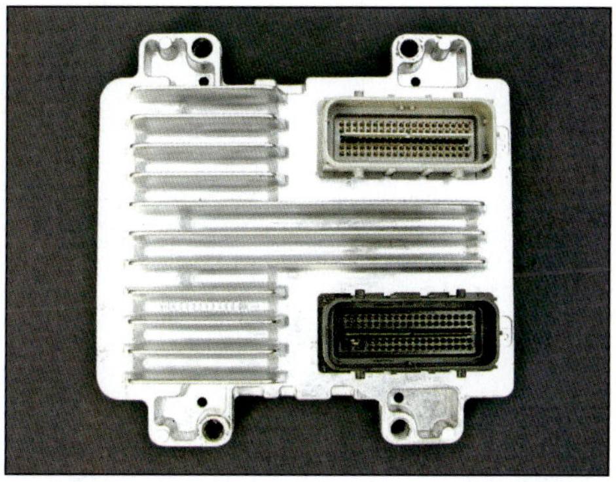

This is a 58x reluctor computer; the ancillary parts are very expensive, so make sure to get all of them from the donor car. Otherwise, you will spend a lot of money to buy these components individually. (Photo Courtesy Street & Performance)

Changing the reluctor wheel also requires changing the cam timing gear. The reluctor wheel and the cam gear work in tandem to monitor the ignition system. If they don't match, the engine doesn't run. (Photo Courtesy Street & Performance)

The following engines have the 58-tooth reluctor:

- 2006–up Corvette LS7
- 2008–up Corvette LS3
- 2007-up 4.8, 5.3, and 6.0 Vortec truck engines

Gen III/IV Engines with 24-Tooth Reluctor Wheels

Year	Engine	Part Number
1997–1998	Corvette, Camaro, Firebird, and Vortec	16238212, 16232148 (red and blue plugs)
1999–2000	Corvette, Camaro, Firebird, and Vortec	09354896, 16263494
2001–2002	Camaro, Firebird, Vortec, 2001–2003 Corvette LS1 and LS6	12200411
2003	Vortec truck	12576106
2004	Corvette LS1 and LS6	12586242
2004	Vortec truck	12586243
2004	GTO and SSR	12598343
2005	GTO and SSR	12603892
2005	Corvette LS2	12597191, 12597883
2005–2006	Vortec truck	125862432
2006	Vortec truck	12583560, 12583561
2006	5.3 SSR	12596679
2006–2007	LS2 and LS7	12603892
2007-up	Vortec truck	12597121

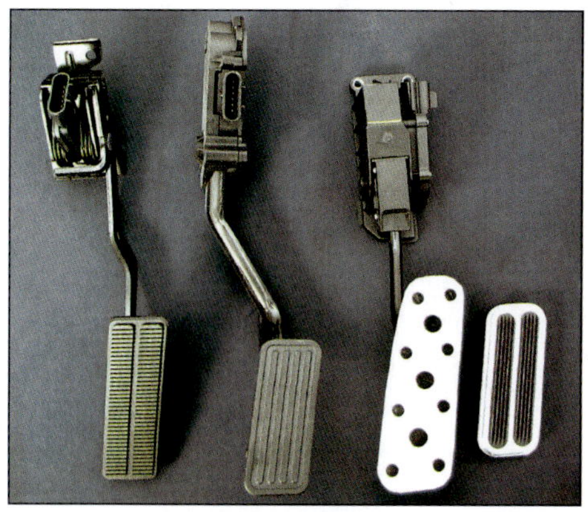

There are several different drive-by-wire pedals. Shown from left to right: a 2005–up Corvette, 2005–2006 SSR, 2005–2006 GTO, and Lokar pedal replacement pad. Not shown are pedals for the 1997–2004 Corvette, CTS-V, 2007 Trailblazer, and the rest of the trucks, which interchanged through the years. (Photo Courtesy Street & Performance)

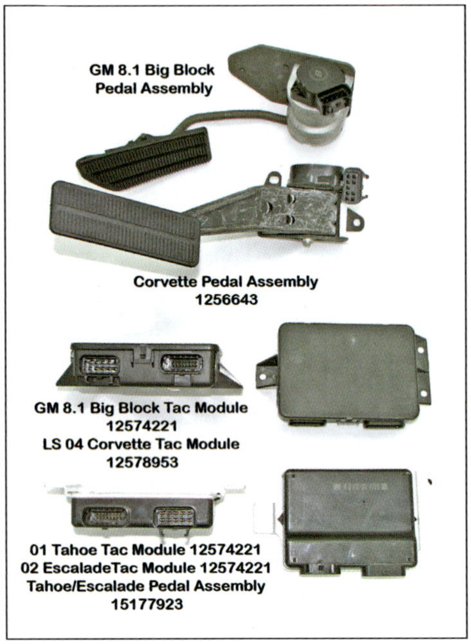

The pedals and TAC modules are a matched set. You need both units to properly operate a drive-by-wire throttle. (Photo Courtesy Street & Performance)

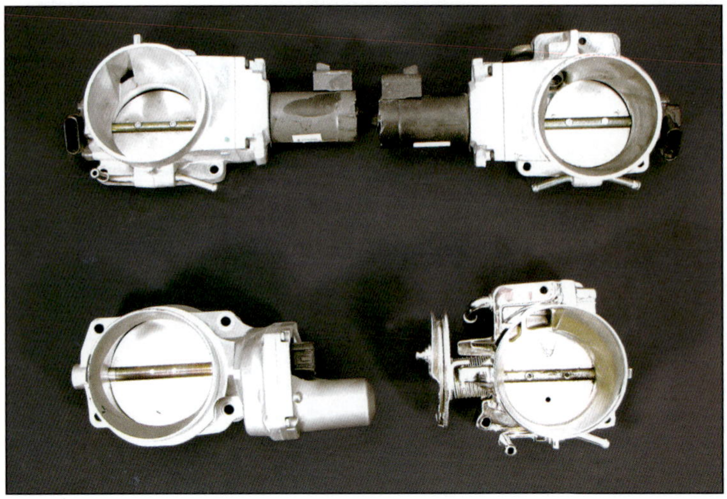

These throttle bodies are: 1997–2004 Corvette (top left), Vortec trucks (top right), drive-by-wire assembly (bottom left), and LS2 2005 GTO (bottom right). (Photo Courtesy Street & Performance)

Each engine uses a specific computer. The wiring harnesses are dedicated to each computer, so it's very important to get all of the components when pulling an engine from a salvage vehicle. If you do not have the proper computer, you can find a wide range of used LS computers from various retailers.

ECM Programming

The 24x ECMs can be programmed for either drive-by-cable or drive-by-wire. For instance, a 1999 F-Body LS1 with a drive-by-cable throttle body can be wired to a 2000 Corvette drive-by-wire ECM, but the ECM must be reprogrammed to reflect the drive-by-cable change.

You can also convert an engine to drive-by-wire by reprogramming the original computer for drive-by-wire, but you must be able to plug the wiring harness into the particular computer. The 1998 F-Body computers and harnesses are not compatible with 1999-up harnesses or computers because the plugs are different. If you plan on running the stock harness and computer, make sure to get them from the donor vehicle, or buy used if you can't.

Programming the stock ECM can be done several ways. Home-based programs, such as HP Tuners and EFI Live, are designed to work with the Gen III/IV computers. Most of the aftermarket tuning modules and software are locked, meaning they lock themselves to a particular computer on the first use. To unlock them, you must purchase pass codes or VINs for additional vehicles. Some products include two passes to tune two separate vehicles. When purchasing tuning software, you typically have unlimited tuning capability (or "tunes") on the same vehicle.

ECM Tuning Packages

Do-it-yourself tuning packages are very efficient and handy to have. They allow you to tune the engine for a multitude of parameters, help identify trouble codes, and add some personalization to the engine without getting greasy. But there are some things that home-based tuning software can't do. Most software packages can't make significant changes to the programming of an ECM, so you can tune the engine, but you cannot change the ECM from drive-by-wire to drive-by-cable or vice versa.

Tuning an aftermarket ECM is easy with supplied software. Some are simple programs using pre-determined options, and some are full-blown custom tuning packages that allow you to control every aspect of the tune.

ECM Mounting

Mounting a stock ECM can be tricky, as they do not have any mounting holes from the factory. You can use one of the factory assembly screws or make a bracket. The bracket shown here was made from 18-gauge steel for a C2 Corvette. ■

Attach a couple of foam pads to the bracket to absorb vibration and to provide some grip. Bend a piece of strap to fit into the cooling fins of the LS1 ECM to secure one side.

Lay another piece of foam into the fin and a form second strap bracket. The foam provides grip for the bracket. It also prevents the bracket from rattling under the dash.

To put the brackets under tension, bend the strap so it is spaced away from the base bracket. A bolt pulls it together, securing the computer.

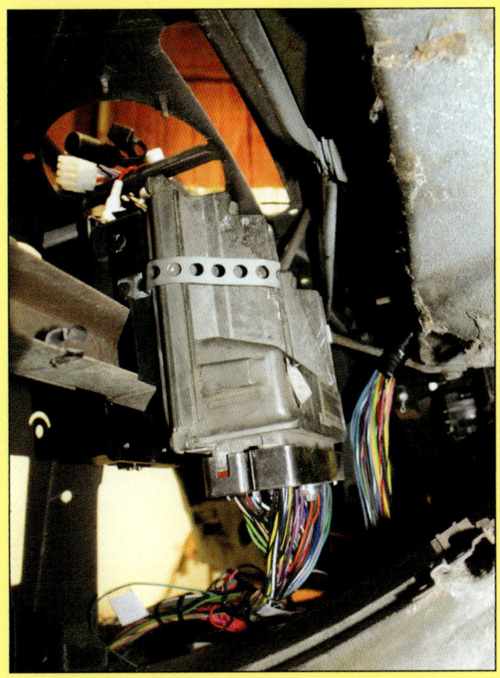

Mount the assembly under the dash of the car (here, a Corvette). The ECM can be mounted under the hood as well, as they are fully sealed.

Aftermarket ECMs such as this Holley are easier to mount with built-in tabs. Most are supplied with rubber isolators as well. Holley computers now come with extra stickers, in case you have to mount yours upside down, as seen here.

The software also is not the best way to swap a computer from a different year to a different engine; this requires more significant programming beyond what the tuning software was designed for. These programs are great for what they do: tune the existing programming to better suit your application and needs.

HP Tuners

This comprehensive tuning software allows you to fully tune and adjust a stock ECM. Available in a base or pro form, the HP VCM Suite adjusts Gen III/IV computers. HP works on the credit system and allows you to tune up to four specific vehicles or unlimited tunes for the same year and model vehicle (any 2000 Camaro LS1, for example), or even unlimited Gen III/IV vehicles.

Each option costs credits. A single vehicle license costs 2 credits per year, model licenses cost 6 credits, and unlimited LS1 tunes cost 70 credits. The basic software purchase includes 8 credits and additional credits are always available, adding to the flexibility of the software. This home-based software costs a good deal more than a handheld tuner or shipping your computer off, but it has much more flexibility and is likely worth the extra cost in the end.

However, the HP software cannot load programming from different model years to any given computer. Therefore, you need to start with the right-year computer for your engine application.

The HP VCM Tuner Suite comes with the handheld scanner required to upload the tunes to the vehicle, but does not come preloaded with tunes. The software gives you access to hundreds of tunes, and you can even build your own. The HP tuner software is also easy to upgrade to the most up-to-date information and calibrations.

EFI Live

EFI Live offers several versions of their products including FlashScan and FlashScan and Tune. The tuning version allows to you build your own ECM tunes, controlling all aspects of the ECM programming. The FlashScan software works on a VIN licensing system, which requires each vehicle to be licensed. The main kit includes two VIN licenses; additional licenses can be purchased.

The EFI Live software is capable of tuning Gen III and Gen IV computers. The FlashScan software features more than 600 engine calibrations for in-depth ECM tuning, as well as fixes for issues with stock computers such as VATS, MAF, and TCS (traction control system) fault codes. The software is constantly upgrading and evolving, ensuring the product you purchase not only serves its current purpose, but is up-to-date as the technology changes.

Handheld Tuners

These are an alternative to the home-based software programs and offer more portability for tuning the engine. Handheld engine tuners allow you to tune the computer on the fly and run diagnostics whenever the need strikes and regardless of location. Upper-end handheld tuners are typically comparable in price to the entry-level, home-based software programmers.

Handhelds usually control the basic functions and parameters needed to tune the engines, but only the basics; computer-based software programs have many more variables and options. The biggest advantage of the handheld tuners is their ease of use. The simple user interface makes tuning easier than the home-based software.

Reprogramming Services

If you need to change from drive-by-wire to a throttle cable or swap a newer ECM to an older engine, you need to work with a reprogrammer. Shops such as Street & Performance and Speartech offer reprogramming services to precisely

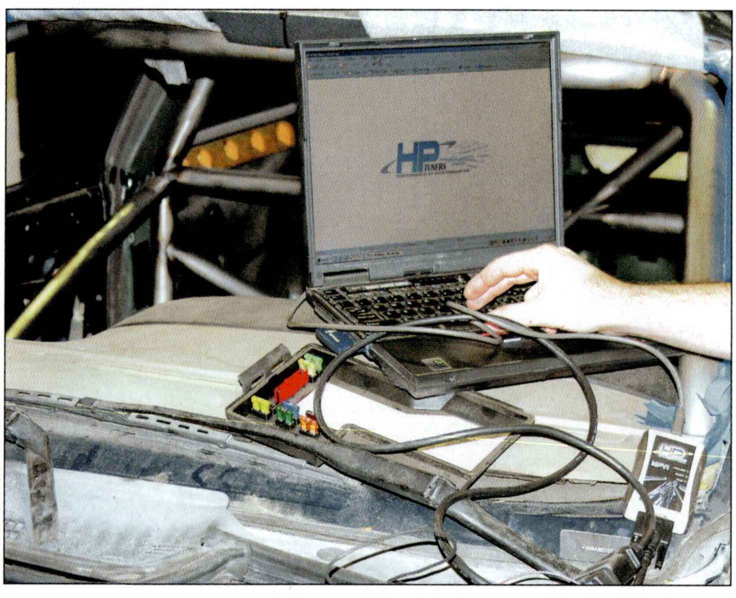

For factory computers, HP Tuners software is the most complete of all of the aftermarket software available to consumers. It allows you to change just about all parameters of the ECM programming. (Photo Courtesy HP Tuners)

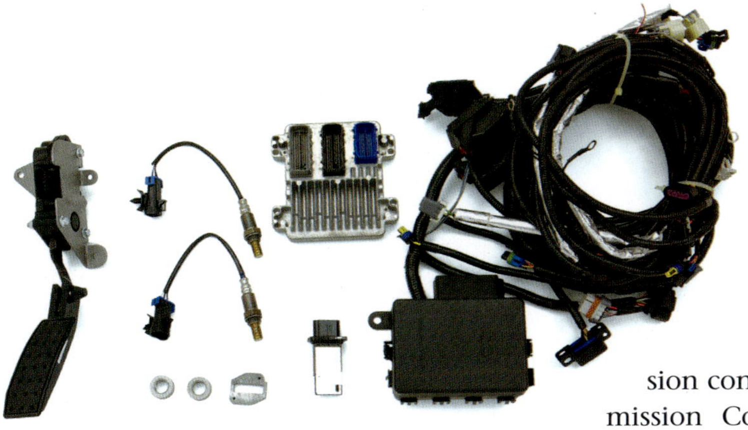

If you buy a used engine, the wiring harness, computers, and peripheral equipment are there for the taking. But if you buy a crate engine, this equipment may need to be purchased separately. This engine controller from Chevrolet Performance offers the best of both worlds: a factory-backed computer with performance tuning built in. (Photo Courtesy General Motors)

program the ECM to your requirements. If you plan on just keeping a stock or slightly modified tune in the computer, having the stock ECM reconfigured is usually cheaper than buying a tuning package. It is also the only way to make certain changes.

Other considerations also need to be addressed on some pull-out engines. Most vehicles built with Gen III/IV engines use the ECM to control automatic transmissions, but not all of them. The LS2 GTO uses a transmission control module (TCM) to send information to the PCM. Both of these components are necessary if you are going to use the stock computer. Vortec platforms began using the TCM module on all the automatic transmission trucks in 2005.

In addition, if you change the style of transmission, automatic to manual or vice versa, the tune should be changed in the computer.

If running an electronically controlled automatic such as a 4L60E, use the tuning software to enter the VIN (on the side of the case) into the ECM or TCM module so the computer has access to the transmission.

Transmission Controller

If you use an electronically controlled transmission without the stock computer, the engine management may not support the transmission. In this situation, you need a transmission controller. TCI's Transmission Control Unit (TCU) and Painless Performance's Perfect Torc offer greater tuning capability of the GM electronically controlled transmission than the factory controller. These units are compatible with most GM electronically controlled automatic transmissions. They provide load, gear, RPM, and speed-based programming with the click of a mouse.

The TCI unit is also fully compatible with CAN 2.0B engine management systems, such as the FAST XFI system, which makes it easy to integrate the TCU with the engine controller.

Transmission controllers come with tuning software and wiring harnesses. The software allows you to change many parameters, even allowing paddle and push-button shifting configurations along with manifold-pressure-based shift firmness, greatly adding to the ability to tune the transmission far beyond the capabilities of a stock TCM or ECM.

Chevrolet Performance offers a factory-tuned transmission controller for carbureted and aftermarket-EFI LS engines. This is essentially the same control found in factory ECMs. (Photo Courtesy General Motors)

Aftermarket Engine Management

Aftermarket engine management has many benefits that go far beyond the factory computer capabilities. Some builders say the stock computer is more than enough to control their LS engine, and they're correct: the factory computer works very well for a stock engine. Simple tuning changes and adjustments are made fairly easily and quickly show improvements in performance. Even entry-level performance mods such as to the exhaust, a larger throttle body, and mild cams can be tuned in with the stock computer.

But once you get out of the mild performance arena and get into more serious mods such as big cams, superchargers, or turbos, the stock computer simply can't keep up. Even a bunch of smaller components that add up to bigger gains can overwhelm the stock computer and start to show its weaknesses. Ultimately, the computer can't adjust the fuel maps and timing curves to compensate for the new air and fuel requirements on heavily modified engines.

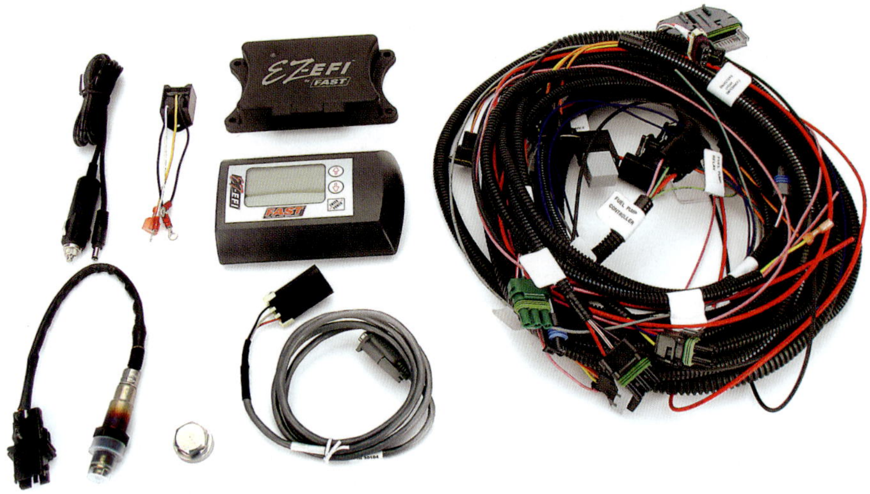

For a simple aftermarket solution that does not require advanced tuning skills, the FAST EZ-EFI is a simple-to-use system that comes with all the wiring required to control the engine. This does not control the transmission; however, they are compatible with the TCI transmission controllers. (Photo Courtesy FAST)

However, aftermarket engine management can, and they offer an array of tuning options.

Aftermarket controllers are an important consideration when using a crate engine. Chevrolet Performance crate engines do not come with a computer or wire harness, leaving it up to the buyer to get a harness and a computer. Chevrolet Performance does, however, offer a very good controller and harness for each of their crate engine offerings, including one for the carbureted LS364 and LS376 engines.

If you need complete control over every aspect of your LS engine's tune and have an electronically controlled transmission, the Dominator EFI ECM from Holley has everything in one box. (Photo Courtesy Holley Performance Products)

Chevrolet Performance Plug-and-Play Engine Controller

General Motors designed these controllers to help take the guesswork out of a Gen III/IV engine swap. Offered for the Gen IV–series engines, this controller works with the LS2 (PN 19166568), LS3 (PN 19201861), and LS7 (PN 19166567) crate engines. These controllers are complete stand-alone systems that allow the builder to simply plug the factory-style wire harness connections into the new controller and start the engine. No tuning, no removing codes or parameters—just fire it up. It's a great option for builders who want a factory-based system and a specialized tune for a crate engine.

The Chevrolet Performance controller is based on the factory ECM, but features custom calibration of the electronic throttle control, EFI, and ignition systems. The Gen IV controller features an OEM-style fuse and relay center, with additional positions for other elective components, 12-wire bulkhead with outputs for the tachometer, VSS, oil pressure, malfunction indicator light (MIL), water temperature, and others. These signal outputs are compatible with aftermarket gauges only, and do not control factory electronic gauges.

The cooling fans and fuel pump can be controlled through the controller as well with the included outputs. Each controller comes with a compatible drive-by-wire gas pedal, MAF sensor, and oxygen sensors. This controller regulates any LS-series engine that uses the Gen IV air/fuel components.

Using the Chevrolet Performance controller gives you the benefit of the vast testing labs available to General Motors, ensuring that this controller performs flawlessly with aftermarket components. It is also backed by the Chevrolet Performance warranty.

Chevrolet Performance LSX Ignition Controller

All OEM-installed engines are fuel injected but not all LS engines are fuel injected. Chevrolet Performance offers two carbureted LS engines for those who like the simplicity of a carburetor. The LS364/440 and LS376/515 engines are based on the LS2 and LS3, respectively, but are cammed up and topped off with Chevrolet Performance's carburetor LS intake. The LS376/515 is the most powerful LS crate engine to date, pushing 515 hp at the flywheel.

Although these powerhouse engines run a classic carb on top, they use the LS distributorless ignition, which means that they need an ignition controller. The Chevrolet Performance LSX ignition controller module (PN 19171130) was developed for use with these carbureted engines, but works for any carbureted LS engine with a 58x reluctor wheel. The controller has several

Carbureted LS engines are distributorless, so you need an ignition controller such as this one from FAST. The XIM is also used with the XFI system on EFI engines. (Photo Courtesy FAST)

pre-programmed timing curves, along with software to create custom curves and adjust the rev limiters and step retard functions. The controller includes the MAP sensor and is compatible with all LS-series ignition coils.

Self-Learn Tuning

If you want to increase the tuning potential for your LS engine, there are quite a few options. The current entry-level controller for LS-series engines shares one key feature that greatly simplifies any LS swap: self-learning tuning. By eliminating the finer points of EFI engine tuning, the self-learn ECMs use data collected by the sensors to constantly tweak how the engine runs. This means automatic changes as the environment around the vehicle changes.

Let's say you take a trip across the country. With a static tune, the engine runs differently at various elevations. With self-learning, the tune adapts to the environment much better than a static-tuned ECM. Once the engine is running, the ECM starts learning; within just a few miles, it has already begun to tune the engine automatically. This means less time working on a laptop trying to get your engine running at its best and more time enjoying the drive. FAST's EZ-EFI and Holley's HP EFI systems both feature self-learn, and they are reliable controllers for the LS-series EFI systems.

If you want more control, you can have it. Even the basic self-learn systems have some user controls. The Holley HP EFI ECM can be manually tuned in addition to having the self-learn function. Where these entry and mid-level systems drop off is in the boost department. These controllers may not be compatible with superchargers or turbos; some are, while others are not. Just keep that in mind when making your decision.

Advanced Tuning

Although most aftermarket controllers are excellent in terms of engine management, most do not have transmission control for late-model electronic transmissions. A few, such as the Holley Dominator ECM, feature advanced tuning capability and include a built-in transmission controller. Others require a separate transmission controller.

Several aftermarket transmission controllers, such as the TCI Transmission Control Unit (TCU) and Painless Performance's Perfect Torc, offer greater tuning capability of GM electronic controlled transmissions than the factory controller. These units are compatible with most GM electronically controlled automatic transmissions. They provide load, gear, RPM, and speed-based programming with the click of a mouse.

The TCI unit is also fully compatible with CAN 2.0B engine management systems, such as the FAST XFI system, which makes it easy to integrate the TCU with the engine controller. Transmission controllers come with tuning software and wiring harnesses. The software allows you to change many parameters, even allowing paddle and push-button shifting configurations and manifold-pressure-based shift firmness, greatly adding to the ability to tune the transmission far beyond the capabilities of the stock TCM or ECM.

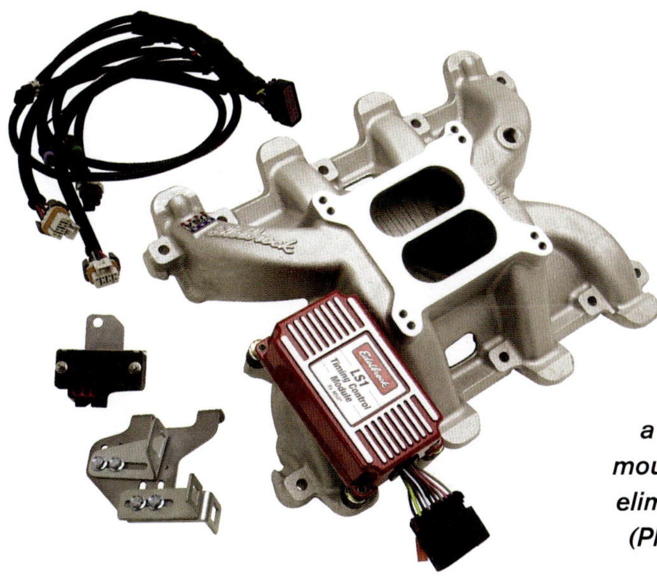

This carbureted intake and controller from Edelbrock comes with a controller from MSD that mounts directly to the intake, eliminating mounting issues. (Photo Courtesy Edelbrock)

1967 Chevy Pickup

One of the most popular swap platforms is also one of the most popular classic trucks ever produced. With millions made between 1967 and 1972, the classic C10 of this era is an extremely popular truck, and for good reason. They had excellent styling, great work, and haul potential, and are plentiful to say the least. Available in everything from a short wide-bed to Suburbans, there is a Classic C10 for everyone.

This 1967 C10 built by Red Dirt Rodz is a prime example of a restomod truck, using modern suspension updates, four-wheel disc brakes, and, of course, an LS-series engine. Here, a 2001 Chevy Vortec 5.3 and 4L60E automatic transmission were chosen. Not settling on just a stock swap, the 5.3 was treated to a host of aftermarket goodies from Holley, including a mid-rise modular intake, accessory drive, and Dominator EFI system.

This truck is different from many others because it does not have the typical short, wide body. It is a 1967 long step-side truck that had the perfect patina. Having spent most of its life as a farm truck in Montana, the truck was well used, but structurally intact. A four-wheel disc brake system was installed on the front drop spindles and factory 12-bolt rear end. Completing the suspension is a Ridetech air-ride system with tubular control arms and electronic controls.

When the 327 under the hood developed a knock, it was swapped rather than rebuilt. The 5.3 with 65,000 miles on the odometer was sourced from a salvage yard. With these engines commonly reaching into the mid-250,000 range without much issue, this is a fairly fresh engine.

The block was mounted to the stock frame rails using a set of Hooker LS motor mounts. Even though the stock Vortec components work quite well with this era of Chevy truck, most of them were swapped out for high-performance components. The accessory drive was changed to accommodate the modular Holley intake system that positioned the 90-mm LS3-type throttle body farther forward than the Vortec intake.

As this generation of Chevy truck uses an in-cab fuel tank, it was removed for a frame-mounted fuel cell from Summit Racing. This eliminated any potential safety issues and freed up some room in the cab for the Kicker audio system. To push the fuel to the engine, an Aeromotive A1000 in-line fuel pump was used.

Even though the truck looks as if it just drove out of the field, everything underneath and inside is brand new. Getting more than 20 mpg while churning the tires into a furious rage of white smoke isn't a problem for this once-abandoned piece of Detroit iron. Another Red Dirt Rodz classic.

Above: *After the truck's 327 went down, the only choice was to do an LS swap. With the affordability of the 5.3, there was plenty of room in the budget for some performance goodies.*

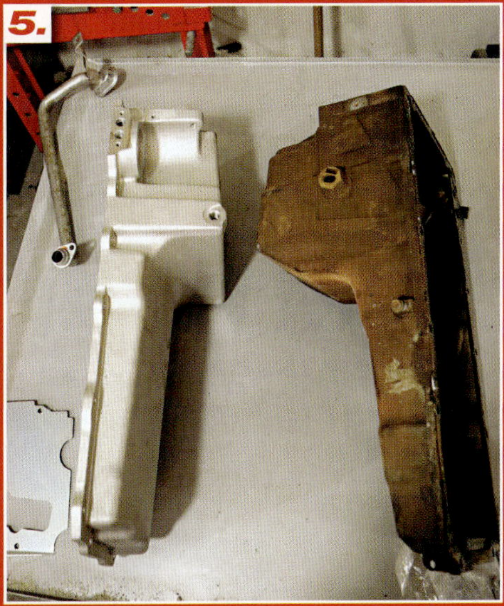

Photo ***1:*** *Stock frame stands worked perfectly for this swap, but the Hooker LS manifolds needed some additional clearance, so the stands were altered with a torch and knocked down with a hammer.* ***2.*** *The clearance gained was significant, adding a good 1/2 inch for engine twist. Once the fabrication was complete, the truck was disassembled and all the parts were painted.* ***3.*** *The Hooker manifolds clear everything else and provide a unique look for the truck. Hooker manifolds are available in several finishes, but the cast gray is perfect here.* ***4.*** *Under the truck, the oil pan hung about 2 inches below the stock engine crossmember. Because the C10 is on air suspension, this does not work, especially considering the crossmember could touch the ground before the swap. The Vortec pan is just too low.* ***5.*** *Holley's swap pan (left) uses the factory-style oil filter mount, and comes with a new pick-up tube and an oil baffle. You can see here how much deeper the factory truck pan (right) is in comparison.* ***6.*** *Once installed, the Holley pan sat about an inch above the bottom of the crossmember.*

7.

8.

9.

10.

11.

7. *Part of the modular intake system is the dual-quad base. This intake can be used as a stand-alone with two carbs and an ignition controller, or you can add more Holley components as was done on this truck to make it a throttle-body intake.* ***8.*** *Thirty-six-pounds-per-hour fuel injectors were mounted to the aluminum rails. They use the STD-type injector clips. Be careful to keep the ends of the injectors (the part that fits into the intake) clean. Oil can degrade the injector.* ***9.*** *Topping off the intake system is an EFI top hat and an LS3-style 90-mm four-bolt drive-by-cable throttle body. There are two parts to this top section: an adapter plate that bolts to the dual-quad base and the top hat, which fits the LS3 throttle body.* ***10.*** *You can see the tight clearance of the truck accessory drive: the throttle body hits the upper idler pulley and the alternator barely clears the fuel rail.* ***11.*** *The solution was the Holley accessory system, which is loosely based on the CTS-V design. This kit can be used for all three water pump/crank pulley lengths when used with the correct hardware. A/C will be added later.*

12.

13.

14.

15.

16.

12. *The stock valve covers were also swapped out for a set of Holley's custom valve covers. They use LS3-type coils, but Vortec coils were reused for now.* ***13.*** *Stock sensors were installed into the throttle body and plugged in using the Holley EFI wiring harness, which features stock LS-type plugs.* ***14.*** *Holley's Dominator EFI ECM controls the engine and the 4L60E transmission for a simple computer system. The ECM was mounted under the dash behind the glove box for easy access.* ***15.*** *The fuel-pressure regulator was mounted at the rear of the fuel rails, plumbed to the return line to the fuel cell. This allows the rails to have maximum fuel pressure at all times.* ***16.*** *The clearance between the Vortec accessory drive and the driver-side fuel rail is so tight that the alternator had to be removed just to get the line threaded in.*

17.

18.

19.

20.

17. *With the new drive, there is no issue at all. The crossover line is -8 AN made from Earl's Plumbing hose with fittings. The rest of the line is -6, but the crossover eliminates any potential restriction.* ***18.*** *Mounted between the rear frame rails is a Summit Racing 16-gallon fuel cell. The cell came with -8 fittings, but the Aeromotive pump requires -10, so one side was drilled out to take a -10 bulkhead.* ***19.*** *Every electric fuel pump requires a pre-filter. This high-flow 100-micron unit from Aeromotive does not restrict the gravity feed as smaller filters do. Note that the 90-degree fittings are of the tube-type variety and not squared off. This allows for free flow.* ***20.*** *The pump was mounted vertically on a bracket next to the cell. The pump should be as close to the tank as possible, and the inlet should be level or below the lowest point of the tank. That can be tricky in some cases, but this works perfectly.*

Fuel Systems

Fuel-injection systems require careful planning and component selection. There are many components that go into a fuel system (including tank, fuel pump, lines, fittings, and filters) and each one has multiple replacement/upgrade options. So, simply installing an electric fuel pump is not going to work. The fuel-pressure requirements alone necessitate some detailed planning.

In-Tank Fuel Pump

When it comes to fuel pumps, there are two categories: in-tank and external. In-tank pumps tend to last longer, hold higher pressure, and run quieter. However, in-tank pumps are also more complicated to install, and retrofitting an in-tank pump costs more. Virtually any aftermarket EFI in-tank pump that can supply the 60-psi fuel-pressure requirement is suitable. Many builders suggest the Walbro 340 in-tank pump because it holds higher pressures and has proven to be very reliable for supplying LS engines. The key is to buy a pump that is suited for your application. The stock F-Body fuel-pump assembly can be purchased from GM dealers and used for retrofit applications.

There are two ways to add an in-tank pump to your vehicle: buy a tank with a pre-installed EFI pump, either custom or OEM from a different vehicle, or retrofit the tank. Both options can be pricey, but there are ways to keep it on the cheap as well.

Buy a New Tank

New tanks can cost upward of $1,000. Companies such as Rock

New tanks from Rock Valley come well packaged and ready to install. They are available for most popular cars and trucks, or you can have your existing tank modified. The tanks are recessed to allow clearance for large AN-style fittings. (Photo Courtesy Street & Performance)

One of the newest alternatives to complete tank modification is the Aeromotive Phantom in-tank system. Everything is included for the install, even the foam baffle and a drill jig for the mounting holes.

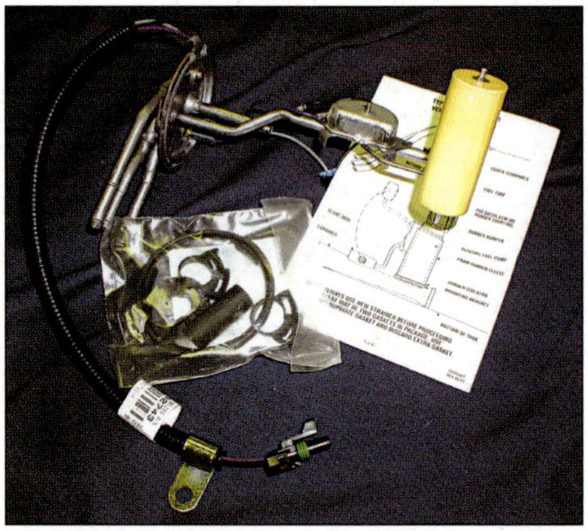

Most GM stock sending units, such as this one, can be modified with an electric pump, but the pump needs a filter sock touching the bottom of the tank.

Valley Antique Auto Parts build custom stainless-steel gas tanks for street rods, hot rods, muscle cars, and trucks. If your car is not on the list, Rock Valley can build a custom tank. These new tanks are very slick, well built, and easy to install, but they come with a high price tag.

Each Rock Valley EFI fuel tank features a dropped sump in the top of the tank. This allows for adequate floor clearance. Each EFI tank comes with a new high-volume, high-pressure fuel pump to feed your engine.

Refit the Current Pump

There are several ways to alter your stock tank to take an EFI fuel pump. The bargain-basement method is to take the stock sending unit assembly out of the tank, cut off a short section of feed line (about 1½ inches, depending on the depth of the tank and the length of the pump), and fit the pump to the stub using fuel line and hose clamps. The important thing here is to make sure the pump is mounted about 1/4 inch off the floor of the tank, with a filter sock resting on the bottom of the tank. This keeps the impurities out of the pump while getting the most fuel out of the tank. The pump needs to be supported, so a piece of steel rod can be welded to the underside of the assembly plate. The pump is then clamped to the rod, so it remains stationary.

This method doesn't work for all tanks, especially shallow tanks, and clearance may be hampered by the diameter of the stock assembly. Additionally, the fuel-level sending unit may be in the way, depending on application. This method keeps the stock feed lines in place and eliminates any floorpan clearance issues. One more drawback is the complete lack of a fuel sump feature, which traps fuel around the pump inlet, ensuring it does not run dry. Running an in-tank pump dry is very destructive; they don't last long when run dry.

Modify the Tank with Welding

Welding on the tank is extremely dangerous and should not be attempted in haste or by novices. *All* of the old fuel must be removed and the tank thoroughly rinsed, drained, and rinsed again until there is absolutely no possibility of any remaining fuel vapor.

If you smell a hint of gas, clean it again. Some people even suggest filling the tank with water or inert gas, such as argon, while the welding is being performed. In any event, when in doubt, seek the help of a professional. Most fuel tank builders also offer their services for retrofitting tanks.

Installing a custom in-tank pump in the top of the tank often requires a recessed panel on the top. The fittings clear the floorpan and provide a flat surface to mount the new assembly. If the top sump is placed to the side of the original, the stock sending unit can be used, simplifying the process. This requires a boxed section to be built and welded to the top of the tank.

Then a fuel-pump assembly unit is built with both wiring and inlet and outlet fittings. This unit should have a bar or rod on the inside portion of the tank to mount the pump. Using 90-degree hose barb fittings is usually the easiest way to get the fuel in and out of the assembly. These fittings must be sealed tight so they do not leak. The entire assembly bolts to the sump.

In addition, by installing baffles on the inside of the tank, fuel surrounds the pump at all times. The baffles should be added before the top sump is installed.

The other option is to weld in a sump in the bottom of the tank. This sump is placed directly below the pump, but the pump is installed in the lowered section, with the filter sock on the floor of the sump. Tanksinc.com offers an upper tank mount, complete with a fuel pump and baffle. This option reduces some of the building legwork and ensures the pump is covered with fuel at all times.

Install a Pump Kit

You can install a truly high-performance fuel pump into a stock fuel tank without welding. Aeromotive offers two retrofit in-tank pump kits: the Phantom and the A1000 Stealth.

For basic street performance use, the Phantom 340 kit is suitable. This kit allows you to simply cut a hole in the top of the tank, drop in the pump, bolt it down, and hook up the lines. The kit comes with the seals, hardware, and a drill jig to ensure the holes are in the right place. The 340

Sumping a Gas Tank

EFI engines require lots of fuel; this is not because they are inefficient, but rather because they typically run a return-style fuel system that requires more volume. Most modern cars have in-tank fuel pumps, but that is not always practical for a retrofit.

In-line fuel pumps need a free-flowing gravity feed in order to survive. When the fuel flow is limited through either a loss of siphon feed or line restrictions, the pump cavitates and fails in very short order. One of the ways to eliminate this is to add a sump to the fuel tank.

There are all kinds of fuel sump designs, but for this project we went with the full-blown trap-door-style sump from Aeromotive. The sump comes preassembled with -10 AN fittings for feed and return lines. Although this sump is designed for an external pump, Aeromotive offers this same sump with an in-tank A1000 fuel pump.

WARNING: the following process requires welding on a gas tank. Take adequate precautions before cutting the tank, or take it to a professional. ■

1 ***This is an old trick, and I stand by it. I have used it several times with great success. In this step I am hanging the gas tank so it's safe to work on. The goal is to push out any residual fuel vapor by filling it with an inert gas.***

2 ***With the tank on the bench, outline the sump on the bottom of the tank. The top is narrower than the base, so cutting to the line is not an issue.***

3 ***Drill a couple of holes into the bottom of the tank for the saw blade.***

4 ***Use a jigsaw with a fine-tooth metal-cutting blade to open up the tank. The key here is to make the holes line up so the blade fits.***

5 ***There may be quite a bit of junk and trash in the tank from years of use. Also note that the fuel-level sender may be in the way. If so, spin it 180 degrees.***

Sumping a Gas Tank *CONTINUED*

6 *The sump sits in the hole, but may not go in far enough. The sump needs to be inside the tank to about the midline of the sump, which is the point that it angles in on the right side, just under the fitting. More trimming is needed.*

7 *This is as far as the sump fits in the tank. A clearance of at least 1 inch is required from the sump to the top of the tank. The sump can be trimmed, but this one did not need any trimming.*

8 *Use a body hammer to tap the metal around the sump until it's flush. This helps with sealing. This only requires light tapping, as you don't want to crush it inside the joint.*

9 *Remove the sump and drill it with a 3/8-inch drill bit just above the lowest point of the tank. This allows fuel to fill the sump even when the fuel level is below the top.*

10 *Remove all the paint at the edges of the tank with a sanding pad for the welding process.*

11 *Use a screw-driver to push the metal together while welding the sump to ensure a clean metal-to-metal seal.*

12 *You can weld the tank with a TIG welder or a MIG welder. Work in short 1-inch areas, skipping around the tank to avoid warpage. TIG welding is better as it provides the best joint with less likelihood of leaks.*

13 *Once the sump is fully welded, set the tank on a stand. Plug the fitting and fill the tank with water to look for leaks. Don't be surprised if it leaks. They usually do.*

14 *There are almost always a few pinholes that require more welding. This tank had two that were resolved with a couple of additional welds. The final step: paint and reinstallation.*

supports up to 700-hp supercharged EFI engines, or 1,000-hp supercharged carbureted systems. That means there is plenty of room to power a stock 400-hp LS3. The Phantom system can fit in just about any tank, so this is a really good option that takes out the guesswork.

For more serious performance engines, the Stealth A1000 system feeds up to 1,300-hp EFI systems and 1,500 hp for carbureted engines. Installing these systems takes slightly more effort than the Phantom kit, but not much.

Adding a Return Line

1 *Adding a return line to a non-return fuel tank is not that tough; it does not even have to be welded. This is the tank for a 1967 Corvette that received an LS1. You can see a recess in the upper passenger's side that will be used for a return line fitting.*

2 *Starting with a 3/8-inch barbed brass fitting, check to make sure it fits.*

3 *Drill the tank with a bit that is two or three times smaller than the suggested bit size for the thread size. Make sure the gas tank is empty before working on it. Even a small spark from drilling could cause an explosion.*

4 *Here is a trick: Use a punch for an air hammer with a heavy taper. You can buy the same tool as a dedicated sheet-metal thread punch too. The shank should match the drill size for the pipe thread on the fitting.*

Adding a Return Line *CONTINUED*

5 *Tap the punch into the hole using a hammer. Go slowly so the metal stretches. You don't want to tear it.*

6 *The result is an inverted section of sheet metal about 1/4 inch deep, which is enough for a good seal and several threads.*

7 *Using a tap, thread the hole to match the fitting. Whenever you use a tap, make sure to go slowly and use cutting fluid or penetrating oil.*

8 *The fitting threads in easily. Make sure to thoroughly vacuum out the tank after drilling and tapping the hole. Neither metal shavings nor contaminants can remail in the tank.*

9 *To seal the hole, coat the fitting with Teflon paste. This is all you really need for return lines because they are not under much pressure.*

External Fuel Pump

External, or in-line pumps, are simpler to install and are usually cheaper than in-tank fuel pumps. In-line pumps are *much* easier to change, making roadside swaps bearable. The main gripe with in-line pumps is the noise. The relatively quiet and smooth-running Gen III/IV engines do not drown out many external sounds, including these in-line pumps. Therefore, drivers hear the whir of the electric pump sound over the engine with a stock-style quiet exhaust. For most builders, the added noise isn't a problem but merely an inconvenience; for a show car, a noisy pump might be considered a serious drawback.

Installing an in-line pump is easier than installing an in-tank pump. Just be sure to install a large-capacity pre-filter and secure the high-pressure side with EFI-rated fuel line.

The real drawback for an in-line pump is that the fuel line is only pressurized after the pump, meaning the tank to the pump is gravity fed. Anyone who has dealt with a modern high-performance external fuel pump can tell you that life is really difficult when you lose the siphon feed in the fuel tank. Simply having the pump in the tank maintains a constant supply of fuel to prevent those hard-cornering and acceleration woes that come with a stock tank and an in-line electric fuel pump.

In-line fuel pumps also require a more substantial return line system because of the long distance between the regulator and the fuel tank. In-line pumps are also subject to failure through heat. The only thing that cools the pump is the gas flowing through it.

Assembling Steel-Braided Hoses

Although regular rubber hoses are adequate for factory installations, braided lines and hoses provide the best look, performance, and fit for a custom install. For decades, steel-braided lines have been the standard for muscle cars and trucks, but it takes more skill and work to cut and install fittings on steel-braided lines. There are a few tips and tricks, however, that can take the strain out of plumbing your ride and getting the best look possible.

Earl's Performance Plumbing, a division of Holley Performance, offers a few products that bring the braided look under the hood while reducing the strain of stainless steel. The Pro-Lite 350 hose is a high-quality rubber hose with a black nylon braid that protects the rubber from chaffing, flying debris, and cuts. The nylon is easy to cut, saves your fingertips, and really cleans up the engine bay. The Pro-Lite 350 can be used with all the AN fittings and simple hose clamps, adding to its versatility.

Working with AN fittings requires some extra knowledge and planning for each system. Typically, the local parts store doesn't carry AN fittings, so without quick access to a speed shop, ordering fittings is the only option. Plan out the system beforehand to prevent wasting time with unnecessary parts or ending up waiting for parts.

The aerospace industry developed AN fittings, and each AN size directly correlates to a specific outer diameter of metal tubing. Each size is listed as "-X," and each number after the "-" indicates a 1/16-inch increase in size: a -3 fitting is 3/16 inch, a -4 is 1/4 inch, and so on.

If a car sees a lot of street time, running hard fuel lines is recommended. Even braided lines can collapse over time, but a properly routed steel line lasts almost forever. Depending on the stock system, it might be possible to reuse the stock hard lines. A 3/8-inch feed line and 1/4-inch return line (if using a return-style system) are the minimum requirements for a high-performance fuel system. These sizes are good to about 500 hp. If your LS engine produces more than 500 hp, upgrade to 1/2-inch lines.

Converting to Braided

There are two ways to convert from hard lines to braided lines with AN fittings. A hose clamp can be installed on a bare hose, or it can be done the proper way by using a tube sleeve, tube nut, and an AN fitting. There is a trick to it, though, and if not done properly, the fitting leaks.

The automotive industry standard flare is 45 degrees. This is the angle of the inside lip of the flare, and is what seals against the fitting. All commonly available flaring tools come in 45-degree kits. AN fittings, however, require 37-degree flares. Those 8 little degrees can mean the difference between a proper seal and a nasty leak. Finding a 37-degree flare tool might prove to be difficult, however, as most parts store don't carry them. A basic double flare is all you need.

Planning

Careful measuring is important. Using a simple drawing of a car and marking out the route for the lines and hoses can greatly simplify the task.

Determining the placement of the fuel pump is key.

For the transmission cooling lines, route the hoses through the frame whenever possible to reduce the amount of exposed line.

If the lines need to make a sharp turn, figure in an angled fitting, such as a 45- or 90-degree fitting, instead of trying to bend the hose. A 3-inch radius is the maximum bend for rubber hose.

Often, there are things that don't fit, or additional fittings are needed. Remember that ordering parts online or from a catalog takes time for delivery and can delay the planning process. Discuss all plans with the tech advisors because they can offer advice that saves both time and money.

Component Selection

Choosing which components to use depends on the budget and desired level of performance. Earl's Performance Plumbing offers several different types of fittings and hoses to suit each system's needs.

Black Ano-Tuff hard-anodized fittings resist corrosion and wear better than the more common red and blue anodizing, and these fittings are perfect for Earl's Pro-Lite nylon braided hose. Pro-Lite 350 hose is best suited for the fuel, heater, and transmission because of its light weight and flexibility.

Stainless-steel Teflon lines or nylon braided high-pressure hose are needed for power steering lines.

Swivel-Seal hose ends add flexibility to the lines because these ends prevent the hose from twisting when assembling the lines in the car; otherwise, they can collapse.

Once all lines are installed, be sure to test each system for leaks before setting out on a road trip. ■

Assembling Steel-Braided Hoses *CONTINUED*

1 *Running AN lines means assembling the fittings to the lines through a specific process. Here is a set of -8 fittings, -8 hose from Earl's, some Royal Purple assembly lube, and some AN wrenches.*

2 *Lube the main fitting to accommodate the hose and the threads on the collar. It is much more difficult to install the hose dry.*

3 *Install the collar on the hose. The hose should be 1/16 inch from the threads on the inside of the collar. Wrap tape around the hose at flush with the base of the collar.*

4 *Clamp the main fitting into a vise. You can use a set of Earl's aluminum jaws to protect the finish of the fitting.*

5 *Installing the hose to the fitting takes a little effort. Push the hose into the fitting and then start spinning the entire hose/collar assembly until it can't be threaded by hand anymore. Then use the AN wrenches to seat the collar 1/8 inch from the end of the fitting.*

6 *The hose should not push out from the collar more than 1/16 inch. If it does, it needs to be reinstalled.*

Not all in-line pumps are created equal. They come in different shapes and sizes, with the majority consisting of low-pressure units designed for carburetors. These pumps deliver 6 to 14 psi, not nearly close enough to the 60 psi required to operate an LS engine. Any less than 60 psi and it leans out and does not run well, if at all. Thankfully, there are plenty of in-line EFI pumps to choose from. Many builders prefer the Walbro GSL 392 external pump. These pumps are well suited for Gen III/IV engines and can supply the pressure needed.

Installation

It's pretty simple to install an in-line pump, but there are a few caveats. The first is to *always* install a pre-filter before the pump, so the pump does not get clogged and ruined. A pre-filter is basically a screen-style filter that traps the big stuff.

A micron filter should be placed after the pump to catch small contaminants. Do not install a micron post filter in front of the pump (between the tank and the pump) because it impedes the gravity feed and there is not enough force to push the fuel through it.

7 *Most people just stop here, but the fitting needs to be pressure tested. Using a kit from Summit Racing, cap the ends. One end has a Schrader valve for adding air.*

8 *Pressurize the line to the capacity of the system: in this case, about 65 psi. The hose needs to be checked at or above the pressure of the system.*

9 *While holding pressure, place the assembly in a jar of water. Test both fittings. You can also let the hose sit for 5, 10, and 20 minutes, checking to see if the hose loses pressure over time.*

Make sure the pre-filter is large enough to free-flow the fuel. A small pre-filter restricts the flow to the pump, causing cavitation, and burns up the pump. A stock-type metal canister pre-filter works great, but they are not pretty. Most aftermarket fuel-pump makers have large-capacity pre-filters if you want a good-looking filter. Most aftermarket pre-filters are re-buildable.

When using a brand-new pump, it is a good idea to pump a little fuel into the pump from the feed line. This ensures the pump is not dry when it is first fired up. (Photo Courtesy Street & Performance)

These AN-style lines on the Rock Valley tanks are a little larger than a hose with a clamp. The fuel-sending unit was wired up as well. (Photo Courtesy Street & Performance)

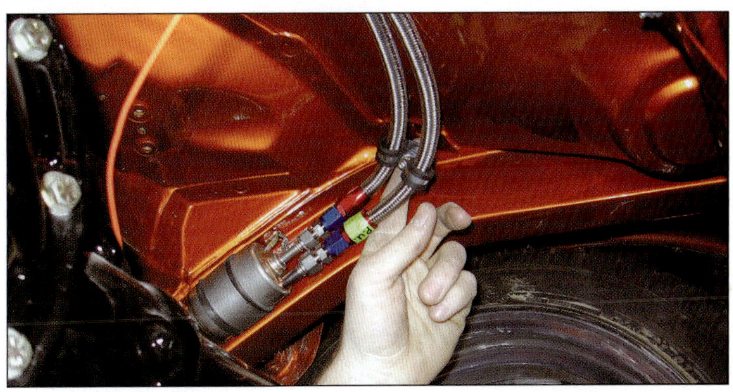

It is a good idea to use some rubber-lined cable clamps to keep the fuel lines in place as they will prevent the lines from snagging on something or hanging loose. (Photo Courtesy Street & Performance)

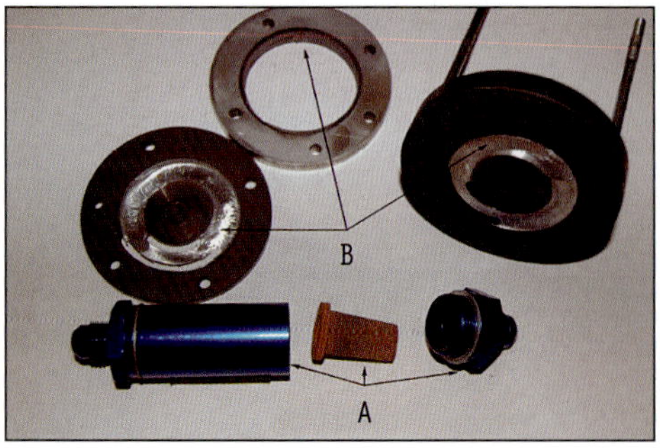

These parts show what happens when the pump cavitates. A shows a typical off-brand filter. The small sintered metal filter restricts flow to the pump. B shows the actual damage inside the pump. The cavitation grooves out the aluminum, sending shavings into the system and ruining the pump. (Photo Courtesy Aeromotive)

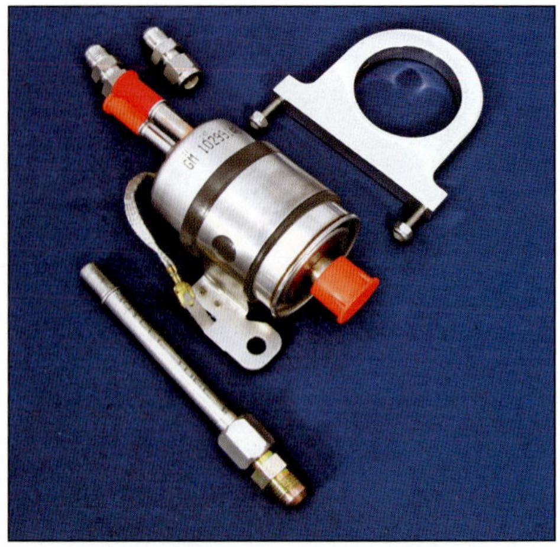

Installing a Corvette-style filter regulator is a simple option. This unit acts as both the fuel filter and fuel pressure regulator. (Photo Courtesy Street & Performance)

Cavitation

Cavitation is a natural process that occurs when vapor bubbles are introduced into liquid under pressure. All electric fuel pumps are susceptible to this force. Its most common cause is installer error, where an inadequate fuel supply increases the suction on the inlet side.

Cavitation is literally boiling the fuel through pressure. Vapor bubbles form and then split, causing a micro-explosion. This is extremely damaging, as even a few minutes of cavitation can ruin a fuel pump.

Another cause of failure is overheated fuel. Not running a return line (dead-head style) or attempting to plumb the return line into the feed line (not into the tank) causes hot fuel to cycle back through the pump, heating it up more. The hotter the fuel, the easier it is to cavitate or even vapor lock. Yes, EFI systems can vapor lock too. This is why a proper return system is so important for EFI.

Wiring

The most important aspect of any electric fuel pump is the wiring. In addition, it is most difficult to get solid grounds because paint, rust, and scale inhibit the ground. *Always* be sure to remove the paint and anything else from the ground location so you have clean metal.

Electricity requires equal grounding and positive current flow. A bad ground is just as bad as a faulty positive feed. Electric fuel pumps require a lot of current, so it's important to run a relay circuit from the pump trigger lead and to run 12-gauge positive and negative wires to the fuel pump. This ensures the pump gets the required amperage without overheating the wires.

Do not run a 16- to 24-gauge primary wire to a fuel pump, because it will cause a fire. All fuel pumps require at least a 12-gauge power wire.

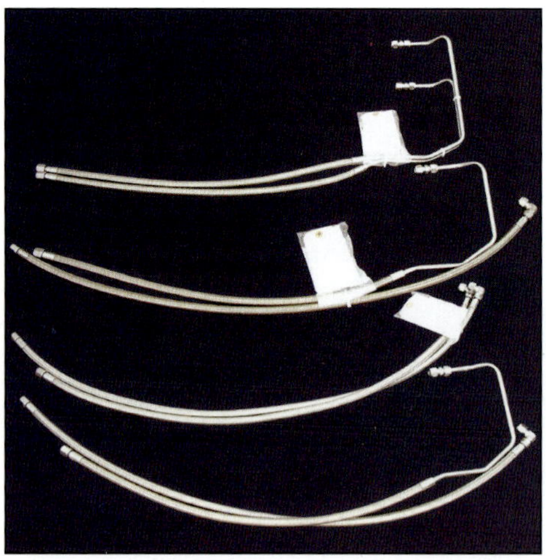

These Street & Performance braided steel lines are for the stock LS engine fuel rails, which use the full-length return line. The regulator for these lines is located at the rail, and this requires a second line for the unused fuel to return to the tank. (Photo Courtesy Street & Performance)

The Corvette filter regulator mounts under the car and near the tank, so the return line is very short. This design is simpler, but some prefer a dual-line system to keep the fuel cooler. However, the performance difference is negligible in a street car application. (Photo Courtesy Street & Performance)

Stock fuel rails use a snap-on clip fitting, but these rails have been modified to accept AN-style fittings. (Photo Courtesy Street & Performance)

This compression fitting bolts on in two pieces. It clamps the inner section to the outer ring, holding the fitting tight and giving it a good seal. (Photo Courtesy Street & Performance)

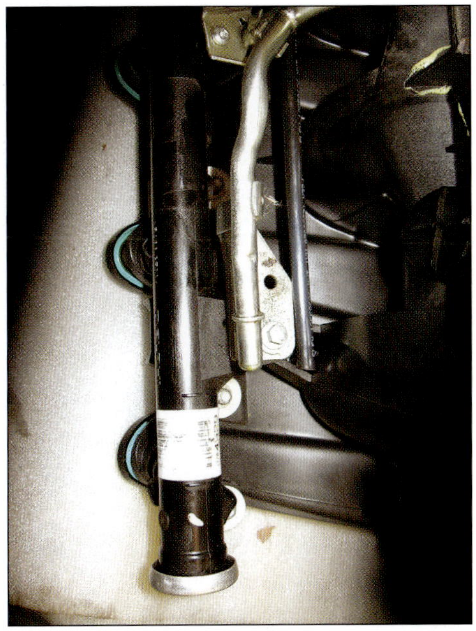

The stock rail tube fitting does not have any threads. You can use the stock-type line, but most opt for AN adapters. (Photo Courtesy Street & Performance)

After the compression fitting is secured in place, the AN fuel lines can thread on. AN fittings do not require much torque; in fact, if you tighten them too much, the flare can crush, leading to leaks. (Photo Courtesy Street & Performance)

Return Lines

All EFI engines require return lines. This can sometimes be confusing because Gen III/IV engines use a single-line fuel rail. The 1997–1998 Corvettes and 1998–2002 F-Body LS1s used a dual-line fuel rail. In 1999, the Corvette LS1 went to a single-line rail, using a filter regulator near the fuel tank and running a short return line back to the tank. This configuration is much simpler and requires only a single line run the length of the vehicle.

Many builders prefer to run two lines the distance of the vehicle with the dual-line fuel rails. The benefit of running a full-length return system is cooler fuel. The fuel does not sit in the lines, heating up from the pressure. Instead, a constant flow of fuel is running through the lines, ensuring cooler fuel and therefore more power.

This of course requires two sets of fuel lines: a 3/8-inch line for the feed and a 5/16-inch line for the return. Some muscle cars and trucks came with return-style mechanical pump fuel systems, but these are not the norm for older vehicles; most were dead-head systems, meaning that the fuel simply stops at the pump until it is sent on to the engine.

If you choose the simple one-line route, you need the 1999-up Corvette filter regulator. This unit has two lines (an input and an output) on one side for the fuel tank, and one

Stock fuel rails exit through the side of the engine cover. Street & Performance offers several fuel rail conversions, depending on the application, or you can use log-style rails from Holley, FAST, or any other performance brand. (Photo Courtesy Street & Performance)

The fuel system needs to be tested before firing up the engine. The magic number for LS engines is 60 psi at the rails. Make sure to check for leaks! (Photo Courtesy Street & Performance)

output on the other side that goes to the engine. This pre-set regulator provides the correct 60 psi to the engine, which pressurizes the entire fuel line while pumping the excess fuel back to the tank. This is typically mounted as close to the tank as possible to minimize the length of feed and return lines to the tank. For a dual-line system with the pump in the tank, a filter is needed between the pump and the fuel rails. It is best to filter the fuel as soon as possible to keep the fuel lines clean.

Installation

Installing new lines is simple, but it can be nerve-wracking at the same time. There are three ways to accomplish this task: install pre-bent hard lines, bend new hard lines, or run braided hose.

Using pre-bent hard lines is the simplest method if the vehicle has the fuel tank in the stock location. Pre-bent lines, such as those from Classic Tube and Tube Tech, are patterned after the original lines in the car and should fit just like the originals. That is not to say that there are not compromises and tweaks that must be made along the way.

Bending and installing custom lines most effectively transports fuel the length of the vehicle, but it is much easier said than done. This is a challenging task that requires some metalworking skills, and therefore the task is frustrating at best for the novice. Tubing makers such as Classic Tube offer custom-bending services using coat hangers or other wire, where a pattern is bent by hand and sent to the maker. They, in turn, can bend a set of hard lines to those specifications. This ensures quality bends with proper flare where you want them; without kinks and without the aggravation of doing it yourself.

The third option is to use flexible hose for the long runs. This works; however, braided hose is preferable to plain rubber hose to prevent road debris damage. The chance of debris snagging a long braided fuel line is much higher than with a hard line. Rubber lines are not the best option, either. Rubber lines dry out and crack much faster than hard lines corrode, so you have to replace the rubber lines eventually.

Feature Vehicle

1966 Mustang

Photos courtesy Mike Magnuson

When Mike Magnuson was looking to build a new project, he knew it had to be an early Mustang. Growing up a Ford fan, Blue Ovals were at the top of the list. Then Mike saw a 1969 Camaro with an LS swap and became very intrigued. He then found the original version of *How To Swap GM LS-Series Engines Into Just About Anything* and was hooked. After a trip to the Holley LS Fest, Mike realized that any vehicle could be LS powered for far less money, time, and effort than just about any other modern engine. After some searching, he eventually landed a pair of LQ4 6.0L Vortec engines for $1,400. When it came to the car, Mike went back to his Ford roots. When he found a clean 1966 coupe that had been dismantled for restoration, the deal was made.

Mike began by reassembling the car with modern performance in mind. The front strut-style suspension was removed, along with the strut towers, in favor of a Total Cost Involved front clip. This opened up the engine bay for the wider LS engine to fit where the 289 once lived. The 2002 Denali LQ4 was stripped to the long block. A 2002 Camaro intake was installed, along with an accessory bracket from KWiK. The alternator is a 2002 Camaro unit, and the power steering pump comes from a 1994 Cavalier with a 1998 Pontiac Montana pulley. The truck oil pan was retained.

The 4L60E transmission was rebuilt with a Beast sunshell gear, Raybestos clutches, Corvette servo, and a stage two shift

Above: *The 1966 Mustang is a beautiful example of Dearborn, Michigan's finest creations. Pop the hood, however, and the blue-oval faithful might not be quite so pleased.*

Photo 1: A 289 was originally installed in the pony car, but Mike had different plans. Dropping the LQ4 Vortec between the fenders was a bold choice. **2.** *The LQ4 looks right at home in the Mustang. KWiK's accessory drive kept the running gear under the hood. Note the heater hoses: this was done to keep the coolant flowing, as the heater is not installed in the car yet.* **3.** *Rather than purchase pre-made motor mounts, Mike fabricated a set using 1/8-inch plate steel.* **4.** *Headers for a Mustang LS swap are non-existent. These Hedman headers are supposed to fit a 2002 Camaro, but Mike cut them up and used some sections of header J-pipe from Jegs to walk the pipes around the steering gear.* **5.** *Once the headers fit as needed, they were wrapped with CoolTec header wrap to keep the underhood temperatures down.* **6.** *The factory strut towers are often the major issue in fitting a larger engine in Mustangs. The TCI front suspension allowed removal of the towers. Changing spark plugs is much easier now. The TCI suspension is a custom design that greatly simplifies the underhood area of early Mustangs; using coil-over shocks eliminates the strut design. The strut towers are in the way for an LS otherwise.* **7.** *This is a new replacement Mustang fuel tank. Although it could work with the system as is, Mike wanted a quiet-running pump, which meant it needed to be in the tank.*

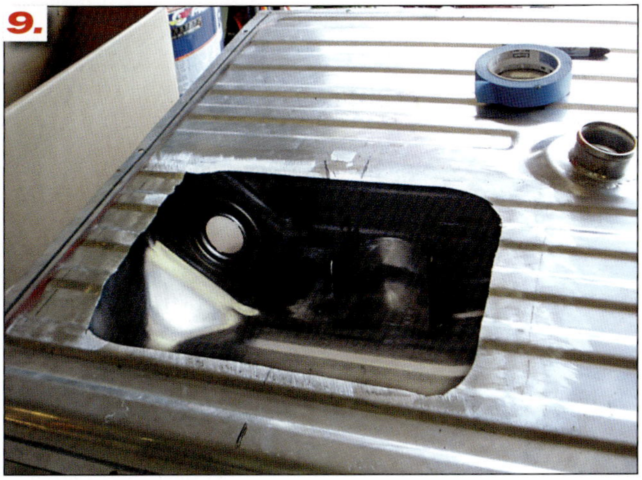

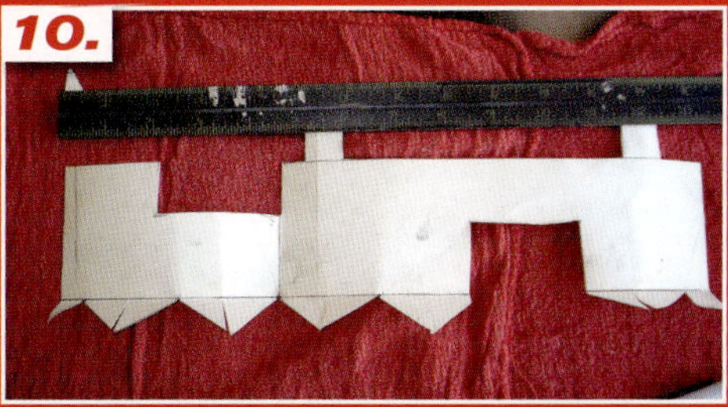

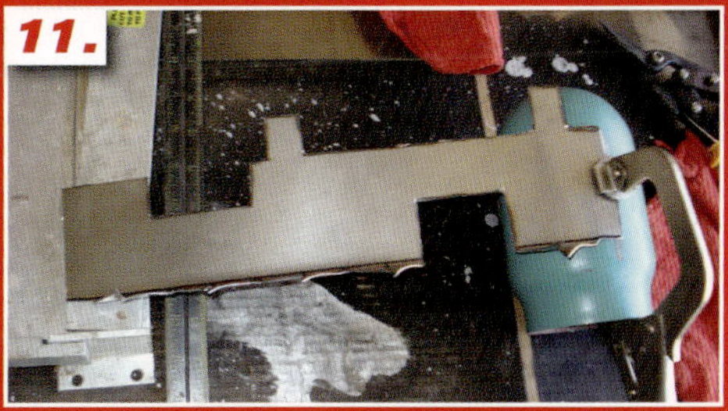

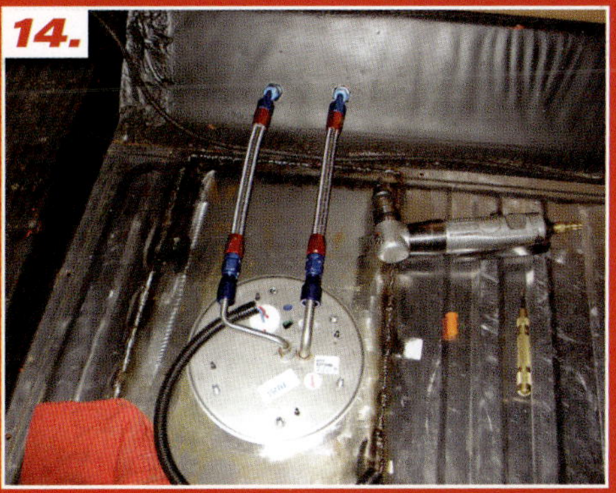

kit. The stock Mustang shifter was modified to control the shifts. Under the dash, the Mustang retains the drive-by-wire throttle. The exhaust is handled by a set of Hedman 2002 Camaro headers that were modified to fit around the steering shaft. To handle the increased power and torque, a 1996 Ford Explorer 8.8-inch rear was narrowed 3 inches and installed under the Mustang, along with a set of 3.73:1 gears on an Eaton limited-slip differential.

The fuel system uses the stock Mustang tank with a 2003 Ford F350 in-tank fuel pump and module. Mike built a custom sump to help keep the inlet covered with fuel. Outside the tank, the lines continue with -8 AN braided hose feeding a Corvette combo filter/regulator running to the factory fuel rails.

The results of Mike's efforts are quite nice. The Mustang was driven to the 2012 Holley LS Fest, averaging 23 mpg on the 1,300-mile trip. This first-generation Mustang was the only one at the show and garnered a lot of comments. The car was even featured on Chuck Hanson's television show, *Horsepower TV*.

8. *Sticking with Ford parts, a Ford F350 pump module was ordered from the local parts supply. The F350 pump provides the amount of fuel the LS needs with lots of headroom for upgrades.* **9.** *Here, Mike cut a giant hole in the brand-new tank. That may seem counterintuitive but it is a necessary step for installing an in-tank fuel pump. A reciprocating saw or die-grinder works well for this task.* **10.** *Using poster board, Mike made a template for the baffle that goes inside the tank. Note the little triangles at the bottom; these serve as welding tabs when the template is rolled up.* **11.** *The soon-to-be baffle was cut from steel and clamped to a gas bottle cap. The cap was used to form the sheet metal into a U shape. Just about any round pipe works for this.* **12.** *Mike welded the baffle into the tank. The pump module mounts to the baffle so it doesn't slosh around in the tank when there is gas in it.* **13.** *Next, Mike welded the top of the tank with some sheet metal. Note the studs welded to the top for the fuel pump mount. In the end, he decided to remove all of the ribbed section from the original cut-out section to simplify the process of sealing the tank.* **14.** *The lines were hooked up with -8 AN fittings and braided steel line. The Mustang fuel tanks double as the trunk floor, so the braided lines are really a necessity here.*

Exhaust Systems

The Gen III/IV engines have the same basic requirements for the exhaust system as other automotive engines, but these high-performance engines have specific EFI system requirements that must be met for the system to perform properly. All EFI systems require oxygen sensors to read the oxygen gas levels in the exhaust and tell the computer if the engine is running rich, lean, or just right. But that is not all. LS engines come with catalytic converters that burn up the exhaust gases to reduce emissions. This is a very important factor to consider and requires a bit of homework.

Most states have a classic car provision that exempts older vehicles from emissions standards and/or safety inspections, but it is absolutely imperative to research the current laws in your state before completing your swap. Some states require the vehicle emissions to match the standards for the year of the engine, not the vehicle, which requires the engine to retain all of the original smog equipment (including the EGR, AIR, and catalytic converters) in working order. Every state is different, and the laws are constantly being revised. It is up to you to make sure your LS swap is legal in your state.

Exhaust Manifolds

Stock Gen III/IV exhaust manifolds are fairly efficient and can keep up with 400-plus hp for most engines. The trick is finding a pair that fits your vehicle's specific chassis, as motor mounts and engine installation typically determine exhaust manifold compatibility. One set of manifolds may fit one installation and not another. Test fitting is the only way to verify clearances.

Flange Compatibility

Stock exhaust manifolds need a compatible flange that can be welded to the rest of the exhaust system. Several different flanges are used on the stock exhaust manifolds, but not all of them are reproduced. The trick here is to make sure to get some of the stock exhaust when the engine is first pulled from the donor

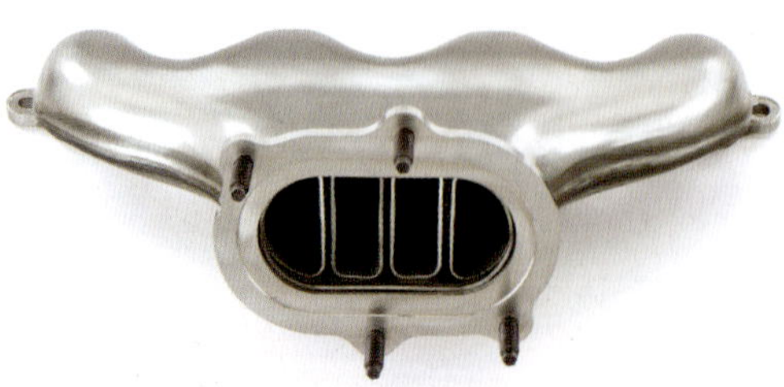

These LS7 flanges are very different from the classic three-bolt flange used for years. Get a fair section of the downpipes with the donor LS engine to ensure you have the new-style flange. (Photo Courtesy Street & Performance)

The stock manifolds may or may not fit your application; information on stock manifold fitment is sketchy at best. Truck manifolds are usually too big to clear the firewall in most muscle cars. (Photo Courtesy Street & Performance)

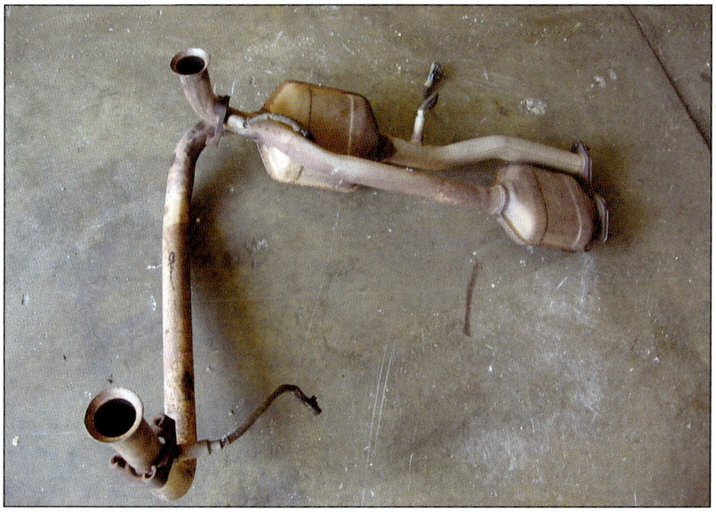

Stock downpipes also usually have catalytic converters. If they're usable, it will save some cash down the road. (Photo Courtesy Street & Performance)

The truck manifolds fit most GM trucks, and clear the steering column. You can retain the heat shields or take them off. (Photo Courtesy Street & Performance)

vehicle. The section just below the flange is all that's needed to match the exhaust manifolds being used. If your engine does not have the correct flange available, fabrication is your only option.

Speedway Motors reproduces exhaust flanges for LS1 and Vortec manifolds. Another source for flanges is used catalytic converters. Although you can't buy a used converter, you can buy the flanges. Most salvage yards gladly cut them off and sell them.

Steel Flanges

Using the exhaust gasket as a pattern, you can cut a flange using a plasma cutter. An acetylene torch certainly cuts the steel, but it's not the correct tool for this job because it also warps the steel to the point where it isn't usable as an exhaust flange. Depending on the installation, there are a couple of ways to cut new flanges.

The most common material for flanges is mild steel. For a good seal, 1/8-inch or thicker material should be used. This yields a high strength while being easier to cut than thicker steel. With a good basic outer dimension measured from the manifold or exhaust gasket, any local metal supply shop should be able to cut a plate to fit. Depending on the shop, they may be able to cut out the entire part needed.

Otherwise, using the basic plates, trace the inside of the gasket to the plate and then trim out the plate to the outside edge of the line with a plasma cutter. Any metal overhang can cause some turbulence, impede airflow, and reduce horsepower, but does not significantly affect performance if the overhang is small. If you do not have access to a plasma cutter, the following procedure also removes any metal overhang.

Using a drill bit, drill to the inside of the line marking the exhaust opening. If you are using Z06 manifolds, do this in each corner. Then place the flange in a vise and use a reciprocating saw, air body saw, or hack saw to cut out the center section. It may take awhile, but it does work. A plasma cutter, of course, certainly makes the quickest work of the job.

Aluminum Flanges

An aluminum flange looks great with a stainless, chrome, or polished exhaust. Cutting aluminum is easier than cutting steel, and you can cut a set of aluminum flanges from

Although factory manifolds fit a lot of applications, they don't necessarily have the right look. These Hooker LS manifolds fit many applications and come with 2010 Camaro-type flanges for a good seal without searching for parts or gaskets.

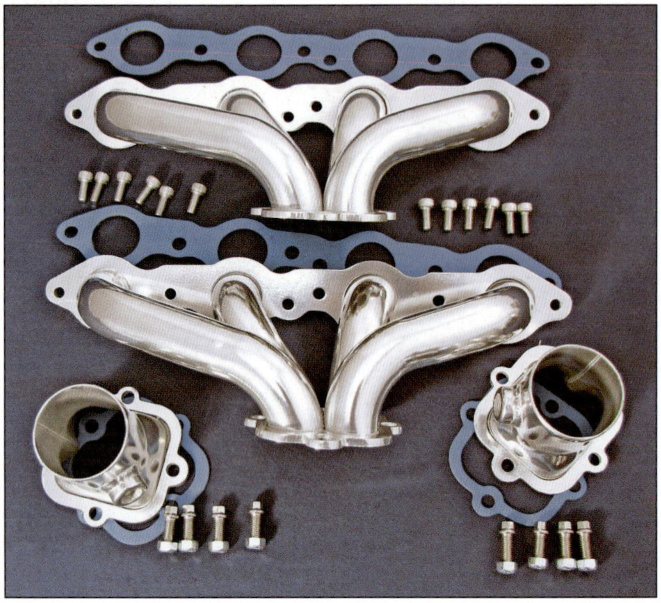

These are tight-tuck block-hugger headers in Chromex. This coating helps dissipate heat for maximum efficiency and horsepower output. (Photo Courtesy Street & Performance)

plate aluminum with a band saw and a scroll saw pretty easily. Aluminum is softer than steel, so aluminum flanges have to be thicker than their steel counterparts. Aluminum flanges should be made from at least 1/4-inch or 3/8-inch plate.

The cutting process is the same. Plasma torches quickly cut aluminum, so be careful. If you hand-cut flanges, aluminum is softer, so it is a little easier. Also, aluminum cleans up nicely with carbide tips and a die grinder.

Custom Flanges

Local shops may use CNC, plasma, or water jet equipment to cut the parts. The cutting process is usually not very expensive, but the program-writing time is typically around $50 per hour. Because flange design is really simple, it shouldn't take a shop longer than an hour. Once the program has been written, a shop can make as many as needed. If you are doing multiple swaps, you can amortize the cost to several engines.

Bridging the gap between the factory manifold's fitment and the performance of the headers are Hooker's cast-iron LS manifolds. These manifolds provide tight fitment coupled with better flow performance, and they use 2010 Camaro-type flanges. The manifolds come with flanges and use OEM gaskets for a leak-free seal.

Headers

With all of the challenges of modifying stock manifolds, most swappers prefer aftermarket headers that are designed for engine swaps. Street & Performance offers several custom-fit headers for the most popular LS swap vehicles, as do several other manufacturers, including Hooker, Edelbrock, and Dynatech.

Choosing headers requires taking some measurements and doing some research, so be careful and do it right. Some headers might fit, but have the stock-style flange, and present the same mounting difficulties. Sure, the stock flange could be cut off and a new one welded on, but isn't avoiding modification part of the reason for buying aftermarket headers? Some vehicle-specific headers fit late-model chassis and are designed for LS engines. These headers do not have the stock-style flange, making them excellent candidates for swap applications.

Vehicle-specific swap headers come with the universal three-bolt triangular flange that has been used for decades. This ensures the headers easily mate up to the rest of the exhaust. Some kits are available for specific vehicles that include the headers and exhaust, all in one package.

Street & Performance

Street & Performance makes headers for all the popular GM swap vehicles. They are designed for non-emissions-controlled vehicles. All their headers feature smooth-ground welds, optional

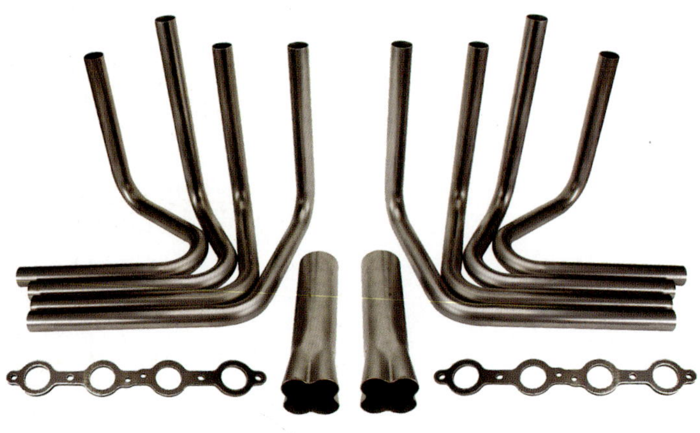

If custom headers have to be made, this kit from Speedway Motors is a great way to go. It comes with LS flanges, primary tubes, and collectors. (Photo Courtesy Speedway Motors)

Installing a Pypes Exhaust System in a GM A-Body

Swapping an LS engine is a lot of work. One of the most overlooked components of the job is the exhaust system. When it gets the attention it deserves, it is often over-built, producing less than superior performance. The most common mistake is running an exhaust that is simply too big for the engine.

Scavenging

Exhaust piping is not solely intended to eject spent gases from the engine to the back of the car. In fact, the exhaust is an essential system that can actually create horsepower through scavenging. In basic terms this is the effect of pulling exhaust out of the engine by means of positive and negative pulses. As each pulse of the engine pushes exhaust out, there is an opposite pulse toward the engine. These pulses create a vacuum that actually draws additional gases out of the combustion chamber and can even draw fresh air/fuel into the chamber.

The scavenging effect is directly proportional to the heat and tubing size. As the diameter of tubing increases, the pressure is reduced, dropping the temperature inside the pipe, which slows the gases, reducing scavenging. On the opposite end of the spectrum, pipes that are too small restrict flow, produce high temperatures, and cause power loss. There is a compromise that yields the best flow and scavenging.

Muffler Shop Option

For a typical sub-500-hp street car, a 2½-inch exhaust is more than enough to support the flow of the engine while maintaining proper scavenging. As the horsepower increases and surpasses the 500-hp mark, engines need a 3-inch exhaust to maintain proper flow. These numbers are for mandrel-bent pipe, not for compression-style pipes found at most local muffler shops. Compression-bent pipes require larger diameters as the diameter changes drastically when bent.

Having the local muffler shop create and install a set of pipes gets the job done, but the cost of the system can far outweigh its benefits. Many local muffler shops are more interested in quantity, not quality, and use inferior products and tools. The welding is often poor, with large gaps between the pipes. To get a properly tuned exhaust system for your specific model, choose a system that was designed to fit your vehicle.

With the Buick GS up on a set of Race Ramps (which are much safer than jack stands), there is enough room to work comfortably.

Pypes Option

Pypes Performance Exhaust offers engineered systems for just about every vintage muscle car available, as well as trucks, SUVs, and modern muscle applications. Each system is designed to produce efficient flow and properly fit the car. Pypes uses 409 stainless-steel tubing for all of its systems, ensuring a rust-free finish that lasts. For builders who want to take a step up, Pypes offers the 304 polished stainless kits.

Most Pypes systems come with a basic X-pipe, which balances the exhaust system. As an added option, you can upgrade to the X-Change X-pipe, which adds open-exhaust dumps after the X-pipe crossover. This not only offers the ability to bypass the mufflers for racing, it also keeps the benefits of the X-pipe. Another unique feature of the X-Change X-pipe is that the exhaust dumps are straight out of the pipe,

The key feature of the Pypes kit is the optional X-Change kit. This kit adds well-designed dumps, sending the open exhaust straight out rather than making it turn as with most other dump pipe kits.

Installing a Pypes Exhaust System in a GM A-Body *CONTINUED*

instead of on the curve, which reduces the flow restriction when running the system open.

Pypes offers three levels of muffler performance: Street Pro, Race Pro, and The Violator. For the project Buick GS shown here, Street Pro mufflers were chosen. These are great for cruising and not attracting the local law enforcement, but still have a nice mellow rumble. For a more vocal exhaust, the Race Pro units are the way to go. Installing the 2½-inch 409 stainless system with Street Pro mufflers and an X-Change X-pipe on this 1971 Buick GS convertible was fairly simple. (The money saved by not paying shop labor allows you to buy a better system.) The pipes are slip fit, and can be installed using the included clamps. However, welding the exhaust is the best method, and the 409 stainless is easily welded with a standard MIG wire welder. The vehicle must be safely raised off the ground because this job requires working room under the car. Jack stands or ramps are a suitable replacement for a lift if you don't have access to one.

Installation

The first step is to lay out the kit parts on the floor according to the included diagram. That's the easy part but remember that they might not fit up that way. Make sure to test fit the pieces together because they don't always fit out of the box, and you don't want to fight it under the car.

Remove the old exhaust and install the new components. Start with the new hangers, then the rear pipes, going up and over the rear end. One person can do the job, but a second pair of hands always helps.

The mufflers should go on next, but that depends on the particular application and where the mufflers are located.

Install the X-pipe assembly. This piece is important and comes unwelded. It should be centered under the driveshaft, and is directional; the arrow should point toward the engine, not toward the back of the car (read the instructions; it is a serious pain pulling it out and switching it around).

Place the shorter front X-pipe tubes. These tubes may require trimming for the best fit, depending on the motor mounts and headers used.

The next step requires some fitting, measuring, cutting, and welding. Use a chop saw with a fresh blade. It makes things easy and much cleaner.

Bolt or clamp the header collector reducers to the headers. Slip on the tubes from the exhaust. With everything else in position, carefully measure the length of the tube. Mark the tube with a Sharpie and pull the assembly from the car. Measure twice, if not three times. Cut off the excess tube and weld the tube to the reducer.

Reinstall the assembly and make sure everything fits. At this point, you can use clamps to hold the system together, but you should weld it for the utmost strength and durability. The slip-fit design does not require welding the entire circumference of the pipes, which is nice, because it is a tight fit. A few well-placed tack welds suffice and ensure there are no leaks and that the pipes hold together. Standard MIG wire welds the 409 stainless tubing without issue.

The following steps are a general overview of the process. ■

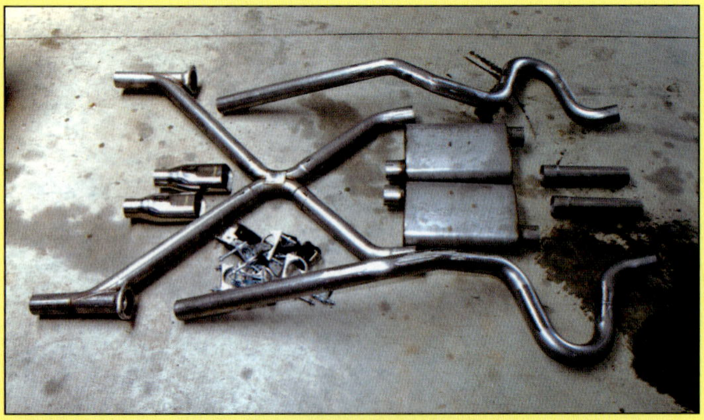

1 ***The Pypes exhaust is very simple to install and includes all the hardware. The optional polished stainless tips go on after the car is painted and the freshly chromed bumpers are installed.***

2 ***The stainless-steel mufflers feature slotted ends that facilitate the slip-on fit. You may have to open these up a bit with a hammer to get the pipes to fit together. Don't worry; it only takes a couple of taps. Once resized, you tap the tabs to form fit the tubing.***

3 *The kit comes with a bunch of body clips and bolts to mount the new hangers. They work on one side, but not the other. You have to place the rear hanger just behind the gas tank on the frame.*

4 *The muffler hanger mounts to the rear crossmember in front of the rear end. These have to go on just like this or the pipes don't hang correctly.*

5 *The most difficult task is routing the over-axle tailpipes. The weight of the body needs to be taken off the suspension to gain the necessary clearance. Make sure to look at the diagram on the instructions. The pipes are side-specific, and you don't want to have to do this twice.*

6 *The mufflers go on the tailpipes in front of the rear end. The clamp mounts to the muffler, then the remaining thread pushes through the hanger and the nuts go on. These only need to be hand tightened for now.*

7 *The X-Change X-pipe assembly is the key to the Pypes system. The rear section with the dumps connects to the mufflers and the X-pipe through a second Y-pipe on each side. This allows the X-pipe to be used regardless of whether the dumps are open or not.*

8 *The X-pipe center section has an arrow that must point toward the front of the car. It is easy to mistake this as meaning the direction of flow. It's important to read the instructions.*

Installing a Pypes Exhaust System in a GM A-Body *CONTINUED*

9 *Remove all paint from the collectors before welding.*

10 *Weld the collector pipes to the collector flanges. Whenever you weld thin metal, it is important to go slowly to avoid burning through.*

11 *With the collector reducers in place, mark the header-to-X-pipe tubing for length. This piece must be trimmed to fit, as different headers need different-length pipes. If you are running manifolds or short headers, order a downpipe for this section.*

12 *Using a Sharpie, mark the pipes for fitment. Measure twice, cut once. It is easy to make a mistake, hence the scribbled-out mark you can see here.*

13 *Cut down the pipe using a chop saw. Measure twice, cut once because it is a lot harder to put it back on. Each side is likely different, so measure both sides.*

14 *The trimmed and welded header-to-pipe assembly completes the fitting stage. Bolt and torque down the reducer before you begin welding. Although the kit comes with clamps and can certainly be clamped together long term, it is highly recommended that the system be welded together. Standard MIG wire easily welds the 409 stainless tubing.*

15 *All done. The new exhaust system is much more neighbor-friendly than open headers. The entire job should take one person about four hours. You can leave the mufflers clamped in place so that they can be removed more easily if you choose to take them off for a driveline maintenance/upgrade such as transmission repairs.*

Chromex coating inside and out, and matching flanges. Each header features stainless-steel head and exhaust flanges. These four-bolt flanges are a square design and have built-in oxygen bungs. There are separate applications for Gen III/IV engines and LS7 engines.

Applications include: 1954–1996 Corvette, 1978–1987 G-Body, 1967–1969 F-Body, 1964–1972 GM A-Body, 1962–1979 Chevy Nova, 1955–1957 Tri-Five Chevy, 1955-up GM trucks, street rod mid-length, and street rod block hugger.

Oxygen Sensor Bungs

The most important detail for an LS exhaust, other than fitment, is to have properly working oxygen sensors. It is a good idea to replace the oxygen sensors because they wear out and don't cost that much. The front oxygen sensors are required, but the rear sensors are not. If you don't use rear oxygen sensors, they need to be programmed out of the ECM. ■

1 *This downpipe is being prepped for an oxygen sensor bung.*

2 *The bung is really just a large nut. Some have a hex shape; most are round. Position the bung at least 18 inches from the cylinder heads.*

3 *Using a step-drill bit, drill the pipe to accept the sensor tip. Step bits work great here as you don't have to change the bit when you need a bigger hole.*

4 *Don't cut it too big. The bung should sit on the outside of the pipe with just enough clearance for the sensor.*

5 *Weld the bung to the pipe with a MIG welder. There is a gap that must be filled on the edges.*

Oxygen Sensor Bungs *CONTINUED*

6 *The welds must completely seal the bung to the pipe. You don't want it to leak, which can cause faulty readings due to the cold air coming in after each exhaust pulse.*

7 *Because the tubing was originally wrapped with exhaust wrap, the last step is to re-wrap it and clamp it back in place. The oxygen sensor is now ready to go. Don't forget to put anti-seize on the threads.*

EGR Plugs

The exhaust gas recirculation (EGR) system is a component of the engine's emissions controls. By recycling a low percentage (typically 5 to 15) of the exhaust gases back through the engine, the fuel burn is slowed, which ensures a more complete burn cycle and the engine has fewer exhaust emissions. Not all LS-series engines have the EGR system. For example, the 98-00 LS1 has EGR, but the 01-02 LS1 does not. In swap situations, most states do not require maintaining the factory emissions controls, so you can remove the EGR system. Removing it from your LS-series engine can increase its overall performance and efficiency, especially in older engines when the EGR valve is plugged. If you remove the EGR, the ECM needs to be tuned to reflect the removal, otherwise it produces a trouble code. The code doesn't alter performance, but it keeps the engine light on. ■

1 *The EGR system can be disabled by using an EGR plug, which is available from many aftermarket sources. (Photo Courtesy Street & Performance)*

2 *Apply a little silicone to the plug. The O-ring seals the hole, but the silicone keeps it from popping out under pressure. (Photo Courtesy Street & Performance)*

3 *Next, pop the plug into place. The plugs are available with several logos milled in the top. Although not necessary, this is an easy way to customize the look of your LS engine. (Photo Courtesy Street & Performance)*

Edelbrock

The conversion kit from Edelbrock includes headers made of 409 stainless-steel tubing with 3/8-inch-thick port and collector flanges. The collectors use graphite donut gaskets instead of the leak-prone three-bolt collector and gasket. The kit fits 1964–1972 GM A-Body cars, including the Chevelle, Malibu, El Camino, Cutlass, 442, Skylark, Buick Special, GS350, GS455, GTO, LeMans, and Tempest. The Gen III/IV swap headers have 1¾-inch primary tubes stepped up to 1⅞ inches for maximum flow and power.

Edelbrock recommends using its LS-series engine-mount kit (PN 6701) with Edelbrock swap headers. If you have Edelbrock E-Tec-series LS heads or Vortec Fast Burn heads, the Edelbrock swap headers (PN 65083) have the correct port flange configuration, so they are compatible with stock A-Body motor mounts. The Edelbrock LS swap exhaust system matches the headers and motor mounts, although the system also works well with other mounts and headers.

The exhaust system is constructed from 2½-inch 409 stainless-steel tubing with an X-pipe assembly and includes a pair of Edelbrock SDT-series mufflers and a pair of polished stainless-steel tips.

This kit fits the same vehicles listed at left for the header conversion kit.

Hooker Headers

Hooker builds a couple of vehicle-specific LS swap headers (first-generation Camaro/Firebird and GM A-Body) in addition to its universal block-hugger LS headers.

1967–1969 F-Body, 1966–1972 GM A-Body: These headers are built with lightweight, 18-gauge tuned-length 1¾-inch primaries, with 3-inch smooth transition slip-fit-style collectors. This yields a leak-free fit to the rest of the exhaust. The headers are designed to fit tight to the chassis, giving increased ground clearance, from 1 to 3 inches, which is especially helpful for lowered vehicles.

The cylinder head flanges are made from 5/16-inch machined steel for a good seal. To accommodate the oxygen sensors, the headers include 3- to 2½-inch slip-fit reducers with oxygen sensor bungs welded in, plus a set of extra bungs for running a 3-inch exhaust system.

Hooker LS swap headers fit most manual and automatic GM

Filter Options

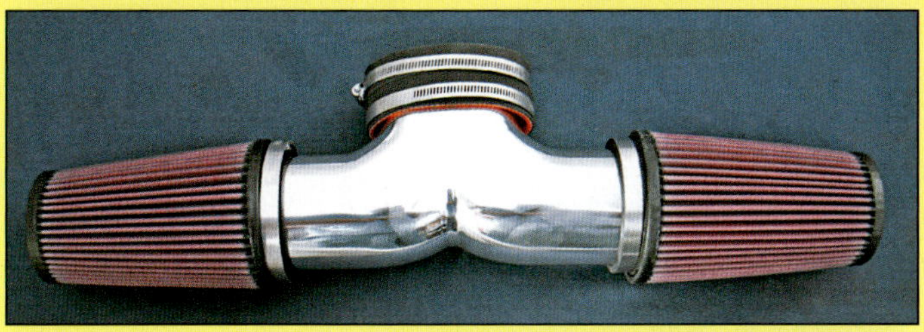

This twin-filter setup looks beautiful on any LS engine, and allows the engine to breathe properly. When using a tight 90-degree elbow, the airflow is restricted. By adding two filters, that restriction is eliminated. (Photo Courtesy Street & Performance)

These filters look great, and fit in tight applications, but they can actually cost as much as 20 to 30 hp because the air must make such a sharp turn so quickly. The air they are pulling is heated from under the hood. Ideally, a longer tube with fresh, cool air is optimum for performance. (Photo Courtesy Street & Performance)

The 90-degree elbow kits like this one allow for a much smoother transition if you can fit it. Early Corvettes may have issues with this setup, depending on the motor mounts. (Photo Courtesy Street & Performance)

Building Custom Headers

Photos by Blane Burnett

Engine swaps can be challenging, especially when it comes to the exhaust. Although there are a million header designs out there, it can be really expensive to use the trial-and-error method when trying to find one that works for your application. Sometimes the only real choice is to build a custom set at home. There are several ways to do this: kits, custom header shops, etc. There are even a few kits with plastic tubes that work like big-boy Legos; you assemble and then send them off to the manufacturer to copy for an exact fit.

This is all fine if you have the cash to spend for a set of $2,000 headers. Most swappers have a tight budget and cannot afford to spend that amount of money on a set of headers, so they have to build their own.

Headers have a bit of mystery surrounding them, but they really are not that hard to build: you just need some patience. The Nissan 240SX from Chapter 1 was used for this project.

The following steps are a general overview of the process. ■

1 ***The process begins with a header flange and a set of J-bends tacked to the flanges. These can be cut at whatever angle necessary to put all four pipes where they need to be.***

2 ***Under the car, tack a pair of collectors to a crossbar that is clamped to the frame. This ensures the collectors don't move.***

3 ***Arrange other tubes under the car, working around the various obstacles. You want an assortment of bends, including 45, 90, and some intermediates. These kits are available separately from Summit Racing, or they can be bent at a local exhaust shop.***

4 ***Once you decide on the general arrangement, connect the primary tubes to the collectors with sections of straight pipe. This is time consuming and usually requires a lot of trial and error. Once set, tack weld them in place.***

5 *Remove the entire assembly for some welding to keep the pipes in place. A Sharpie is great for making marks to help line up the tubes if they move while you take them out of the car.*

6 *Reposition the tubes under the car and connect other tubes. You may have to do this several times during the process.*

7 *The passenger-side header is almost finished; it just needs to be welded up.*

8 *Keeping an eye on ground clearance is a good idea, too, especially on low-profile vehicles such as this Nissan 240SX.*

9 *Start working on the driver-side header using the same process, working to clear all the critical areas, such as the starter.*

10 *Once the fabrication is finished, take the header to the bench and complete the final TIG welding.*

Building Custom Headers *CONTINUED*

11 ***The trickiest part of welding up headers is the collector tube. The gaps have to be filled with either weld or plates.***

12 ***With the headers fully welded, fabricate the rest of the exhaust from stainless-steel tubing and install it.***

13 ***The last step is to take the fabricated headers and make seamless one-piece bends for each of the primary tubes, weld them up, and ceramic coat them to match the rest of the exhaust. This step is not required but it certainly makes for a killer look.***

transmissions, including the Tremec 5-and 6-speed manual transmissions.

Block Hugger: Hooker's block-hugger LS swap header design is tuned for low- and mid-range street performance from idle to 3,500 rpm. The primaries are made from 18-gauge, 1⅝-inch mild steel tubing that is mandrel-bent and tuned by length to reduce backpressure and increase exhaust velocity. This design delivers more power, torque, and crisp throttle response; the 2½-inch collectors with a 3/8-inch-thick three-bolt flange make installation simple.

The head flange is machined to ensure a flat surface for a tight seal. The tight-tuck tube design was used to fit within narrow street rod frames and provide a good fit in most vehicles that do not have a dedicated swap header. The collectors exit parallel with the oil pan for maximum ground clearance in lowered vehicles and are positioned to clear the starter and motor mounts.

Doug's Headers: Designed for Tri-Five Chevy, Olds, and Buick cars, these shorty-style headers feature 1⅞-inch primaries with a 3-inch collector made from 16-gauge steel. They are available in ceramic coated or natural finish.

1932 Ford Coupe

Photos courtesy Gearhead Garage

There is no hot rod platform more iconic than the 1932 Ford. From the very beginning of hot rodding, these cars have been at the forefront. Ever since 1955, people have been slapping small-block Chevys between the rails. What you don't see very often is an LS under the hood. These rods are typically built with a lot of thought and emphasis on form rather than function.

Frankly, the Gen III/IV engines don't have the same aesthetics as a classic small-block Chevy, but that doesn't mean it can't be done. Matt Diamond of Gearhead Garage in Gilbert, Arizona, planned to do just that. "The goal of the build was to give the customer a reliable daily driver with some modern amenities built on a vintage platform," Matt told me. "The car has A/C, a killer stereo, and makes 400 hp on pump gas." I think he nailed it.

The project began with a fiberglass 1932 Ford coupe body and frame from Atlanta Hot Rods. The front suspension consists of Pete & Jake's components. The engine is an LQ4 salvage take-out from a 2002 Chevy Silverado, along with the matching 4L60E transmission. Mounting the engine to the frame is a set of motor mounts by Dirty Dingo Motorsports. Matt

Above: *No other car screams "hot rod" like a 1932 Ford. This coupe was custom built by Gearhead Garage and features a 400-hp LQ4 Vortec engine.*

Photo ***1:*** *The project started out as an Atlanta Hot Rods fiberglass body and steel frame. The front suspension is a Pete & Jake's buggy-spring, while the rear is a 9-inch Ford with a triangulated four-link.* ***2.*** *The LQ4 was painted the same brandywine color as the body before it was dropped into the frame. It uses a set of Dirty Dingo motor mounts.* ***3.*** *The headers were a bit of a challenge, as even stock manifolds ran into the steering and kept the hood sides from closing. Gearhead Garage chopped up a set of block huggers to make it work.* ***4.*** *Using some J-bend tubing, the headers were fabricated to clear all the important parts, such as the steering linkage and frame.* ***5.*** *The passenger's side was less of an issue; the headers fit out of the box.*

used an F-Body oil pan for ground clearance. The accessory drive features components from the Vortec system, an F-Body tensioner and water pump, mounted to Street Shop brackets. The water pump was machined so it could rotate 90 degrees, placing the outlet facing downward rather than out the side in order to provide clearance for the lower radiator hose. Gearhead Garage tuned the LQ4 ECM using HP Tuners software through a modified stock wiring harness.

One of the key issues for LS engines versus the typical small-block Chevy in a 1932 Ford is the look and fit of the exhaust. The owner of this car wanted the option to run hooded or with the hood sides removed, so the exhaust had to match. This is not an issue for a small-block Chevy, but the LQ4 proved to be tricky. None of the off-the-shelf headers or factory manifolds cleared the hood sides.

Matt built a custom set of headers to clear the frame and the hood sides while retaining the look. He added a set of electric cutouts on the headers with side dumps so the owner could choose when to get loud.

Once completed, the 1932 runs like a brand-new car with all the goodies expected on a high-end hot rod. It even features keyless push-to-start technology. Weighing just under 2,500 pounds, the 400-hp LQ4 makes this a beast on the drag strip too.

6. *Without the hood sides, the LQ4 looks right at home, even though it is far from the traditional small-block Chevy or Ford V-8.* **7.** *Once the header fabrication was complete, Gearhead ceramic-coated the headers for a bright finish. Ceramic coating not only looks good, but it helps push the heat from the exhaust out the pipes instead of into the engine bay.* **8.** *The 1932 looks as if it belongs in a ZZ Top video. With 400 hp on tap, the 2,500-pound coupe is a rocket.*

Source Guide

Accel Ignition
10601 Memphis Ave., #12
Cleveland, OH 44144
216-658-6413
accel-ignition.com

Advance Adapters
4320 Aerotech Center Way
Paso Robles, CA 93446
800-350-2223
advanceadapters.com

American Touring Specialties
3685 S. Highland Dr., Unit #10
Las Vegas, NV 89103
702-245-6305
americantouringspecialties.com

AutoKraft
5020 W. Folsom St.
Eau Claire, WI 54703
715-874-5921
autokraft.org

AutoMeter
413 West Elm St.
Sycamore, IL 60178
866-248-6356
autometer.com

Billet Specialties
500 Shawmut Ave.
La Grange, IL 60526
800-245-5382
billetspecialties.com

B&M Racing & Performance
100 Stony Point Rd., Ste 125
Santa Rosa, CA 95401
707-544-4761
bmracing.com

BRP Muscle Rods
5849 Rogers Rd.
Cumming, GA 30040
770-751-0687
brphotrods.com

BowTie Overdrives
17359 Darwin Ave., Unit C
Hesperia, CA 92345
760-947-5240
bowtieoverdrives.com

Canton Racing Products
232 Branford Rd.
North Branford, CT 06471
203-481-9460
cantonracingproducts.com

Car Shop Inc.
421 12th St.
Moline, IL 61265
309-797-4188
carshopinc.com

Classic Tube
80 Rotech Dr.
Lancaster, NY 14086
716-759-1800
classictube.com

COMP Cams
3406 Democrat Rd.
Memphis, TN 38118
800-999-0853
compcams.com

Crane Cams
1830 Holsonback Dr.
Daytona Beach, FL 32117
386-310-4875
cranecams.com

Current Performance
6330 Pine Hill Rd., #16
Port Richey, FL 34668
727-844-7570
currentperformance.com

Dakota Digital
4510 W. 61st St. N.
Sioux Falls, SD 57107
800-593-4160
dakotadigital.com

Detroit Speed and Engineering
185 McKenzie Rd.
Mooresville, NC 28115
704.662.3272
detroitspeed.com

DiabloSport
Corporate Headquarters
1865 SW 4th Ave., Ste. D-2
Delray Beach, FL 33431
561-908-0041
diablosport.com

Doug's Headers
440 E. Arrow Hwy.
San Dimas, CA 91773
909-599-5955
pertronix.com

Dynotech Engineering
1731 Thorncroft Dr.
Troy, MI 48084-5302
800-633-5559
dynotechengineering.com

Earl's Performance Plumbing
1801 Russellville Rd.
Bowling Green, KY 42101
270-782-2900
holley.com

Edelbrock
2700 California St.
Torrance, CA 90503
310-781-2222
edelbrock.com

ESAB Cutting and Welding Equipment
411 South Ebenezer Rd.
Florence, SC 29501-0545
843-669-4411
esabna.com

EFI Live Limited
121 Elliot St., Unit 2
Howick
Auckland 2014, New Zealand
+64 (9) 534 1188
efilive.com

FAST
3400 Democrat Rd.
Memphis, TN 38118
877-334-8355
fuelairspark.com

Flex-a-lite
7213 45th St. Ct. E
Fife, WA 98424
800-851-1510
flex-a-lite.com

Gearhead Garage
1021 N. Gilbert Rd., Ste. 104
Gilbert, AZ 85234
480-497-8811
gearheadaz.com

GMPP
P.O. Box 33170
Detroit, MI 48232
800-222-1020
gmperformanceparts.com

Granatelli Motor Sports
1000 Yarnell Pl.
Oxnard, CA 93033-2454
805-486-6644
granatellimotorsports.com

Griffin Thermal Products
750 Estes Dr.
Piedmont, SC 29673
800-722-3723
griffinrad.com

Holley
1801 Russellville Rd.
Bowling Green, KY 42101
270-782-2900
holley.com

Hooker
1801 Russellville Rd.
Bowling Green, KY 42101
270-782-2900
holley.com

HP Tuners
725 Hastings Ln.
Buffalo Grove, IL 60089
hptuners.com

JBA Headers
440 E. Arrow Hwy.
San Dimas, CA 91773
909-599-5955
jbaheaders.com

Jaguars That Run
P.O. Box 66
Livermore, CA 94551
925-462-3619
jagsthatrun.com

Jet Performance
17491 Apex Cir.
Huntington Beach, CA 92647
800-535-1161
jetchip.com

Lokar Performance Products
10924 Murdock Dr.
Knoxville, TN 37932
865-966-2269
lokar.com

LS1Tech.com

Koul Tools
Lake Havasu City, AZ 86405
928-854-6706
koultools.com

March Performance Pulleys
16160 Performance Way
Naples, FL 34110
239-593-4074
marchperf.com

Mezeire
220 S. Hale Ave.
Escondido, CA 92029
800-208-1755
meziere.com

Milodon
2250 Agate Ct.
Simi Valley, CA 93065
805-577-5950
milodon.com

Moroso
80 Carter Dr.
Guilford, CT 06437-2116
203-453-6571
moroso.com

MSD
1350 Pullman Dr.
El Paso, TX 79936
915-857-5200
msdignition.com

P-Ayr Products
719 Delaware St.
Leavenworth, KS 66048
913-651-5543
payr.com

Painless Performance Products
2501 Ludelle St.
Fort Worth, TX 76105
817-244-6212
painlessperformance.com

Pypes Performance Exhaust
2705 Clemens Rd.
Hatfield, PA 19440
800-421-3890
pypesexhaust.com

Red Dirt Rodz
4518 Braxton Ln.
Stillwater, OK 74074
405-880-5343
reddirtrodz.com

Rock Valley
Route 72 and Rothwell Rd.
Stillman Valley, IL 61084
815-645-2271
rockvalleyantiqueautoparts.com

Speartech
3574 E. State Rd. 236
Anderson, IN 46017
765-378-4908
speartech.com

Steeroids
1901 S. FM 129
Santo, TX 76472
970-731-1381
steeroids.com

Street & Performance
#1 Hot Rod Ln.
Mena, AR 71953
479-394-5711
hotrodlane.cc

Superchips
1790 E. Airport Blvd.
Sanford, FL 32773
888-227-2447
superchips.com

Tanks Inc.
260 Welter Dr.
Monticello, IA 52310
877-596-3842
tanksinc.com

TCI
151 Industrial Dr.
Ashland, MS 38603
888-776-9824
tciauto.com

V8 Archie
11411 Summerwood Dr.
Machesney Park, IL 61115
800-891-3608
v8archie.com

Vorshlag Motor Sports
6913 K. Ave., Ste. 307
Plano, TX 75074
972-422-7170
vorshlag.com

Zoops Products
931 E. Lincoln St.
Banning, CA 92220
951-922-2396
zoops.com